Unlocking Excellence

A Blueprint for Achieving Business Success

Business Lessons: Book One

GEORGE BICKERSTAFF

FEBRUARY 2024

Table of Contents

Foreword 3
Introduction 4
About This Book 5
Book Summary 6
Key Book Lessons 8
Ten Actions to Take 12
Ten Mistakes to Avoid 13
Part One: Foundations of Business 14
   Chapter 1: Understanding Business Fundamentals 14
   Chapter 2: Crafting a Vision and Mission Statement 26
   Chapter 3: Building a Strong Organizational Culture 38
   Chapter 4: Navigating Legal and Regulatory Compliance 49
   Chapter 5: Embracing Ethical Business Practices 62
Part Two: Strategy and Planning 74
   Chapter 6: Developing a Business Strategy 74
   Chapter 7: Conducting Market Research and Analysis 85
   Chapter 8: Creating a Comprehensive Business Plan 96
   Chapter 9: Setting SMART Goals for Success 107
   Chapter 10: Implementing Effective Change Management 121
Part Three: Marketing and Sales 132
   Chapter 11: Identifying Target Markets and Customers 132
   Chapter 12: Developing a Brand Identity and Positioning 143
   Chapter 13: Leveraging Digital Marketing Channels 154
   Chapter 14: Mastering the Art of Selling 166
   Chapter 15: Cultivating Customer Relationships and Loyalty 177
Part Four: Finance and Operations 188
   Chapter 16: Managing Finances and Budgets 188
   Chapter 17: Understanding Financial Statements 200
   Chapter 18: Securing Funding and Investment 213
   Chapter 19: Optimizing Supply Chain and Logistics 225
   Chapter 20: Enhancing Operational Efficiency and Productivity 237
Part Five: Innovation and Growth 248
   Chapter 21: Fostering Creativity and Innovation 248
   Chapter 22: Harnessing Technology for Competitive Advantage 260

Chapter 23: Expanding into New Markets and Industries..........271
Chapter 24: Scaling Your Business for Growth..........282
Chapter 25: Nurturing a Culture of Continuous Improvement..........293
Epilog..........304
Glossary of Terms..........305
About the Author..........310

Foreword

In the journey of business, the path to success is often as intricate as it is fascinating. This book, "Unlocking Excellence," is a compass for navigating that journey, offering insights that illuminate the way forward. As you turn these pages, you are about to embark on an adventure that transcends the conventional boundaries of business wisdom.

The essence of business, at its core, is not merely about transactions or the bottom line; it is about the people it serves and the lives it touches. This book is a testament to that truth, weaving together stories of resilience, innovation, and leadership that inspire and instruct. Each chapter is a beacon, guiding entrepreneurs and business professionals through the complexities of the marketplace with clarity and purpose.

What sets this book apart is its unwavering commitment to the reader's growth, both personal and professional. The authors have meticulously crafted a narrative that is not only informative but also profoundly motivational. Through a blend of expert analysis, real-world examples, and actionable strategies, "Unlocking Excellence" empowers you to elevate your business acumen to new heights.

As you delve into the insights and lessons contained within, you will find yourself equipped with the tools to craft a vision for success that is uniquely yours. This book challenges you to think differently, to embrace change, and to pursue excellence with relentless determination. It is a call to action, urging you to transcend limitations and to forge a legacy of achievement.

To the aspiring moguls, the innovative thinkers, and the leaders of tomorrow: this book is for you. May it serve as a source of inspiration, a fountain of wisdom, and a roadmap to success in your entrepreneurial voyage. Let the journey begin.

Warm Regards,

George Bickerstaff

Introduction

Embark on an inspiring journey into the realm of business mastery, where success emerges from the synergy of strategic foresight and unyielding effort. This ever-evolving landscape beckons with a promise of excellence, transforming the mastery of business nuances into a perpetual adventure. Here, a world brimming with potential awaits those bold enough to seize it, yet it is also a world that demands astute navigation through its myriad challenges.

This guide is your compass on the path to unparalleled business acumen, crafted to be an indispensable asset for ambitious entrepreneurs, leaders seeking to hone their skills, and anyone intrigued by the pillars of business success. It interlaces the insights of industry pioneers, trailblazing entrepreneurs, and thought leaders to light your way through the complexities of achieving business excellence. More than just a compilation of knowledge, it shines as a beacon guiding you towards strategic growth and personal development.

Within these pages, you will find a comprehensive roadmap to business success, addressing key aspects such as cultivating an entrepreneurial mindset, leveraging technological progress, and embracing the global marketplace. It explores the critical importance of strategic choices, innovation, and agility in a rapidly changing business landscape. By sharing expert perspectives and real-world experiences, this book equips you with the tools to navigate and conquer the challenges of the modern business environment.

True business mastery, however, extends beyond mere financial gains. It is rooted in the principles of integrity, resilience, and an unwavering commitment to adding value. This narrative champions a holistic approach, emphasizing the empowerment of individuals, the nurturing of impactful relationships, and the pursuit of a significant, positive influence. It challenges us to rethink the conventional metrics of success, advocating instead for a legacy defined by meaningful contributions and societal betterment.

As we embark on this voyage together, prepare to question established norms, broaden your perspectives, and unlock your full potential. The wisdom encapsulated here is set to redefine industry standards and leave a lasting mark on the world. By committing to the journey of business mastery, you are not only charting a course for personal achievement but also laying the foundations for a legacy of innovation and community enrichment.

Let this book be your guide as you venture towards mastering the art of business. It is not just about reaching the pinnacle of individual success but about forging a path that benefits society at large. Through dedication, insight, and the strategies outlined in these pages, you are embarking on a journey that promises to transform not only your life but also the world around you.

About This Book

Crafted with meticulous attention to detail, the book captures the reader's attention from the very beginning, offering a clear and compelling journey through its pages. It is divided into five distinct parts, each comprising five engaging chapters, presenting a well-structured path toward enlightenment. The content is enriched with motivational quotes, heartwarming stories, and insightful wisdom, making complex subjects more understandable and relatable for those on a quest for personal growth. This thoughtful organization ensures that readers can easily navigate through the book, finding both inspiration and practical advice that resonate with their own life experiences.

Each chapter of the book is deeply influenced by the author's personal journey, adding a layer of authenticity and relatability to the narrative. The author's experiences serve as a foundation for the actionable advice provided, allowing readers to see real-world applications of the concepts discussed. At the end of each chapter, readers are presented with a concise summary of key points and strategies for incorporating these insights into their daily lives. This approach not only makes the content more digestible but also serves as a constant companion for readers, guiding them away from common mistakes and encouraging ongoing personal development.

The book transcends its status as a mere literary piece, becoming a potential catalyst for profound transformation in its readers' lives. Its growing popularity online, particularly for the chapters that have had the most significant impact, attests to its ability to touch the lives of many. Readers inspired by the book's insights often find themselves adopting new viewpoints and pursuing personal growth, highlighting the deep and lasting influence the book has on its audience. The testimonials of individuals who have been moved to change their paths underscore the powerful and transformative nature of the book's message.

At the heart of the book is a structured framework that demystifies complex concepts through engaging storytelling and actionable advice. It acts as a mentor, guiding readers towards making wiser choices and fostering both personal and professional growth. By offering a roadmap for navigating life's challenges, the book encourages readers to pursue self-discovery and improvement. This guidance is instrumental in empowering individuals to take steps toward change, reinforcing the book's role as a valuable tool for personal transformation.

Book Summary

"Unlocking Excellence" is an indispensable roadmap for those poised to conquer the modern business world, authored by a seasoned expert in entrepreneurship and business strategy. It meticulously unpacks the foundational principles and tactics essential for triumph, beginning with an insightful analysis of the latest market trends, technological breakthroughs, and consumer behavior shifts. The book underscores the pivotal role of adaptability, encouraging businesses to remain agile and responsive to the rapid changes that define today's economic environment, setting the groundwork for a deeper understanding of business success.

The narrative stresses the critical importance of goal setting in the business arena, guiding readers through the formulation of SMART (Specific, Measurable, Achievable, Relevant, Time-bound) objectives. It further emphasizes the necessity of regular goal review to maintain alignment with the dynamic nature of business aims. Focusing on leadership, the text offers an exhaustive examination of various leadership models, the transformative power of a constructive organizational culture, and the profound effect of leading by example, aiming to empower leaders to motivate their teams and cultivate a setting where excellence is the norm.

"Unlocking Excellence" delves into strategic planning as an essential mechanism for navigating a business towards its overarching aspirations. It outlines a methodical approach for conducting SWOT (Strengths, Weaknesses, Opportunities, Threats) analyses and crafting potent growth strategies. The discourse extends into financial stewardship, addressing critical topics like budget formulation, cash flow management, and prudent investment, crucial for fostering business growth and sustainability, thereby arming readers with the acumen to make savvy financial choices that drive their ventures forward.

In discussing marketing and branding, the book provides a thorough examination of modern strategies, spotlighting the transformative influence of digital marketing and social media in establishing brand credibility and consistently delivering value to customers. It accentuates the significance of customer relationship management, offering strategies for customer engagement, feedback acquisition, and loyalty enhancement. Concluding with a call for relentless pursuit of learning and adaptation, "Unlocking Excellence" positions these principles as the bedrock of sustained success in the fluid business landscape, marking the publication as an essential compendium for emerging entrepreneurs and seasoned business leaders alike.

Each chapter of this guide is a beacon for those navigating the complex terrains of the business world, illuminating the path to success with strategic insights and actionable advice. It invites readers to embrace a mindset of growth and resilience, essential for thriving amidst the challenges and opportunities of today's business environment. By integrating the lessons from "Unlocking Excellence," readers are equipped to chart a course of continuous improvement and strategic innovation, essential for achieving and surpassing their business goals.

The book's exploration of leadership and organizational culture serves as a reminder of the profound impact that visionary leadership and a positive work environment have on achieving business objectives. It provides a blueprint for leaders to inspire, influence, and drive their teams towards shared success. Through its comprehensive analysis and expert recommendations, "Unlocking Excellence" acts as a catalyst for transformational leadership and organizational excellence.

Financial acumen is highlighted as a cornerstone of business mastery, with the book offering invaluable guidance on navigating the complexities of financial planning and management. It prepares readers to tackle financial challenges head-on, ensuring the financial health and growth of their enterprises. This section is a treasure trove of wisdom for those looking to secure their business's financial future and achieve long-term success.

The emphasis on marketing and branding reiterates the importance of connecting with customers and building lasting relationships in today's digital age. "Unlocking Excellence" showcases strategies that leverage technology and innovation to meet customer needs and exceed their expectations. It serves as a comprehensive guide for creating a powerful brand presence and securing a competitive edge in the marketplace.

"Unlocking Excellence" champions the ethos of continuous learning and adaptation as indispensable to navigating the ever-changing business landscape. It inspires readers to remain curious, open to new ideas, and resilient in the face of adversity, ensuring their businesses not only survive but thrive. This book is not just a guide to business success; it's a manifesto for building a legacy of innovation, impact, and enduring achievement.

Key Book Lessons

1. **Understanding Business Fundamentals**: It's crucial to grasp the core concepts of how businesses operate, including understanding the market, knowing your competitors, and being clear on what your business offers. This foundation is essential for any successful business strategy.

2. **Crafting a Vision and Mission Statement:** A compelling vision and mission statement not only guide a company's strategic direction but also inspire and align the team towards common goals. It's the backbone of a company's identity and influences all decision-making processes.

3. **Building a Strong Organizational Culture:** The strength of a business is often rooted in its culture. Cultivating an environment where employees are motivated, values are shared, and teamwork is emphasized can lead to increased productivity and satisfaction. Organizational culture is a key factor in attracting and retaining top talent.

4. **Navigating Legal and Regulatory Compliance:** Understanding and adhering to the legal and regulatory framework of your industry is non-negotiable. Compliance protects the company from fines, penalties, and reputational damage. It also ensures ethical standards are maintained.

5. **Embracing Ethical Business Practices:** Ethical practices are at the heart of long-term success. They foster trust among customers, employees, and stakeholders. Ethical behavior should be a core aspect of a company's strategy, influencing how products are developed, how customers are treated, and how problems are solved.

6. **Developing a Business Strategy:** A strong business strategy is crucial for setting the direction and scope of a company over the long term. This involves defining your unique value proposition, understanding your competitive advantage, and identifying your target market. A well-crafted strategy aligns all aspects of the business towards common goals and objectives, driving growth and profitability.

7. **Conducting Market Research and Analysis:** Knowledge is power in the business world. Conducting thorough market research and analysis helps you understand your industry, competition, and customer preferences. This insight is vital for making informed decisions, identifying opportunities for innovation, and tailoring your products or services to meet the needs of your target audience.

8. **Creating a Comprehensive Business Plan:** A comprehensive business plan is a roadmap for success. It outlines your business goals, strategies, financial forecasts, and the steps needed to achieve your objectives. This document is

essential not just for guiding your own decision-making process, but also for communicating your vision to potential investors, partners, and stakeholders.

9. **Setting SMART Goals for Success:** Goals provide direction and motivation, and setting SMART (Specific, Measurable, Achievable, Relevant, Time-bound) goals ensures they are clear and attainable. SMART goals help break down your vision into actionable steps, enabling you to measure progress and adjust your strategies as needed to stay on track towards achieving your business objectives.

10. **Implementing Effective Change Management:** In a rapidly evolving business environment, the ability to manage change effectively is critical for sustaining success. This involves preparing your organization to adapt to changes, managing the transition process smoothly, and minimizing resistance from employees. Effective change management ensures your business remains agile, competitive, and aligned with your strategic goals.

11. **Identifying Target Markets and Customers:** Understanding who your ideal customers are and what markets they occupy is foundational to business success. Identifying your target market involves analyzing demographic, geographic, psychographic, and behavioral characteristics to tailor your products, services, and marketing efforts. This focused approach ensures that your business resources are used efficiently to attract and serve the customers most likely to purchase from you.

12. **Developing a Brand Identity and Positioning:** Your brand is more than just your logo or product; it's the emotional and psychological relationship you have with your customers. Developing a strong brand identity and clear positioning helps differentiate your business in a crowded market. It involves defining your brand's personality, values, and the unique benefits you offer, making your business memorable and appealing to your target audience.

13. **Leveraging Digital Marketing Channels:** In today's digital age, leveraging online marketing channels is crucial for reaching and engaging your target audience. This includes utilizing social media, email marketing, SEO, and content marketing to build brand awareness, generate leads, and drive sales. Digital marketing offers the advantage of targeting specific demographics with precision and measuring the effectiveness of your campaigns in real time.

14. **Mastering the Art of Selling:** Sales are the lifeblood of any business, making it essential to master the art of selling. This involves understanding the needs and pain points of your customers, building strong relationships, and effectively communicating the value of your products or services. Successful selling is not just about closing deals but about solving problems and creating value for customers, leading to repeat business and referrals.

15. **Cultivating Customer Relationships and Loyalty:** Lasting business success comes from not just acquiring new customers but retaining them over time. Cultivating strong customer relationships and loyalty involves providing exceptional customer service, listening to customer feedback, and consistently exceeding expectations. Loyal customers are more likely to make repeat purchases and become brand advocates, driving word-of-mouth referrals and sustainable growth.

16. **Managing Finances and Budgets:** Effective financial management and budgeting are crucial for the sustainability and growth of any business. This involves planning your finances to ensure that you can cover your costs while investing in growth opportunities. Proper budgeting helps you forecast future revenue, manage cash flow, allocate resources efficiently, and prepare for unforeseen expenses. Staying on top of your finances enables you to make informed decisions and keeps your business financially healthy.

17. **Understanding Financial Statements:** Financial statements are essential tools for analyzing the financial health of your business. They provide a snapshot of your company's financial performance and position at a given time. Mastering the ability to read and interpret income statements, balance sheets, and cash flow statements gives you insights into your business's profitability, liquidity, and cash flows. This knowledge is vital for strategic planning, identifying trends, and attracting investors or lenders.

18. **Securing Funding and Investment:** Access to capital is critical for starting and growing your business. Securing funding and investment can come from various sources, including loans, venture capital, angel investors, or crowdfunding. Understanding the pros and cons of each funding source and what investors look for in a potential investment can help you prepare a compelling pitch, demonstrating the viability and potential of your business to secure the necessary capital.

19. **Optimizing Supply Chain and Logistics:** An efficient supply chain and logistics operation can significantly impact your business's bottom line. Optimizing these areas involves coordinating and streamlining processes to reduce costs, improve speed, and ensure the quality of goods from suppliers to customers. Strategies may include negotiating better terms with suppliers, investing in logistics technology, and adopting just-in-time inventory management to reduce waste and enhance customer satisfaction.

20. **Enhancing Operational Efficiency and Productivity:** Improving operational efficiency and productivity is key to maximizing profits and staying competitive. This can be achieved through process optimization, technology adoption, and workforce management. Identifying bottlenecks, automating repetitive tasks, and empowering employees through training and development can lead to significant

improvements in productivity. Continuous improvement should be a goal in all operations to reduce costs, improve quality, and increase output.

21. **Fostering Creativity and Innovation:** Creativity and innovation are the lifeblood of any successful business. Encouraging an environment where new ideas are welcomed and risk-taking is supported can lead to breakthrough products, services, and business models. This involves empowering employees, investing in research and development, and staying open to external sources of innovation. Companies that continuously innovate can differentiate themselves in the marketplace and stay ahead of the competition.

22. **Harnessing Technology for Competitive Advantage:** Technology can be a powerful tool to gain a competitive edge. Leveraging the latest technological advances, such as AI, blockchain, or IoT, can improve efficiency, enhance customer experiences, and open up new revenue streams. Businesses need to stay abreast of technological trends and assess how these can be integrated into their operations and offerings to stay relevant and competitive.

23. **Expanding into New Markets and Industries:** Growth often requires looking beyond current markets and industries. Expanding into new areas can diversify revenue streams and reduce dependency on a single market. This strategy requires thorough research to understand new customer needs, regulatory requirements, and competitive landscapes. Successful expansion strategies might include partnerships, acquisitions, or developing new products tailored to these markets.

24. **Scaling Your Business for Growth:** Scaling a business involves more than just growing sales; it requires building the capacity to support larger operations without compromising quality or efficiency. This can include investing in systems and infrastructure, developing scalable processes, and hiring the right talent to manage growth. Strategic planning and careful management are crucial to ensure that scaling efforts align with the company's long-term vision and capabilities.

25. **Nurturing a Culture of Continuous Improvement:** A culture of continuous improvement helps businesses remain agile and responsive to changes in the market. This involves regularly evaluating and improving processes, products, and services. Encouraging feedback from employees and customers, learning from failures, and celebrating successes are all part of fostering a mindset geared towards constant betterment. This culture ensures that the business can adapt and evolve over time, sustaining its success.

Ten Actions to Take

1. **Grasp Business Fundamentals:** Understand core business operations, market dynamics, and competitor landscapes to build a solid foundation.

2. **Define Vision and Culture:** Create clear vision and mission statements to guide your strategy and foster a strong organizational culture that promotes teamwork and productivity.

3. **Comply with Regulations:** Ensure adherence to legal and regulatory requirements to protect your business from penalties and maintain ethical standards.

4. **Strategize and Plan:** Develop a comprehensive business strategy and plan, outlining your value proposition, target market, and financial projections to direct growth.

5. **Set and Achieve Goals:** Implement SMART goals to break down your vision into actionable steps, providing clear direction and measurable outcomes.

6. **Engage in Market Research:** Conduct thorough market research and analysis to understand customer needs and preferences, informing product development and marketing strategies.

7. **Build Brand and Sell Effectively:** Develop a strong brand identity and master the art of selling to communicate value, build customer relationships, and drive sales.

8. **Manage Finances Wisely:** Practice effective financial management, understand financial statements, and secure appropriate funding to ensure sustainability and facilitate growth.

9. **Innovate and Utilize Technology:** Foster creativity and innovation while harnessing the latest technology to gain a competitive edge and improve efficiency.

10. **Expand and Scale:** Explore new markets for expansion and carefully manage scaling efforts to grow your business sustainably, ensuring long-term success.

Ten Mistakes to Avoid

1. **Neglecting Core Business Principles:** Do not overlook the fundamentals of your business, including market understanding and competitive analysis, as it leads to strategic errors.

2. **Disregarding Vision and Culture:** Avoid ignoring the development of clear vision and mission statements, as well as nurturing a positive organizational culture, which are critical for guiding and motivating your team.

3. **Ignoreing Legal and Ethical Standards:** Never bypass legal compliance and ethical considerations; such actions can result in severe legal and reputational consequences.

4. **Overlooking Strategic Planning:** Do not operate without a coherent business strategy and a comprehensive business plan, as these are essential for directing growth and securing funding.

5. **Setting Unclear Goals:** Avoid setting vague or unrealistic goals, which can lead to confusion and inefficiency within your organization.

6. **Resisting Change and Innovation:** Do not resist adapting to changes in the market and industry, and avoid stifling creativity and innovation, as these are necessary for staying competitive.

7. **Misunderstanding Your Audience:** Do not misidentify your target market or neglect the development of your brand and customer relationships, which are crucial for effective marketing and sustained business growth.

8. **Failing in Financial Management:** Avoid poor financial management practices, including neglecting financial statements and budgeting, which are vital for maintaining the financial health of your business.

9. **Underutilizing Technology and Digital Marketing:** Do not ignore the benefits of leveraging technology and digital marketing strategies, as they are key to operational efficiency and reaching your target audience.

10. **Mishandling Scaling and Expansion:** Avoid improper scaling and not considering expansion opportunities, as these actions can limit growth potential and lead to operational strain.

Part One: Foundations of Business

"Foundations of Business" immerses participants in the vital principles of business, including management, marketing, finance, and operations. Through interactive case studies and exercises, it enhances critical thinking and offers insights into market dynamics and strategic planning essential for success. This hands-on approach ensures learners can apply theoretical knowledge to real-world challenges, preparing them to make strategic decisions and foster growth in their organizations.

Chapter 1: Understanding Business Fundamentals

Embarking on the journey of business success in today's competitive market requires a solid grasp of its fundamental principles. These core concepts act as a sturdy foundation, allowing entrepreneurs to navigate through the ebbs and flows of market dynamics with confidence and agility. This chapter is crafted to equip you with the critical knowledge and skills needed to steer through the complexities of the business world with assurance and expertise.

A deep dive into strategic planning, financial management, and marketing unveils the inner workings of thriving businesses. This exploration provides you with a holistic view, empowering you to spot opportunities, mitigate risks, and drive your venture towards sustainable growth. The insights gained here are invaluable, offering you the foresight to make strategic choices that resonate with your overarching goals.

The significance of comprehending business fundamentals cannot be overstated, especially in an era where adaptability is key to survival and success. It lays the groundwork for informed decision-making and flexibility, which are indispensable in responding to market changes. This chapter aims to arm you with the essential tools for a confident and proficient journey through the business landscape.

By mastering these essential business concepts, you position yourself to face the challenges and seize the opportunities that lie ahead. This knowledge becomes a beacon, guiding your path to strategic and informed choices that propel your venture forward. In doing so, you not only navigate the present landscape but also pave the way for future success in the ever-evolving world of business.

Understanding the fundamentals of business is pivotal for anyone aiming to make their mark in today's marketplace. This chapter offers a roadmap to acquiring the necessary knowledge and skills for navigating the business world with confidence. Embracing these principles sets the stage for a rewarding journey of growth, innovation, and enduring success.

Inspirational Quote

> *"Success in business requires training and discipline and hard work. But if you're not frightened by these things, the opportunities are just as great today as they ever were."* - David Rockefeller

Vision and Purpose

A well-defined vision acts as a beacon for businesses, illuminating the path ahead with clarity and direction, especially during tough times. It instills a deep sense of purpose, sparking a fire of passion within team members, motivating them to push through obstacles with grit and determination. This drive, rooted in a clear purpose, enables entrepreneurs to establish a unique presence in the competitive world of business.

Entrepreneurs with a clear commitment to their vision navigate the complexities of the marketplace with skill and agility. Their determination to succeed drives continuous adaptation and innovation, essential for staying relevant in the dynamic business environment. This relentless pursuit of their goals not only helps them withstand challenges but also flourish, setting a strong foundation for lasting success.

The strength of a vision lies in its ability to unify and inspire, creating a collective force moving towards a common goal. This unity fosters an environment of innovation and creativity, where every challenge is viewed as an opportunity for growth and learning. It's the shared commitment to this vision that transforms ordinary individuals into extraordinary teams, capable of achieving remarkable feats.

In the world of business, a strong vision and purpose act as the cornerstone for building enduring enterprises. They provide the strategic focus needed to make informed decisions, prioritize actions, and allocate resources effectively. This strategic clarity is what differentiates successful businesses from the rest, enabling them to capture opportunities and scale new heights.

Ultimately, the journey of entrepreneurship is about more than just financial gain; it's a quest for impact and fulfillment, guided by a compelling vision. This journey challenges entrepreneurs to remain resilient and visionary, no matter the obstacles. It is this unwavering commitment to a greater purpose that leads to true success, leaving a lasting legacy in the world of business.

Value Creation

In the journey to business excellence, placing the emphasis on creating real value is a foundational strategy. Entrepreneurs excel by pinpointing gaps in the market and ingeniously crafting solutions to fill these voids, setting the stage for enduring growth. Every new product or service launched should aim to significantly improve customer experiences, building a strong base of loyal supporters and securing the business's future.

Focusing on value creation not only ensures customer contentment but also strengthens a company's competitive position. By reliably presenting solutions that meet genuine needs and elevate user experiences, businesses build a solid reputation for innovation and dependability. This unwavering commitment to prioritizing value helps to maintain a loyal customer base while simultaneously drawing in new patrons, propelling the company towards ongoing success and development.

Moreover, businesses that consistently center their strategies around value creation stand out in their industries. This approach not only meets but often exceeds customer expectations, setting a high standard for competitors. The ripple effect of prioritizing value creation is profound, leading to enhanced brand perception and increased market share.

In addition, a value-centric business model encourages a culture of continuous improvement and creativity among employees. Staff members are motivated to innovate and push boundaries, knowing their contributions lead to meaningful customer experiences. This internal drive fosters a dynamic workplace atmosphere, further amplifying the company's ability to innovate and grow.

Ultimately, the commitment to value creation is a powerful catalyst for building a sustainable and thriving business. By consistently focusing on enriching customers' lives through innovative products and services, companies not only achieve financial success but also make a positive impact on society. This virtuous cycle of value creation and delivery is the hallmark of truly successful businesses, setting a beacon for others to follow.

Strategic Planning

Strategic planning stands as the cornerstone for businesses aiming for lasting growth and the ability to adapt to change. Through detailed analysis and forecasting future trends, organizations can strategically position themselves to thrive in the competitive market landscape. This forward-thinking approach not only opens doors to new opportunities but also provides the agility needed to overcome potential obstacles with grace.

In the realm of strategic planning, flexibility is an invaluable trait for entrepreneurs. This adaptability allows them to swiftly adjust their course in reaction to shifts in market conditions or unforeseen events. Merging strategic vision with the capacity to adapt ensures businesses remain at the forefront, securing their place in an ever-changing environment.

By embracing strategic planning, companies can forge a path that leads to sustainable advancement and resilience against market volatilities. This process empowers them to identify and seize opportunities that align with their long-term objectives. Consequently, businesses are better prepared to face the future, equipped with the knowledge and flexibility to tackle challenges head-on.

A well-crafted strategy acts as a roadmap, guiding businesses through the complexities of the market with clarity and purpose. It fosters an environment where quick adaptation is not just possible but encouraged, enabling companies to pivot effectively when necessary. Such agility is crucial for sustaining competitiveness and fostering innovation in a dynamic business world.

Ultimately, strategic planning is about envisioning the future and preparing to meet it with confidence. It combines analytical insight with the readiness to evolve, creating a powerful formula for enduring success. For businesses committed to making a mark, the integration of strategic foresight and adaptability is the key to navigating the uncertain waters of the global market with assurance and prowess.

Financial Literacy

Mastering financial literacy is a key to unlocking the potential of any entrepreneurial journey. It equips business owners with the ability to steward resources wisely, make strategic decisions, and confidently step through the intricacies of financial markets. This knowledge lays the groundwork for maintaining a healthy financial state for their businesses, ensuring long-term growth and stability.

Furthermore, a deep understanding of finance opens doors to new opportunities and safeguards against unforeseen pitfalls. It allows entrepreneurs to strategically allocate funds, streamline their cash flows, and boost their bottom lines. This financial acumen becomes a powerful lever for growth, positioning businesses to capitalize on opportunities and navigate through economic challenges with agility.

Financial literacy is not just about numbers; it's a language of business that, when fluently spoken, can lead to unparalleled success. Entrepreneurs who are adept in financial principles can foresee potential financial hurdles and strategically steer their ventures away from them. This proactive approach to finance is essential in crafting a resilient and flourishing business.

In today's fast-paced and competitive business environment, being financially literate is more important than ever. It enables entrepreneurs to not only survive but thrive, adapting to market changes and emerging stronger. Financial literacy lays a solid foundation upon which businesses can build innovative strategies, foster growth, and achieve sustainable success.

At its core, financial literacy is a critical asset for anyone looking to make a mark in the entrepreneurial world. It offers the clarity needed to make informed decisions, the confidence to pursue ambitious goals, and the capability to turn visions into reality. For entrepreneurs, investing in financial literacy is investing in the future of their businesses, setting the stage for success in an ever-evolving economic landscape.

Adaptability and Resilience

Adaptability and resilience are essential for achieving success. Entrepreneurs view change as an opportunity to innovate and move forward. Their ability to stay flexible in their approaches and operations allows them to confidently tackle challenges, transforming obstacles into opportunities for development.

Entrepreneurs understand that change is not something to fear but an engine for progress. By embracing change, they can stay ahead of the curve, continuously evolving their business models and strategies. This mindset helps them to not only survive but thrive in dynamic market conditions, setting the stage for long-term success.

Perseverance is a key trait of successful entrepreneurs. They face adversity with a steadfast determination, seeing each failure as a lesson and each setback as a chance to grow. This resilience fuels their ambition, pushing them to keep moving forward despite the odds.

Every challenge encountered on the entrepreneurial path serves as a building block for strength and wisdom. Successful business leaders use these experiences to sharpen their skills and strategies. With each hurdle they overcome, they grow more capable and prepared for future challenges, paving the way for new achievements.

The journey of entrepreneurship is marked by continuous learning and growth. Those who succeed are those who refuse to give up, using every setback as a springboard for success. As they navigate the ups and downs of their ventures, they not only achieve their goals but also inspire others to pursue their dreams with courage and resilience.

Conclusion

Entrepreneurs who adopt key principles lay a strong foundation for enduring success in the dynamic world of business. With a blend of clear vision, defined purpose, and a steadfast commitment to excellence, they skillfully overcome challenges and seize opportunities with enthusiasm. Every choice and action they take is a testament to their entrepreneurial spirit, fueling innovation and advancement in the business sector.

These trailblazers, as they journey forward, continue to redefine the landscape of business with their innovative ideas. Their ability to remain resilient in tough times and adapt to new environments distinguishes them as true innovators in their fields. By living the essence of entrepreneurship, they motivate others and make a lasting impact on the business community.

Their journey is not just about personal achievement but also about inspiring a wave of future leaders. By sharing their knowledge and experiences, they cultivate a culture of continuous learning and growth. This legacy of mentorship ensures that the spirit of entrepreneurship thrives, fostering a community of leaders ready to face tomorrow's challenges.

In navigating the complexities of business, these entrepreneurs demonstrate the power of strategic thinking and ethical leadership. Their decisions are guided by a deep understanding of their market and a commitment to serving their community. This approach not only drives their companies forward but also contributes to the greater good, setting a benchmark for responsible business practices.

The stories of these entrepreneurs serve as a beacon of inspiration for aspiring business leaders worldwide. By embracing resilience, innovation, and ethical principles, they illustrate that success is not just about financial gains but also about making a positive difference in the world. Their legacy encourages others to pursue their entrepreneurial dreams with courage and integrity, promising a brighter future for global commerce.

CASE STUDIES: Understanding Business Fundamentals

Case Study 1: Small Business Startup

Background:

Sarah, a recent graduate with a passion for baking, decides to start her own cupcake business. She has a talent for creating delicious and visually appealing cupcakes and believes there's a market for her products in her local community. With some savings and support from her family, she embarks on her entrepreneurial journey.

Challenges:

- **Market Research:** Sarah initially underestimates the importance of market research. She assumes that because she loves baking and her friends rave about her cupcakes, there will automatically be demand for her products. However, she fails to consider factors such as local competition, target demographics, and pricing strategies.

- **Financial Management:** Sarah struggles with financial management, as she lacks experience in budgeting and forecasting. She overspends on ingredients and equipment, leading to cash flow problems. Without a clear understanding of her costs and profit margins, she finds it difficult to set prices that are competitive yet profitable.

- **Marketing Strategy:** Sarah initially relies solely on word-of-mouth and social media posts to promote her business. While this generates some initial interest, she realizes that she needs a more comprehensive marketing strategy to reach a wider audience and stand out from competitors.

Solutions:

- **Market Research:** Sarah conducts thorough market research by surveying potential customers, analyzing competitor offerings, and studying local trends. This helps her identify gaps in the market and tailor her products and pricing to meet customer needs.

- **Financial Management:** Sarah seeks advice from a small business advisor and enrolls in a basic accounting course to improve her financial literacy. She develops a detailed budget and tracks her expenses diligently, allowing her to better manage cash flow and make informed decisions about pricing and inventory.

- **Marketing Strategy:** Sarah diversifies her marketing efforts by investing in targeted online advertising, collaborating with local businesses for cross-promotions, and participating in community events and farmers' markets. She also enhances her social media presence with professional photography and customer testimonials, showcasing the quality and uniqueness of her cupcakes.

Outcome:

With a solid understanding of business fundamentals and strategic improvements in market research, financial management, and marketing strategy, Sarah's cupcake business experiences steady growth. She builds a loyal customer base and expands her offerings to include custom cakes and catering services. Despite facing challenges along the way, Sarah's perseverance and commitment to learning pay off as her business becomes a beloved fixture in the local community.

Case Study 2: Corporate Expansion

Background:

ABC Corporation, a multinational technology company, decides to expand its operations into a new market to capitalize on emerging opportunities and diversify its revenue streams. After conducting extensive market analysis, the company identifies a growing demand for its products and services in Southeast Asia and sets ambitious growth targets for the region.

Challenges:

- **Market Entry Strategy:** ABC Corporation faces the challenge of choosing the most suitable market entry strategy. The company must decide whether to establish wholly-owned subsidiaries, form joint ventures with local partners, or pursue other modes of entry. Each option comes with its own risks and benefits, requiring careful consideration of factors such as regulatory environment, cultural differences, and competitive landscape.

- **Operational Efficiency:** As ABC Corporation expands into Southeast Asia, it encounters operational challenges related to supply chain management, logistics, and workforce development. Differences in infrastructure, labor regulations, and business practices across countries pose hurdles to achieving operational efficiency and maintaining consistent quality standards.

- **Cultural Adaptation:** To succeed in a new market, ABC Corporation must adapt its products, marketing messages, and corporate culture to resonate with local customs and preferences. Failure to understand and respect cultural nuances could lead to misunderstandings, mistrust, and ultimately, business failure.

Solutions:

3. **Strategic planning serves as a roadmap** for businesses to navigate through uncertainty, identify emerging trends, and capitalize on opportunities for growth and expansion. By setting clear objectives, conducting thorough analysis, and implementing proactive strategies, companies can position themselves for success, adapt to changing market conditions, and stay ahead of the competition.

4. **Financial literacy empowers business leaders** and decision-makers to effectively manage resources, allocate capital, and mitigate risks, enabling informed decision-making and sustainable financial performance. By cultivating a deep understanding of financial principles, metrics, and best practices, organizations can optimize their financial health, drive profitability, and achieve long-term viability.

5. **Adaptability and resilience are indispensable** qualities for thriving in a dynamic and rapidly evolving business landscape, as they enable companies to effectively respond to challenges, pivot in times of uncertainty, and seize new opportunities for growth. By fostering a culture of adaptability, embracing change, and learning from setbacks, businesses can build resilience, drive innovation, and emerge stronger from adversity.

Five Actions to Take

1. **Define a clear vision and purpose** for your business: Establishing a compelling vision and purpose serves as a guiding light for your organization, aligning every action and decision with overarching goals. By articulating your values and mission, you not only inspire stakeholders but also create a strong foundation for growth and sustainability.

2. **Continuously innovate to create value** for your customers: Embrace a culture of innovation to stay ahead in a competitive market, consistently seeking new ways to meet and exceed customer expectations. By prioritizing creativity and experimentation, you can uncover fresh opportunities for product enhancement or service improvement, fostering long-term loyalty and satisfaction among your customer base.

3. **Develop a strategic plan** that aligns with your long-term goals: Craft a strategic roadmap that outlines clear objectives and initiatives, ensuring alignment with your organization's vision and long-term aspirations. Through careful planning and execution, you can navigate complexities and capitalize on opportunities, driving sustainable growth and success over time.

4. **Invest in financial literacy** to effectively manage your resources: Enhance your understanding of financial principles and practices to make informed decisions and optimize resource allocation. By mastering concepts such as budgeting, cash flow management, and investment strategies, you can mitigate risks, maximize profitability, and position your business for long-term financial health and stability.

5. **Cultivate adaptability and resilience** to navigate challenges with grace: Embrace change as a constant in today's dynamic business environment, fostering adaptability and resilience among your team members. By fostering a culture of flexibility and learning, you can empower individuals to respond effectively to unexpected challenges, turning obstacles into opportunities for growth and innovation.

Five Actions Not to Take

1. **Neglecting to define a clear vision and purpose** for your business can lead to confusion among employees and customers alike. Without a defined direction, it's challenging to align strategies and initiatives towards meaningful goals, hindering overall growth and success.

2. **Focusing solely on short-term gains at** the expense of long-term sustainability may provide immediate gratification, but it often results in detrimental consequences down the line. Businesses that prioritize sustainable growth over quick profits are better equipped to weather economic fluctuations and build enduring relationships with stakeholders.

3. **Ignoring the importance of strategic planning** and foresight leaves businesses vulnerable to unforeseen challenges and missed opportunities. By proactively analyzing market trends and anticipating future needs, companies can position themselves for success and stay ahead of the competition.

4. **Overlooking the significance of financial literacy** in business decision-making can lead to costly mistakes and financial instability. Understanding key financial concepts empowers leaders to make informed choices, allocate resources effectively, and mitigate risks, ultimately fostering a healthier bottom line.

5. **Resisting change and failing to adapt** to evolving market dynamics can stagnate business growth and render operations obsolete. Embracing innovation and remaining flexible enables organizations to capitalize on emerging trends, stay relevant in competitive industries, and sustain long-term success.

Unlocking Excellence: A Blueprint for Achieving Business Success   Business Lessons

Chapter 2: Crafting a Vision and Mission Statement

Creating a vision and mission statement is like laying the foundation for a magnificent edifice that stands the test of time. It sets the stage for defining what individuals, teams, and organizations stand for and aspire to achieve. Much like a lighthouse guiding vessels in the dark, a robust vision and mission offer clarity, bring people together, and fuel their resolve to move forward, even in the face of adversity. This process is not just about setting goals; it's about discovering and affirming our deepest values and ambitions.

Embarking on the journey of defining these essential principles is akin to setting sail towards our most cherished dreams. It involves delving deep into the heart of what makes an organization unique and finding the words that capture its true essence and direction. This chapter is dedicated to unraveling the art of creating vision and mission statements that resonate deeply and inspire action. Through careful reflection and alignment with core values, we can forge a common path that unites and propels us toward shared objectives, cementing a culture of collaboration and achievement.

Crafting these statements requires more than just strategic thinking; it calls for a heartfelt commitment to the greater good that an organization seeks to serve. It's about painting a vivid picture of the future we strive to create and the path we will take to get there. By embracing this challenge, we unlock the potential to transform our collective aspirations into reality, setting a standard of excellence and purpose that guides every decision and action.

This endeavor is a testament to the power of shared vision and purpose in driving organizational success. When we articulate a vision and mission that reflect our true intentions and values, we create a strong foundation that supports growth, innovation, and resilience. It empowers every member of the organization to contribute their best, knowing they are part of something larger than themselves, working towards a common goal.

In mastering the craft of developing meaningful vision and mission statements, we not only chart a course for success but also inspire a legacy of impact and transformation. This is the essence of leadership and strategic thinking—envisioning a better future and taking decisive steps to make it a reality. Through this process, organizations can navigate the complexities of the modern world with confidence, inspiring others to join them in their quest for excellence and making a lasting difference in the world.

Inspirational Quote

> *"Vision without action is merely a dream. Action without vision just passes the time. Vision with action can change the world."* - Joel A. Barker

Clarity of Purpose

Creating a vision and mission statement is like laying the foundation for a magnificent edifice that stands the test of time. It sets the stage for defining what individuals, teams, and organizations stand for and aspire to achieve. Much like a lighthouse guiding vessels in the dark, a robust vision and mission offer clarity, bring people together, and fuel their resolve to move forward, even in the face of adversity. This process is not just about setting goals; it's about discovering and affirming our deepest values and ambitions.

Embarking on the journey of defining these essential principles is akin to setting sail towards our most cherished dreams. It involves delving deep into the heart of what makes an organization unique and finding the words that capture its true essence and direction. This chapter is dedicated to unraveling the art of creating vision and mission statements that resonate deeply and inspire action. Through careful reflection and alignment with core values, we can forge a common path that unites and propels us toward shared objectives, cementing a culture of collaboration and achievement.

Crafting these statements requires more than just strategic thinking; it calls for a heartfelt commitment to the greater good that an organization seeks to serve. It's about painting a vivid picture of the future we strive to create and the path we will take to get there. By embracing this challenge, we unlock the potential to transform our collective aspirations into reality, setting a standard of excellence and purpose that guides every decision and action.

This endeavor is a testament to the power of shared vision and purpose in driving organizational success. When we articulate a vision and mission that reflect our true intentions and values, we create a strong foundation that supports growth, innovation, and resilience. It empowers every member of the organization to contribute their best, knowing they are part of something larger than themselves, working towards a common goal.

In mastering the craft of developing meaningful vision and mission statements, we not only chart a course for success but also inspire a legacy of impact and transformation. This is the essence of leadership and strategic thinking—envisioning a better future and taking decisive steps to make it a reality. Through this process, organizations can navigate the complexities of the modern world with confidence, inspiring others to join them in their quest for excellence and making a lasting difference in the world.

Alignment with Values

Your core values are the bedrock upon which your vision and mission should stand, offering a steadfast anchor that defines who you are and the purpose you pursue. In every endeavor you undertake, it's crucial that these values shine through, showcasing the heart and soul of your identity and principles. Above all, integrity must be the keystone of your foundation, acting as the essential trust currency that sustains and nurtures all your relationships and projects.

Creating a vision and mission that truly resonate means tapping into your deepest beliefs, aligning them so closely with your actions that they echo the authenticity of your spirit. This alignment forges a powerful connection with your purpose, kindling the spark of inspiration in others and gathering a community of support around your goals. Your vision and mission then become beacons of light, guiding you and those who follow you towards a future marked by dedication and a relentless pursuit of those values that define you.

In crafting these guiding statements, you're not just setting goals but weaving the very essence of your being into a narrative that speaks to the soul. It's about more than ambition; it's a declaration of your place in the world and a commitment to lead by example. By doing so, you inspire not only yourself but also those around you to strive for greatness, grounded in the values you hold dear.

The journey towards fulfilling your vision and mission is illuminated by the principles you hold sacred. Let these principles guide your steps, ensuring that every decision, every action, is a reflection of your true self. This unwavering adherence to your core values fosters an environment where trust flourishes, paving the way for meaningful progress and impactful achievements.

Your vision and mission are the narratives you choose to live by, a testament to the values that you refuse to compromise. They are your promise to the world and to yourself, a vow to uphold the highest standards of integrity and authenticity. Embrace them as your compass, guiding your way through challenges and triumphs, and watch as they transform not only your life but also the lives of those you touch.

Inspiring Others

Creating a powerful vision and mission is essential to motivate and inspire others towards meaningful action. By vividly describing what the future could look like, you not only attract people to your cause but also inspire them to become part of something greater than themselves. It's important to infuse every word with passion, conviction, and authenticity, as this helps to build real and lasting connections with those you seek to engage. When individuals can see how they fit into the bigger picture, they feel valued and are more likely to contribute their unique skills and insights.

Authenticity in how you communicate is key to building trust and credibility with your audience. It conveys honesty and integrity, which are crucial in forming strong, meaningful connections. Encouraging others to see themselves as vital contributors to a collective endeavor instills a sense of belonging and dedication to the common goal. This shared sense of purpose is what ultimately drives the group forward, bringing the vision closer to reality.

Moreover, when people believe in the genuineness of your mission, they are more inclined to invest themselves fully in its achievement. This belief transforms their involvement from mere participation to passionate commitment. The collective energy and enthusiasm generated by a group of dedicated individuals can significantly accelerate the journey towards realizing the shared vision.

Additionally, a sense of ownership and personal investment in the mission enhances the effectiveness of the team. When each member feels responsible for the outcome, they bring their best efforts and ideas to the table. This collaborative spirit not only enriches the process but also significantly increases the chances of success.

Crafting an inspirational vision and mission, grounded in authenticity and passion, is a powerful catalyst for change. It not only draws people towards your cause but also unites them in a shared journey of transformation. By fostering a culture of trust, commitment, and collaboration, you create a dynamic force capable of achieving extraordinary results.

Adaptability and Resilience

Navigating the ever-changing landscape of life requires adaptability to be at the forefront of success. Establishing a clear vision and mission grounded in resilience offers a solid base in times of uncertainty, allowing for necessary adjustments along the way. Embracing resilience as a core value turns setbacks into powerful learning experiences, pushing both individuals and organizations towards greater achievements.

Facing challenges head-on and cultivating a mindset that views change as a chance for growth significantly boosts one's adaptability. Instead of fearing the unknown, being prepared and proactive opens the door to capitalizing on opportunities that emerge from new situations. In the constantly shifting world we live in, those who prioritize adaptability and resilience do not just survive; they flourish, using change as a springboard for innovation and progress.

Adaptability isn't just about making it through tough times; it's about evolving with purpose and intention. By viewing every challenge as a stepping stone, we position ourselves to leap towards our goals with confidence and agility. This proactive approach not only prepares us for the unexpected but also empowers us to navigate the journey of life with a sense of control and optimism.

The concept of resilience offers a beacon of hope, illuminating the path through the darkest of times. It teaches us that the essence of progress lies in our ability to recover from setbacks stronger than before. With resilience as our guide, we learn that every failure is not a dead-end but a detour towards success.

Adaptability and resilience are indispensable traits in the quest for personal and professional fulfillment. By embracing these qualities, we unlock the potential to transform challenges into victories and uncertainty into opportunity. This mindset not only sets the stage for enduring success but also fosters a culture of continuous improvement and innovation.

Accountability and Commitment

Setting high standards based on your vision and mission is not just important, it's essential for the growth and integrity of your organization. This commitment to excellence becomes real and influential when it's demonstrated through consistent actions. By nurturing a culture where respect and trust are paramount, everyone feels compelled to uphold these standards, creating a strong foundation of collective accountability.

In the journey towards achieving your goals, it's inevitable to encounter challenges and moments of doubt. However, staying true to your path and maintaining accountability even when times get tough is a testament to your dedication to your organization's vision and mission. This steadfastness not only strengthens your resolve but also inspires your team to remain committed to the cause.

Through fostering a sense of responsibility and high standards, you enable a space where mutual respect and trust thrive. This environment encourages each individual to not only hold themselves accountable but also to support their peers in achieving shared objectives. It's in this space that a true sense of community is built, one that is committed to upholding the organization's core values.

By reinforcing the principles of accountability regularly, you empower your team to overcome obstacles with confidence and resilience. This not only ensures that progress is made towards your strategic goals but also that it is done in a manner that aligns with the organization's ethos. This approach fosters a culture of perseverance and dedication, which is critical for sustained success.

Ultimately, the journey towards excellence is a collective effort, requiring every member of the organization to embody the values of accountability, respect, and trust. By doing so, you not only achieve your immediate goals but also lay the groundwork for long-term success and impact. This culture of accountability becomes the driving force behind your organization, propelling it forward in its mission with integrity and purpose.

Conclusion

Creating a vision and mission statement is more than just putting words on paper; it represents a deep dive into who you are and what you aim to achieve. This process is a powerful exploration of one's deepest aspirations and intentions, shedding light on what truly motivates and inspires. By committing to such an endeavor, individuals open the door to a world where their dreams and values align, setting the stage for incredible achievements.

Every great accomplishment begins with a simple idea, a spark of inspiration that resides in the heart of a visionary. This journey of bringing a vision to life is a testament to the power of belief and the courage to dream big. Remember, the most impactful innovations and societal changes were once just ideas, waiting to be brought to fruition by someone with the conviction to see them through.

In aligning with a meaningful vision and mission, one steps onto a path that is both challenging and rewarding. This alignment is not just about setting goals but about connecting with a purpose that transcends everyday life. It encourages individuals to push beyond their limits, achieving what might have seemed impossible.

Embracing the process of defining your vision and mission is an invitation to transform your life. It is an opportunity to move beyond the ordinary, to create something extraordinary. This journey is about becoming a beacon of inspiration and making a tangible impact in the world.

As you embark on this path, remember the transformative potential that your vision and mission hold. Let them be your guide and your motivation, fueling your determination to achieve your dreams. Stay true to your purpose, and let it propel you toward a future filled with achievement and fulfillment.

CASE STUDIES: Crafting a Vision and Mission Statement

Case Study 1: Tech Start-Up Transformation

Background:

A small tech start-up, specializing in green energy solutions, had grown rapidly in both size and scope. Despite its success, the company struggled with a lack of clear direction and purpose, which was affecting its branding and internal cohesion.

Challenge:

The leadership team recognized the need for a unifying vision and mission to better articulate the company's goals and values, both internally to its employees and externally to its customers and stakeholders. The challenge was to encapsulate the start-up's innovative spirit and commitment to sustainability in these statements.

Process:

- **Workshops and Brainstorming Sessions:** The company organized several workshops involving employees from all levels to gather insights, ideas, and perspectives on what the company truly represented.

- **Market and Internal Research:** An analysis was conducted on market trends, competitor positioning, and internal strengths and weaknesses to ensure the vision and mission would be both aspirational and achievable.

- **Drafting and Feedback:** Multiple drafts were developed, with feedback solicited at each stage from a diverse group of stakeholders, including employees, customers, and industry experts.

Outcome:

The final vision statement, "To innovate sustainable energy solutions for a healthier planet," captured the start-up's commitment to environmental sustainability and technological innovation. The mission statement, "Empowering communities with renewable energy technologies for a sustainable future," clearly defined how the company intended to achieve its vision. These statements provided a clear direction for the company, improved employee alignment with corporate values, and enhanced the brand's image.

Case Study 2: Non-Profit Organization Rebranding

Background:

A mid-sized non-profit focused on education for underprivileged children faced challenges in donor engagement and brand recognition. The organization's broad focus made it difficult to communicate its core objectives and impact effectively.

Challenge:

The non-profit needed to refine its vision and mission statements to better reflect its goals, attract more donors, and increase its impact on the communities it served. The challenge lay in capturing the essence of the diverse programs it offered while maintaining a concise and compelling narrative.

Process:

- **Stakeholder Interviews:** Interviews were conducted with beneficiaries, donors, volunteers, and staff to understand the organization's impact from multiple perspectives.

- **Strategic Alignment:** Leadership teams worked to align the new vision and mission with the strategic plan, ensuring it was both aspirational and grounded in the organization's capabilities.

- **Iterative Development:** Through an iterative process, the organization refined its vision and mission statements, ensuring they were inclusive and representative of its core values and objectives.

Outcome:

The non-profit unveiled its new vision statement, "A world where every child has access to quality education," and its mission statement, "To provide transformative educational programs for children in underprivileged communities." These revised statements helped clarify the organization's focus and were instrumental in a successful rebranding campaign. They facilitated improved engagement with donors and volunteers, leading to increased funding and expanded programs.

Conclusion:

In both cases, crafting effective vision and mission statements was a collaborative and strategic process that required deep understanding of the organization's core values, objectives, and the environment in which it operated. These examples demonstrate how well-articulated vision and mission statements can serve as a foundational element in guiding an organization's path forward, enhancing internal alignment, and strengthening external perceptions.

Examples

1. **Apple Inc.:** Apple Inc. is a multinational technology company headquartered in Cupertino, California, known for designing, manufacturing, and selling consumer electronics, software, and services. With a diverse product lineup including the iPhone, iPad, Mac, and Apple Watch, the company continues to innovate and shape the landscape of the tech industry, maintaining a strong focus on user experience and environmental sustainability.

2. **Tesla, Inc.:** Tesla, Inc. is an innovative automotive and energy company led by CEO Elon Musk, specializing in electric vehicles, energy storage solutions, and solar products. With a mission to accelerate the world's transition to sustainable energy, Tesla has revolutionized the automotive industry with its electric vehicles, while also advancing renewable energy technologies through initiatives like the Gigafactory and Powerwall.

3. **The Bill & Melinda Gates Foundation:** The Bill & Melinda Gates Foundation is one of the largest private philanthropic organizations in the world, dedicated to addressing global challenges such as poverty, disease, and inequality. Founded by Microsoft co-founder Bill Gates and his wife Melinda Gates, the foundation funds initiatives in healthcare, education, and economic development, aiming to improve the lives of people worldwide and create lasting positive change.

4. **Amnesty International:** Amnesty International is a global human rights organization that works to promote and defend human rights around the world. Through research, advocacy, and grassroots activism, Amnesty International campaigns against human rights abuses, including those related to freedom of expression, discrimination, and injustice, striving to hold governments and other actors accountable for their actions and policies.

5. **Doctors Without Borders:** Doctors Without Borders, also known as Médecins Sans Frontières (MSF), is an international medical humanitarian organization that provides emergency medical care to people affected by armed conflict, epidemics, natural disasters, and exclusion from healthcare. With a network of volunteer medical professionals operating in over 70 countries, Doctors Without Borders delivers life-saving medical aid where it's needed most, often in challenging and dangerous environments.

Top Five Takeaways

1. **Clarity is a potent force** that propels individuals and organizations towards success. By meticulously defining your purpose with unmistakable clarity, you illuminate the path to achievement, guiding every action and decision with precision and purpose. This clarity serves as a beacon, rallying teams and stakeholders around a common goal, fostering unity and focus amidst complexity.

2. **Aligning with your values** establishes a bedrock of integrity that fortifies your stance and actions. When integrity serves as the cornerstone of your statement, you not only honor your principles but also earn the trust and respect of those around you. This alignment creates a cohesive and authentic identity, empowering you to navigate challenges with conviction and honor.

3. **To inspire others** is to ignite the flames of possibility and transformation. By painting a vivid and compelling picture of the future, you cultivate a shared vision that captivates hearts and minds, compelling others to join you on the journey. This inspirational narrative energizes teams, propelling them towards ambitious goals with passion and purpose.

4. **Embracing adaptability** ensures resilience and relevance in an ever-evolving landscape. By crafting a vision and mission that are both robust and flexible, you equip yourself and your organization to navigate change with agility and confidence. This adaptability enables proactive responses to shifting dynamics, turning challenges into opportunities for growth and innovation.

5. **Accountability is the cornerstone** of high-performance and trust within teams and organizations. By holding yourself and others accountable to the standards set forth, you foster a culture of responsibility and excellence. This commitment to accountability cultivates transparency and reliability, driving continuous improvement and sustainable success.

Actions to Take

1. **Reflect deeply on your core values before crafting your vision and mission:** Take the time to introspect and understand the fundamental principles that drive you and your organization. Your vision and mission should resonate deeply with these values, serving as a guiding light for your actions and decisions.

2. **Involve stakeholders in the process to ensure buy-in and alignment:** Engage with key stakeholders, including employees, customers, and partners, to gather diverse perspectives and insights. By involving them in the process, you not only foster a sense of ownership but also ensure that your vision and mission reflect the collective aspirations and goals of the entire community.

3. **Seek inspiration from other successful vision and mission statements:** Study the vision and mission statements of renowned organizations to gain insights into effective wording and structure. While drawing inspiration, ensure that your statements remain authentic and reflective of your unique identity and objectives.

4. **Regularly revisit and refine your vision and mission as circumstances evolve:** Acknowledge that the business landscape is dynamic and constantly changing. Set aside regular intervals to review and update your vision and mission, ensuring they remain relevant and adaptable to evolving challenges and opportunities.

5. **Lead by example, embodying the principles outlined in your statement:** Demonstrate a commitment to your organization's values and mission through your actions and decisions. Your leadership sets the tone for the entire organization, inspiring others to align their behavior with the principles outlined in your vision and mission.

Actions Not to Take

1. **Instead of rushing through the process**, dedicate sufficient time to introspect and refine your vision and mission. By taking a deliberate approach, you ensure that your goals align with your values and aspirations, setting a solid foundation for future endeavors.

2. **Avoid compromising on your core values** in pursuit of short-term gains or to appease others. While it may seem tempting in the moment, staying true to your principles fosters authenticity and long-term success, establishing trust and credibility within your community.

3. When crafting your vision and mission, **steer clear of vague or generic statements** that lack depth and resonance. Instead, strive for clarity and specificity, articulating a compelling narrative that resonates with stakeholders and inspires action.

4. **Don't overlook the importance of consistently communicating** and reinforcing your vision and mission to stakeholders. Whether through regular updates, strategic messaging, or active engagement, fostering alignment and understanding ensures collective progress towards shared goals.

5. **Resist the urge to rest on your laurels** once your vision and mission are established. Recognize that continuous refinement is essential for adapting to changing circumstances, seizing new opportunities, and sustaining momentum towards your ultimate objectives.

Chapter 3: Building a Strong Organizational Culture

A strong organizational culture stands as the backbone of any successful enterprise, acting as the glue that binds individuals to the shared values and goals that drive progress forward. It demands unwavering commitment, focused efforts, and an ongoing quest for betterment. This chapter unveils the essential principles and tactics for developing a culture that is not only resilient but also adaptable, creating an environment where every team member feels empowered to achieve their best and contribute significantly to the organization's triumphs.

Cultivating a vibrant organizational culture allows for the fostering of an ecosystem ripe with innovation, cooperation, and flexibility. This atmosphere does more than just boost employee morale and satisfaction; it equips the organization with the agility needed to overcome obstacles and capitalize on opportunities in a rapidly changing world. By taking deliberate steps and embracing a collective dedication to greatness, businesses can nurture a culture that stands as a pillar of their strength and a catalyst for continuous improvement.

By setting the cultivation of a dynamic culture as a priority, leaders can lay the groundwork for a setting that not only inspires creativity but also promotes mutual support and the willingness to adapt. Such a culture enhances the organization's cohesion, making it more resilient in the face of adversity and more adept at pursuing new possibilities. The journey towards cultivating this culture is marked by shared visions and the relentless pursuit of excellence, binding the organization's efforts and aspirations.

In fostering an atmosphere where innovation thrives, organizations can unlock the potential of their workforce, encouraging each member to bring forward new ideas and collaborate effectively. This not only drives the organization towards its objectives but also instills a sense of belonging and purpose among employees. The pursuit of a culture that values adaptability and continuous learning is a testament to an organization's commitment to not just surviving but thriving in an unpredictable market.

The path to establishing a culture of excellence is paved with the collective efforts of every member of the organization, guided by visionary leadership and a clear set of values. By embracing these principles, organizations can create a powerful sense of unity and direction that propels them towards their goals. This chapter serves as a roadmap for those seeking to cultivate an organizational culture that not only endures but evolves, ensuring the long-term success and relevance of the enterprise in the global landscape.

Inspirational Quote

> *"Culture is the widening of the mind and of the spirit."* - Jawaharlal Nehru

Vision and Purpose

A compelling vision is not just an idea; it's the heartbeat of organizational triumph, shining a light on the path ahead and guiding every strategic move. When team members grasp their vital roles within this grand vision, their drive for excellence is ignited, pushing boundaries and setting new performance benchmarks. Leaders who master the art of conveying this vision create a powerful sense of unity, seamlessly blending individual goals with the organization's aims, resulting in a harmonious and productive workplace.

Leaders play a crucial role in intertwining personal dreams with the organization's mission, sparking a deep sense of purpose and fulfillment within their teams. This unity of purpose fosters collaboration and resilience, empowering teams to face challenges head-on with courage and steadfastness. The journey towards shared objectives, underpinned by a meaningful vision, enriches team members' sense of belonging and contentment, fueling ongoing success and achievement within the organization.

A well-articulated vision acts as a beacon, guiding and inspiring every member of the organization towards collective success. It transforms the workplace into a field of possibilities where each individual's contribution is recognized and valued. Through effective leadership and communication, this vision becomes a shared aspiration, driving everyone to contribute their best towards the common goal.

This shared vision not only unites team members but also cultivates an environment where innovation and excellence flourish. It creates a space where challenges are met with creativity and resilience, fostering a culture of continuous improvement and growth. As team members align their efforts towards a common purpose, the organization moves forward as a cohesive and dynamic force.

Ultimately, a compelling vision is the foundation of a thriving organization. It is the catalyst for motivation, unity, and achievement, weaving together the diverse threads of individual aspirations into a strong, vibrant tapestry of organizational success. Through dedication, clear communication, and shared goals, leaders and team members together create an unstoppable force, poised for excellence and continual advancement.

Values and Beliefs

Core values are the foundation of an organization's culture, guiding every action and decision like a compass. When embraced by every team member, these values become more than principles; they become the very essence of the organization's identity. Leadership plays a crucial role here, as leaders set the benchmark through their behavior, inspiring everyone to embody these values in their daily work.

Leadership's commitment to these values builds trust and credibility, both internally among team members and externally with stakeholders. This commitment is visible in their day-to-day actions, where consistent application of core values becomes the norm. Such dedication ensures that the organization not only talks the talk but also walks the walk, reinforcing its foundational principles at every level.

At the heart of an innovative and creative workplace is the blend of diverse thoughts anchored by solid core values. Encouraging unique perspectives invites a rich tapestry of ideas, fostering a culture where innovation is not just welcomed but celebrated. This delicate balance is key to staying relevant and competitive, allowing organizations to navigate the complexities of their industries with agility.

Diversity of thought, paired with a strong adherence to core values, propels organizations forward. It allows for the exploration of new avenues while ensuring that every step taken is aligned with the organization's mission and vision. This approach not only nurtures creativity but also ensures that the organization remains true to its identity amidst change.

Ultimately, the integration of core values with a diversity of perspectives is what positions an organization for long-term success. It creates a dynamic environment where innovation thrives within the framework of the organization's principles. This strategic alignment not only drives progress but also cements the organization's place as a leader in its field, ready to meet the challenges of the future.

Communication and Transparency

Creating a workplace that values open and transparent communication is crucial for building trust and integrity within a team. When leaders actively listen and foster an environment where everyone feels comfortable engaging in constructive dialogue, a culture of honesty and collaboration naturally emerges. This approach not only celebrates achievements but also treats setbacks as valuable learning opportunities, encouraging everyone to grow and improve together.

Moreover, being transparent about decision-making processes gives team members a sense of belonging and responsibility. This empowerment allows individuals to fully engage with their tasks and contribute significantly to achieving the organization's goals. It's a powerful way to motivate and inspire team members to take initiative and work collaboratively towards shared objectives.

Consistent and open communication is key to ensuring every team member feels informed and ready to contribute to the organization's success. Leaders who maintain open lines of communication enable the smooth flow of ideas and information, helping teams to work cohesively towards their collective goals. This not only promotes a more inclusive environment but also drives innovation and creativity across the organization.

An organization that prioritizes transparent communication lays the groundwork for long-term growth, adaptability, and achievement. This strategic approach helps in navigating the complexities of the modern business world, ensuring the organization remains resilient and forward-thinking. By valuing each team member's contribution and maintaining open channels of communication, organizations can foster a culture of continuous improvement and excellence.

Embracing open and transparent communication within an organization is a transformative strategy that leads to numerous benefits. It strengthens team dynamics, enhances problem-solving capabilities, and ensures all team members are aligned with the organization's vision and objectives. Cultivating such an environment is essential for any organization aspiring to achieve greatness in an ever-changing business landscape.

Empowerment and Autonomy

Empowering individuals to take charge of their decisions is the cornerstone of building a culture steeped in ownership and responsibility. By allowing freedom within defined boundaries, we lay the foundation for innovation and encourage a forward-thinking approach to problem-solving. It's about leaders placing trust in their team's abilities, guiding them when needed, and fostering an environment ripe for personal and professional growth.

When autonomy is recognized and celebrated, it unlocks the full potential of individuals, igniting creativity and spearheading a wave of innovation throughout the organization. Teams that are given the reins to make decisions become more agile and resilient, better equipped to face challenges head-on and seize opportunities. This empowerment is not just beneficial; it's essential for the enduring success and vitality of the organization.

Providing team members with the authority to make decisions not only bolsters their confidence but also instills a sense of belonging and significance within the organization. This approach cultivates a proactive mindset, encouraging team members to approach challenges with innovative solutions. The role of leadership, then, transforms into one of support and mentorship, guiding teams towards achieving their fullest potential.

Such a strategy of empowerment leads to a dynamic where creativity flourishes, and innovation becomes the norm rather than the exception. Teams feel more invested in the outcomes of their work, driving them to pursue excellence and creativity in every task they undertake. This, in turn, propels the organization forward, fostering a sustainable environment where success is a collective achievement.

Nurturing a culture of autonomy and accountability results in a more motivated, engaged, and innovative workforce. It is a testament to the power of trust and freedom within the workplace, where every individual has the opportunity to contribute to the organization's vision. The path to organizational excellence is paved with the empowerment of its people, making every achievement a shared triumph.

Recognition and Appreciation

Recognizing and celebrating achievements within an organization is crucial for promoting positive behaviors and nurturing a culture of excellence. It's essential that recognition is given promptly, with a focus on the specific details of each achievement, and delivered with genuine sincerity. This approach not only highlights the importance of accomplishments but also ensures that the recognition is meaningful and impactful.

When every team member's unique contributions are valued and celebrated, it creates an atmosphere of inclusivity and belonging. This sense of unity is further strengthened through peer-to-peer recognition, which encourages a spirit of support and teamwork among colleagues. The practice of regularly showing appreciation not only strengthens bonds between team members but also significantly boosts the overall morale and collaboration within the team.

The commitment to acknowledging and celebrating successes plays a pivotal role in shaping an organizational culture that treasures both individual and collective achievements. Immediate and appropriate recognition serves as a powerful motivator, reinforcing the behaviors that lead to innovation and continuous growth. Such a culture of appreciation not only elevates employee engagement and loyalty but also significantly improves job satisfaction and retention rates.

Incorporating a culture of gratitude and recognition into the fabric of an organization can transform the work environment into a more cohesive and productive space. This environment fosters stronger relationships among team members, enhancing their sense of connection and commitment to the organization's goals. The positive energy generated from this culture of appreciation is contagious, leading to a more vibrant and dynamic workplace.

Ultimately, prioritizing the acknowledgment and celebration of achievements is a key strategy for driving organizational success. This approach not only acknowledges the hard work and dedication of employees but also serves as a cornerstone for building a thriving and supportive workplace. By fostering a culture that values recognition, organizations can achieve higher levels of innovation, employee satisfaction, and overall success.

Conclusion

Creating a strong organizational culture is an ongoing journey that demands unwavering dedication, flexibility, and a relentless pursuit of excellence. It's about building on a foundation of a clear vision, core values, open communication, empowerment, and recognition. This framework fosters individual growth, team success, and overall organizational progress, making the workplace a catalyst for achievement and innovation.

To cultivate such an environment, it's crucial to actively encourage involvement, creativity, and continuous learning across all organizational tiers. Promoting teamwork, openness, and a sense of community boosts employee engagement, allegiance, and efficiency. This approach not only enhances the workplace atmosphere but also strengthens the organization's resilience and adaptability in the face of change.

By emphasizing the development of a vibrant and welcoming culture, companies are better equipped to overcome obstacles and seize new opportunities. This strategic focus on culture enriches the employee experience, driving organizational success. In an ever-changing business world, such a culture is an invaluable asset, enabling both individuals and the organization to flourish and stay ahead of the curve.

In this journey, every member of the organization plays a vital role in shaping and sustaining the culture. It's a collective effort that requires contribution and commitment from everyone, from leadership to the newest team members. This shared responsibility ensures that the organizational culture is not just a set of ideals but a living, breathing aspect of daily operations.

A robust organizational culture is the cornerstone of enduring success. It's about creating an environment where excellence is the norm, innovation is encouraged, and every individual feels valued and connected. Such a culture not only attracts top talent but also inspires them to achieve their best, propelling the organization toward its goals with vigor and purpose.

CASE STUDIES: Building a Strong Organizational Culture

Case Study 1: Tech Startup

Background:

A rapidly growing tech startup, Let's Innovate, is revolutionizing the e-commerce industry with its cutting-edge platform. As the company expands its team and operations, the leadership realizes the importance of building a strong organizational culture to maintain cohesion, drive innovation, and attract top talent.

Approach:

Let's Innovate's leadership understands that culture isn't just about perks and benefits; it's about shared values and behaviors. They begin by defining core values that reflect their mission, such as transparency, collaboration, and customer-centricity. These values are not just words on a wall but are integrated into every aspect of the company's operations, from hiring practices to performance evaluations.

To reinforce these values, Let's Innovate invests in regular team-building activities, such as hackathons, cross-departmental projects, and volunteer opportunities. They also encourage open communication through platforms like Slack and regular town hall meetings where employees can ask questions and provide feedback.

Results:

The efforts to build a strong organizational culture pay off for Let's Innovate. Employees feel connected to the company's mission and values, leading to higher levels of engagement and retention. Collaboration and innovation thrive, resulting in the development of new features and products that propel the company's growth. Additionally, Let's Innovate becomes known as a desirable place to work, attracting top talent in the competitive tech industry.

Case Study 2: Healthcare Institution

Background:

A large healthcare institution, MedCare Health System, is facing challenges with employee turnover and morale. Despite offering competitive salaries and benefits, many staff members feel disconnected from the organization's mission and vision. Recognizing the need for a cultural overhaul, MedCare's leadership embarks on a journey to rebuild a sense of purpose and community among its workforce.

Approach:

MedCare Health System begins by conducting employee surveys and focus groups to better understand the underlying issues contributing to low morale. They discover that staff members feel undervalued and disconnected from the organization's mission of providing compassionate care. In response, MedCare redefines its core values to emphasize empathy, teamwork, and patient-centeredness.

To embed these values into the organization's culture, MedCare launches initiatives such as "Patient Stories," where staff members share inspiring anecdotes of their interactions with patients. They also implement regular training sessions focused on communication skills, empathy, and cultural sensitivity. Additionally, MedCare introduces recognition programs to celebrate employees who exemplify the organization's values in their work.

Results:

The efforts to strengthen MedCare Health System's organizational culture yield positive results. Employee morale improves as staff members feel a greater sense of purpose and connection to the organization's mission. Turnover rates decrease, reducing recruitment and training costs for the institution. Patients also report higher levels of satisfaction with the care they receive, as staff members demonstrate increased empathy and commitment to patient-centeredness. Overall, MedCare Health System becomes a more cohesive and effective healthcare provider, driven by a strong organizational culture centered around its core values.

Examples

1. **Google** is renowned globally for fostering an environment where innovation thrives, championing an inclusive culture that welcomes diverse perspectives. Within its walls, employees are encouraged to push boundaries, explore new ideas, and embrace experimentation, resulting in groundbreaking developments across various industries.

2. **Zappos** has earned widespread acclaim for prioritizing exceptional customer service and prioritizing the happiness of its employees. By nurturing a workplace culture centered on employee satisfaction and empowerment, Zappos creates an environment where individuals feel valued and motivated to deliver unparalleled service to customers, ultimately contributing to the company's success.

3. **Southwest Airlines** has built a stellar reputation around its distinctive company culture, characterized by a strong emphasis on teamwork, lighthearted humor,

and a relentless "warrior spirit." This culture not only fosters camaraderie among employees but also fuels the airline's commitment to delivering outstanding service and creating memorable experiences for passengers.

4. **Pixar Animation Studios** is celebrated globally for cultivating a collaborative and imaginative environment that places storytelling at its core. Within its walls, artists and innovators are encouraged to unleash their creativity, pushing the boundaries of animation and storytelling to create beloved films that resonate with audiences of all ages.

5. **Patagonia** stands out for its unwavering dedication to environmental sustainability and its commitment to fostering a culture of activism and purpose-driven work. Employees at Patagonia are not just colleagues but advocates for change, driven by a shared mission to protect the planet and inspire others to lead more sustainable lifestyles.

Top Five Takeaways

1. **Vision and purpose provide a clear direction** for individuals within an organization, helping them understand their roles and how they contribute to the overarching goals. When everyone aligns with the vision and purpose, it cultivates a shared sense of purpose and belonging, driving collective effort towards success.

2. **Values are the fundamental principles** that guide the behaviors and decisions of individuals within an organization, reflecting its culture and identity. By embodying these values in everyday actions and interactions, organizations create an environment where people feel connected and motivated to uphold shared beliefs and standards.

3. **Transparent communication entails sharing information openly** and honestly across all levels of an organization, fostering trust and collaboration. When communication channels are clear and accessible, it enables individuals to feel informed and valued, empowering them to actively participate and contribute to the organization's goals.

4. **Empowering autonomy involves delegating authority** and granting individuals the freedom to make decisions and take ownership of their work. This autonomy not only sparks creativity and innovation as individuals explore new approaches and solutions but also instills a sense of accountability and pride in their contributions to the organization's success.

5. **Recognition and appreciation are powerful tools** for reinforcing positive behaviors and fostering a culture of appreciation within an organization. By acknowledging and celebrating the efforts and achievements of individuals and teams, organizations cultivate a supportive and inclusive environment where everyone feels valued and motivated to perform at their best.

Five Actions to Take

1. **Articulating a compelling vision** involves clearly communicating where the organization is headed and how it aligns with its core values, inspiring stakeholders to actively contribute to its realization. By ensuring that the vision resonates with the organization's values, leaders can foster a sense of purpose and direction among team members, driving collective action toward common goals.

2. **Fostering open and transparent communication channels** entails creating an environment where information flows freely, allowing for honest dialogue and feedback at all levels of the organization. By prioritizing transparency, leaders can build trust and collaboration, enabling teams to address challenges more effectively and make informed decisions that align with the organization's objectives.

3. **Empowering individuals means providing them with the authority** and flexibility to make decisions within clearly defined boundaries, fostering a sense of ownership and accountability. By entrusting individuals with autonomy, leaders can unleash their potential, encourage innovation, and cultivate a culture of empowerment where employees feel valued and motivated to contribute their best.

4. **Recognizing and appreciating achievements regularly** and sincerely involves acknowledging and celebrating the efforts and accomplishments of individuals and teams in a genuine and timely manner. By showing appreciation for their contributions, leaders can boost morale, reinforce positive behaviors, and inspire continued excellence, fostering a culture of recognition and appreciation that motivates everyone to strive for success.

5. **Leading by example** requires embodying the values and behaviors expected of others, serving as a role model for the organization's culture and guiding principles. By demonstrating integrity, accountability, and resilience in their actions, leaders can inspire trust, credibility, and commitment among their team members, setting the standard for excellence and ethical conduct within the organization.

Five Actions Not to Take

1. **Neglecting to communicate the organization's vision and values clearly:** Failure to effectively communicate the organization's vision and values can lead to confusion among employees, hindering their understanding of where the company is headed and what principles guide its actions. When leaders neglect this crucial communication, it can result in disengagement and a lack of alignment with the organization's overarching goals, ultimately impeding progress and growth.

2. **Micromanaging or restricting autonomy, stifling creativity and innovation:** Micromanagement can create a toxic work environment where employees feel stifled and disempowered, hindering their ability to think creatively and innovate. When leaders excessively control every aspect of their team's work, they not only undermine trust and morale but also miss out on the diverse perspectives and fresh ideas that come from empowering individuals to take ownership of their tasks and contribute in meaningful ways.

3. **Failing to recognize and appreciate the contributions of team members:** Neglecting to acknowledge and appreciate the efforts of team members can lead to demotivation and a lack of enthusiasm for their work. By failing to recognize and celebrate achievements, leaders risk eroding morale and diminishing employee satisfaction, ultimately jeopardizing retention and the overall success of the organization.

4. **Allowing values to be compromised for short-term gains**: When leaders prioritize short-term gains over long-term values, they risk damaging the organization's reputation and integrity. By compromising on core values for immediate benefits, leaders set a precedent that can erode trust among stakeholders and undermine the foundation of the organization, ultimately leading to long-term consequences that far outweigh any short-term gains.

5. **Being inconsistent or hypocritical in upholding organizational values and expectations:** Inconsistency or hypocrisy in upholding organizational values sends mixed messages to employees, leading to confusion and distrust. When leaders fail to practice what they preach or hold themselves to different standards, it undermines the credibility of the entire organization, fostering a culture of cynicism and disengagement among team members.

Chapter 4: Navigating Legal and Regulatory Compliance

Navigating the complex world of legal and regulatory compliance is akin to embarking on an intricate journey, filled with challenges that test the wisdom and resolve of professionals. Yet, within these challenges lie unparalleled opportunities for growth, fostering a foundation of integrity and excellence. By delving deeply into the understanding of relevant laws, steadfastly upholding ethical principles, and promoting an ethos of continuous improvement, individuals and organizations can transcend basic compliance to achieve a realm of mutual trust and respect.

Adopting a forward-thinking stance on compliance transcends mere legal adherence, requiring a dedication to perpetual learning and agile adaptation. Engaging in continuous education, conducting thorough self-assessments, and establishing strong compliance frameworks empower entities to navigate through the regulatory maze with confidence. Viewing compliance as a strategic cornerstone, rather than a burdensome duty, positions both individuals and organizations to thrive amid the complexities of the regulatory environment, emerging as stronger, more adaptable entities.

In the heart of complexity, there's a beacon of opportunity for those who choose to see it. This journey through the labyrinth of compliance is not just about avoiding pitfalls but about building a legacy of integrity and excellence. By anchoring themselves in a deep understanding of laws and regulations, and fostering a culture of integrity and continuous improvement, stakeholders stand to gain far more than mere compliance—they forge a path toward enduring success and respect.

The proactive approach to compliance is a testament to an organization's commitment to excellence and resilience. It's about transforming challenges into stepping stones for growth, where continuous learning and self-assessment become the norm. As entities evolve with the regulatory landscape, they not only safeguard their operations but also set new benchmarks for excellence in compliance, showcasing their unwavering commitment to ethical standards and operational integrity.

The intricate journey of navigating legal and regulatory compliance is a profound opportunity for personal and organizational growth. It demands more than just adherence to laws; it requires a culture of integrity, continuous improvement, and strategic foresight. By embracing these principles, individuals and organizations not only navigate the labyrinth with confidence but also emerge as leaders, setting a precedent for excellence in an ever-evolving business world.

Inspirational Quote

> *"Integrity is doing the right thing, even when no one is watching."* - C.S. Lewis

Understanding the Landscape

In the intricate world of legal and regulatory compliance, having a thorough understanding is essential. By mastering the complex web of laws, regulations, and industry standards, organizations can navigate the challenges they face with confidence. Recognizing not just the rules but also their deeper significance and implications ensures that compliance efforts contribute positively to the organization's strategic goals.

Furthermore, keeping up-to-date with the ever-evolving legal and regulatory environment is crucial. The landscape is constantly changing, with laws and regulations frequently being updated or newly introduced. Engaging actively with legal experts and regulatory authorities offers critical insights, enabling organizations to foresee upcoming changes and adapt their compliance measures accordingly.

Adapting and learning continuously in this dynamic field is not just beneficial; it's a necessity. This commitment to staying informed and ready to evolve ensures that organizations remain ahead of the curve. It's about being proactive rather than reactive, which not only minimizes risks but also builds trust among stakeholders and secures a competitive edge.

Proactive engagement and a forward-thinking mindset in compliance management can transform potential obstacles into opportunities for growth and innovation. By leveraging legal and regulatory insights, businesses can devise strategies that not only comply with the letter of the law but also embody its spirit. This approach strengthens the organization's reputation and fosters a culture of integrity and ethical conduct.

Ultimately, navigating the complex regulatory landscape with expertise and foresight paves the way for sustainable success. It enables organizations to turn compliance into a strategic asset, enhancing operational efficiency and fostering an environment of continuous improvement. In this way, businesses can achieve not just compliance but also excellence, setting a benchmark in their industry and contributing to a more transparent and accountable corporate world.

Embracing Ethical Principles

Ethics are the foundation of good conduct, offering a moral compass in the often complex world of rules and regulations. When we weave values like honesty, fairness, and accountability into the very fabric of our organizations, we create spaces brimming with trust and respect. Such commitment to ethical standards not only protects our reputation but also steers us clear of the potential pitfalls that accompany moral quandaries.

In the face of adversity, integrity shines brightly, guiding us towards choices that align with our deepest values. This principle acts as our north star, encouraging us to remain true to ourselves and our principles, even when the road gets tough. By embracing integrity, we not only adhere to ethical norms but also build a foundation of respect and responsibility that strengthens relationships and paves the way for enduring achievement.

Cultivating a culture where ethical behavior is the norm rather than the exception requires dedication and continuous effort. It means setting an example from the top down, where leaders embody the values they wish to see throughout their organization. Such a culture not only enhances the workplace environment but also contributes to a more equitable and just society.

Moreover, ethical practices in business are not just about avoiding negative consequences; they're about creating positive outcomes. They lead to better decision-making, foster innovation, and build stronger teams. When everyone is committed to a high standard of ethics, the organization is better equipped to navigate challenges and seize opportunities.

The pursuit of ethical excellence is a journey that enriches both individuals and organizations. It demands vigilance, courage, and a commitment to doing what is right, even in the face of adversity. By prioritizing ethics, we don't just follow a set of rules; we embark on a path that leads to greater trust, respect, and success in all our endeavors.

Cultivating a Culture of Compliance

Embracing compliance transcends mere adherence to legal standards; it requires a transformative approach to how an organization perceives its mission. By valuing and integrating a culture of compliance, companies enable their workforce to embody values of honesty and strict adherence to both internal and external regulations. This journey begins with clear, open lines of communication, extends through in-depth training initiatives, and is cemented by leadership that consistently models commitment to these high standards.

Making compliance a cornerstone of organizational strategy leads to the creation of an environment characterized by resilience and ethical integrity. When team members grasp the significance of compliance and feel empowered to act in alignment with it, they play a crucial role in protecting the organization's integrity and reducing potential risks. Elevating compliance to this status not only ensures legal and regulatory adherence but also builds a foundation of trust with all stakeholders, paving the way for long-term success.

In this spirit, embedding compliance into the daily operations of a business is not just about following rules—it's about building a legacy of integrity. This transformation requires every employee to see themselves as a guardian of the organization's ethical standards. It's a collective effort that strengthens the fabric of the organization, making it not only compliant but also a model of corporate responsibility.

The proactive pursuit of compliance demonstrates a commitment to ethical excellence that resonates with customers, partners, and the broader community. It signals that an organization is not merely focused on the bottom line but is dedicated to conducting business with unwavering integrity. This commitment lays the groundwork for a culture that attracts talent, encourages innovation, and sustains growth through principled leadership.

The journey towards embedding compliance in the organizational ethos is one of continuous improvement and shared responsibility. It's an investment in creating a workplace where ethical decisions are the norm, not the exception. By fostering an environment where compliance is embraced at every level, organizations not only navigate the complexities of regulatory landscapes but also achieve a competitive edge that is rooted in trust and transparency.

Proactive Risk Management

In the intricate world of legal and regulatory compliance, embracing the principle of prevention over cure can be transformative. By meticulously identifying and addressing potential risks in advance, organizations can protect their valuable time, resources, and reputation from harm. It's crucial to stay vigilant, foresee possible challenges, and tackle issues promptly before they grow, ensuring that regulatory compliance is maintained and potential legal issues are averted.

Adopting a forward-thinking mindset not only reduces the risk of encountering legal problems but also cultivates a culture of accountability and responsibility across the organization. By continuously monitoring, evaluating, and improving compliance processes, companies can stay ahead in the ever-changing regulatory landscape, preserving their competitive advantage. This proactive stance is instrumental in maintaining organizational integrity, earning trust, and ensuring long-term stability in a complex legal and regulatory framework.

Investing in preventative measures is a strategic choice that pays dividends by safeguarding an organization against unforeseen legal challenges. This approach enables businesses to navigate the complexities of compliance with confidence, ensuring they are always prepared for whatever lies ahead. By doing so, organizations can focus on growth and innovation, knowing their compliance framework is robust and responsive.

The commitment to proactive compliance management underscores an organization's dedication to ethical practices and legal integrity. It signals to stakeholders, including customers, employees, and partners, that the organization is trustworthy and committed to upholding high standards. This commitment not only enhances the organization's reputation but also contributes to a positive work environment where ethical practices are valued and promoted.

Prioritizing preventive measures in the realm of legal and regulatory compliance is a wise investment in the organization's future. It not only minimizes risks but also reinforces a culture of responsibility, integrity, and trust. As organizations navigate the complexities of today's legal landscape, adopting such a proactive approach will be key to achieving and sustaining success.

Continuous Improvement

Complacency is a silent hazard in the realm of compliance, often leading to missed details and lapses in regulation adherence. It's crucial to embrace a philosophy of perpetual growth, using lessons from past experiences to refine our approach. By continuously revisiting and updating our policies and practices, seeking out stakeholder feedback, and adapting to the ever-evolving regulatory and industry standards, we position ourselves to proactively tackle new challenges and uphold compliance standards.

Adopting a forward-thinking mindset enables organizations to foster a culture deeply rooted in compliance, aiming not just to meet but to exceed the baseline expectations. This approach not only reduces the risks tied to non-compliance but also builds stakeholder trust, boosts operational effectiveness, and supports sustainable development. The drive for constant improvement is key to navigating the intricate regulatory framework and securing a lasting legacy in the fast-paced business world.

A commitment to continuous improvement acts as a bulwark against the complexities of regulatory demands, ensuring organizations remain compliant and agile. This proactive stance involves a vigilant review of operational protocols, open channels for feedback, and a keen eye on the shifting sands of regulations and industry benchmarks. Through this, we can anticipate challenges before they arise and ensure compliance is seamlessly integrated into our daily operations.

In cultivating a compliance-centric culture, we not only safeguard against potential risks but also unlock opportunities for growth and innovation. This culture encourages an environment where excellence is the norm, and every team member is empowered to contribute to the organization's compliance journey. The ripple effects of this mindset extend beyond mere compliance, enhancing overall business performance and stakeholder confidence.

The dedication to continuous improvement and compliance is foundational to thriving in today's complex and dynamic business environment. It allows organizations to not just survive but flourish, navigating regulatory challenges with confidence and integrity. By placing compliance at the heart of operations, businesses can achieve sustainable success, demonstrating resilience, adaptability, and a commitment to excellence in all aspects of their operations.

Conclusion

In the sphere of legal and regulatory compliance, achieving excellence goes beyond simply avoiding fines or sanctions. It involves creating a solid foundation of integrity, accountability, and dedication to excellence. By embracing ethical principles and gaining a deep understanding of the regulatory environment, businesses lay the groundwork for setting standards and practices that not only meet but exceed compliance requirements. This approach not only safeguards the organization but also elevates its moral and operational standing.

Adopting a culture of compliance is pivotal in this journey. It requires a proactive stance on risk management and an unwavering commitment to ongoing improvement. Such a culture ensures that an organization's compliance strategies remain effective and responsive to both current and future regulatory landscapes. This forward-thinking mindset is crucial for staying ahead of potential challenges and adapting to the ever-evolving demands of compliance.

The benefits of prioritizing legal and regulatory compliance are manifold. By meeting these obligations, individuals and organizations don't just avoid repercussions; they also earn the trust and respect of their peers and stakeholders. This proactive approach not only reduces the risk of non-compliance but also significantly boosts an entity's reputation, enhancing its relationships with partners, customers, and the community at large.

Furthermore, this commitment to compliance and ethical behavior strengthens the organization's credibility. It fosters a positive image that can lead to lasting relationships with stakeholders, contributing to the organization's long-term success and sustainability. The reputation for being a compliant and ethical entity opens doors to new opportunities and serves as a competitive advantage in the marketplace.

Navigating the complexities of legal and regulatory compliance is more than just following rules. It's a strategic choice that plays a critical role in the success of an organization. It aligns with the broader societal values of transparency and accountability, contributing to a fair and equitable business environment. Embracing this approach not only ensures compliance but also positions an organization as a leader in ethical business practices, setting a standard for others to follow.

CASE STUDIES: Navigating Legal and Regulatory Compliance

Case Study 1: Financial Institution Compliance

Background:

XYZ Bank is a multinational financial institution with operations in multiple countries. In recent years, the regulatory landscape for banks has become increasingly complex, with stringent requirements aimed at ensuring financial stability and protecting consumers. XYZ Bank has been proactive in addressing these regulations, but faces challenges in navigating the differences in regulatory requirements across jurisdictions.

Challenges:

- **Compliance with Anti-Money Laundering (AML) regulations:** XYZ Bank operates in countries with varying AML regulations, making it difficult to maintain consistent compliance across all regions. Failure to comply with AML regulations can result in hefty fines and damage to the bank's reputation.

- **Data privacy regulations:** With the implementation of regulations such as the General Data Protection Regulation (GDPR) in Europe, XYZ Bank must ensure that customer data is handled securely and in compliance with applicable laws. This requires significant investments in data protection measures and staff training.

- **Cross-border transactions:** XYZ Bank facilitates cross-border transactions for its clients, which are subject to complex regulatory requirements. Ensuring compliance with regulations governing these transactions, such as the Foreign Account Tax Compliance Act (FATCA) and the Dodd-Frank Act, is a continuous challenge.

Solution:

To address these challenges, XYZ Bank has implemented a comprehensive compliance program that includes the following components:

- **Robust internal controls:** XYZ Bank has established internal policies and procedures to ensure compliance with regulatory requirements. These controls are regularly reviewed and updated to reflect changes in the regulatory landscape.

- **Compliance training:** The bank provides regular training sessions for employees to raise awareness of regulatory requirements and ensure adherence to internal policies. This includes training on AML procedures, data privacy regulations, and cross-border transaction compliance.

- **Technology investments:** XYZ Bank has invested in technology solutions to streamline compliance processes and enhance monitoring capabilities. This includes implementing automated AML screening systems and data encryption technologies to protect customer data.

- **Regulatory monitoring:** The bank closely monitors regulatory developments in all jurisdictions where it operates and adjusts its compliance program accordingly. This proactive approach helps XYZ Bank stay ahead of regulatory changes and minimize compliance risks.

Results:

By implementing these measures, XYZ Bank has successfully navigated the complex legal and regulatory landscape, reducing the risk of non-compliance and protecting its reputation. The bank's proactive approach to compliance has also enhanced trust and confidence among customers and regulators, positioning XYZ Bank as a trusted financial institution in the global marketplace.

Case Study 2: Healthcare Compliance

Background:

ABC Healthcare is a large healthcare provider operating multiple hospitals and clinics across the United States. As a healthcare provider, ABC Healthcare is subject to a myriad of regulations aimed at protecting patient safety, ensuring quality of care, and safeguarding patient data. Navigating these legal and regulatory requirements is essential to maintaining compliance and preserving the reputation of the organization.

Challenges:

- **Compliance with HIPAA regulations:** ABC Healthcare must comply with the Health Insurance Portability and Accountability Act (HIPAA), which sets standards for the protection of sensitive patient information. Ensuring compliance with HIPAA requirements, such as patient consent and data security measures, is critical to avoiding penalties and maintaining patient trust.

- **Medicare and Medicaid billing regulations:** As a provider of services reimbursed by Medicare and Medicaid, ABC Healthcare must adhere to strict billing and coding regulations. Non-compliance with these regulations can result in financial penalties and exclusion from federal healthcare programs.

- **Quality of care standards:** ABC Healthcare is subject to regulatory requirements related to the quality of care provided to patients. This includes adherence to clinical guidelines, infection control protocols, and patient safety measures. Failure to meet these standards can result in sanctions and damage to the organization's reputation.

Solution:

To address these challenges, ABC Healthcare has implemented a comprehensive compliance program that includes the following components:

- **HIPAA compliance training:** The organization provides regular training sessions for staff members to ensure awareness of HIPAA regulations and their responsibilities for safeguarding patient information. This includes training on data security best practices, patient consent requirements, and breach reporting procedures.

- **Billing and coding audits:** ABC Healthcare conducts regular audits of its billing and coding practices to identify and address any potential compliance issues. This proactive approach helps the organization identify billing errors and ensure accurate reimbursement for services rendered.

- **Quality improvement initiatives:** The organization has implemented quality improvement initiatives aimed at enhancing patient care and safety. This includes regular monitoring of clinical outcomes, patient satisfaction surveys, and implementation of evidence-based practices to improve quality of care.

- **Compliance monitoring and reporting:** ABC Healthcare maintains robust monitoring and reporting systems to track compliance with regulatory requirements. This includes regular internal audits, compliance reviews, and reporting of any compliance incidents to regulatory authorities as required by law.

Results:

By implementing these measures, ABC Healthcare has been able to maintain compliance with legal and regulatory requirements, mitigating the risk of penalties and sanctions. The organization's commitment to compliance has also contributed to improved patient outcomes and satisfaction, enhancing its reputation as a trusted provider of quality healthcare services. Going forward, ABC Healthcare remains committed to ongoing monitoring and enhancement of its compliance program to adapt to evolving regulatory requirements and best practices.

Examples

1. **Microsoft Corporation:** Microsoft Corporation is a multinational technology company headquartered in Redmond, Washington. Founded by Bill Gates and Paul Allen in 1975, it is renowned for its development of software products such as the Windows operating system and Office productivity suite, as well as its contributions to the advancement of computer technology worldwide.

2. **Patagonia:** Patagonia is an outdoor clothing and gear company known for its commitment to environmental sustainability and corporate responsibility. Founded by Yvon Chouinard in 1973, the company emphasizes the importance of protecting the planet through initiatives such as donating a percentage of sales to environmental causes and implementing environmentally-friendly business practices.

3. **Ruth Bader Ginsburg:** Ruth Bader Ginsburg was an Associate Justice of the Supreme Court of the United States, serving from 1993 until her passing in 2020. Renowned for her advocacy of gender equality and women's rights, she played a pivotal role in shaping legal precedents and advancing social justice throughout her tenure on the Court.

4. **The Red Cross:** The Red Cross is an international humanitarian organization dedicated to providing aid and relief during times of crisis and disaster. Founded in 1863 by Henry Dunant, it operates across the globe, offering services such as disaster response, blood donation programs, and support for vulnerable communities in need.

5. **Ben & Jerry's:** Ben & Jerry's is an American ice cream company known for its unique flavors and commitment to social activism. Founded by Ben Cohen and Jerry Greenfield in 1978, the company promotes various social causes, including

environmental sustainability, fair trade practices, and social justice initiatives, while delighting ice cream lovers with its innovative flavor combinations.

Top Five Takeaways

1. **Knowledge empowers** individuals and organizations to navigate the complex legal and regulatory frameworks effectively. By staying informed about laws and regulations pertinent to their industry, they can make informed decisions and avoid potential legal pitfalls.

2. **Integrity serves as the cornerstone** of every action, guiding individuals to uphold ethical principles even in the face of challenges. By prioritizing integrity, individuals foster trust, credibility, and long-term relationships, essential for sustainable success.

3. **Cultivating a culture of compliance** entails instilling a deep-seated commitment to adherence to laws, regulations, and ethical standards at all levels of the organization. By embedding compliance into the organizational DNA, businesses not only mitigate legal risks but also foster a reputation for integrity and responsibility.

4. **Proactively managing risks** involves identifying potential threats and vulnerabilities before they materialize into significant issues. By adopting a proactive approach, organizations can implement effective mitigation strategies, safeguarding their assets, reputation, and stakeholders' interests.

5. **Continuous improvement** involves embracing a mindset of learning and adaptation to stay abreast of evolving regulations and industry best practices. By reflecting on past experiences, organizations can refine their processes, enhance compliance efforts, and position themselves for sustained success in a dynamic business environment.

Actions to Take

1. **Invest in ongoing compliance** training for employees: Continuously investing in comprehensive compliance training ensures that employees are equipped with the knowledge and skills necessary to understand and adhere to evolving regulations. By providing regular training sessions and resources, organizations empower their workforce to recognize potential compliance risks and effectively mitigate them, fostering a culture of accountability and integrity.

2. **Conduct regular audits** to assess compliance status: Implementing regular audits allows organizations to systematically evaluate their compliance status, identify any potential gaps or non-compliance issues, and take corrective actions promptly. These audits not only help in maintaining adherence to regulations but also provide valuable insights for enhancing internal processes and improving overall compliance efficiency.

3. **Establish clear policies and procedures** for legal and regulatory compliance: Developing clear and comprehensive policies and procedures ensures that employees have a solid framework to follow when navigating complex regulatory requirements. By clearly outlining expectations and procedures for compliance, organizations minimize ambiguity, reduce the likelihood of violations, and promote consistent adherence to legal and regulatory standards, ultimately safeguarding the organization's reputation and mitigating potential risks.

4. **Foster open communication** channels for reporting compliance concerns: Creating open and accessible channels for employees to report compliance concerns or violations encourages transparency and accountability within the organization. By fostering a culture where employees feel comfortable speaking up about potential issues, organizations can address compliance challenges proactively, mitigate risks, and uphold ethical standards, thereby fostering trust and integrity within the workplace.

5. **Stay updated on changes in laws and regulations** relevant to your industry: Proactively monitoring and staying abreast of changes in laws and regulations pertinent to the industry is crucial for maintaining compliance and avoiding penalties or legal ramifications. By regularly reviewing and analyzing updates in regulations, organizations can adapt their policies and procedures accordingly, ensuring continued compliance and minimizing potential disruptions to operations.

Actions Not to Take

1. **Ignoring compliance requirements** in favor of short-term gains can lead to severe consequences such as legal penalties, reputational damage, and loss of trust from stakeholders. Companies that prioritize short-term gains over compliance risk jeopardizing their long-term viability and sustainability in an increasingly regulated business environment.

2. **Assuming compliance is solely the responsibility of the legal department** neglects the fact that compliance should be integrated into every aspect of the organization's operations. While the legal department plays a crucial role in

interpreting and advising on compliance matters, every department and employee should share responsibility for understanding and adhering to relevant regulations and standards.

3. **Concealing compliance issues** instead of addressing them transparently can exacerbate problems and erode trust within the organization and with external stakeholders. Transparent communication about compliance challenges allows for proactive problem-solving and demonstrates a commitment to ethical conduct and accountability.

4. **Neglecting to document compliance efforts** and decisions leaves the organization vulnerable to legal and regulatory challenges, as well as internal misunderstandings and disputes. Comprehensive documentation of compliance activities provides a clear record of due diligence and helps ensure consistent adherence to policies and procedures.

5. **Relying solely on external** consultants without building internal compliance capabilities can result in a lack of ownership and understanding of compliance requirements within the organization. Developing internal expertise and processes for compliance not only enhances the organization's ability to adapt to changing regulatory landscapes but also fosters a culture of compliance from within.

Chapter 5: Embracing Ethical Business Practices

Ethical conduct is the cornerstone of lasting success in the modern business world. With expectations for transparency and accountability at an all-time high, it's crucial for companies to wholeheartedly embrace ethical principles. This commitment not only builds trust and loyalty among stakeholders but also ensures the company's longevity, creating a legacy that transcends mere profit.

Integrity should always take precedence over short-term gains, for it is the key to establishing meaningful connections that benefit society as a whole. By prioritizing ethical behavior, businesses can contribute to the greater good, making a positive impact that goes beyond the confines of their operations. This approach fosters a sense of community and shared purpose, elevating the company's role in society.

Adopting ethical business practices is a clear sign of a company's dedication to maintaining high moral standards, regardless of external pressures. This steadfast commitment is essential for navigating the complex challenges of today's business environment, ensuring that decisions are made with honesty and respect for all involved. It's not just about doing what's right when people are watching, but maintaining those standards consistently, even in private.

When companies align their strategies with ethical imperatives, they not only boost their reputation but also protect themselves from the risks associated with unethical behavior. This strategic alignment helps to avoid legal and financial pitfalls, reinforcing the company's stability and resilience. Furthermore, it signals a genuine concern for the well-being of all stakeholders, strengthening bonds and reaffirming the company's status as a responsible entity in the business community.

Ethical business practices are the guiding light toward sustainable growth and societal enrichment. They enable companies to navigate the complexities of the market with grace and integrity, contributing positively to the world. By adhering to these principles, businesses can achieve not just financial success, but also a respected place in the tapestry of society, benefiting both themselves and the world at large.

Inspirational Quote

"Ethics is not something you can teach. It's a way of being, a way of living, and a way of conducting oneself in the world." - Anita Roddick

Setting the Foundation

Creating a foundation of ethical business practices is crucial for the development of a robust organizational structure. At the heart of this process is the development of a corporate culture that values honesty, fairness, and respect for everyone involved. Successful leadership is characterized by integrity, acting as a beacon for ethical behavior through a steadfast commitment to moral principles in all forms of communication and actions.

When integrity becomes a core component of an organization, it transforms into the cornerstone of all decision-making and interactions across every tier. This emphasis on integrity allows businesses to create a space where trust flourishes, paving the way for sustained growth and the nurturing of positive relationships with all stakeholders.

Leaders who embody ethical principles inspire their teams to uphold the same standards, setting a powerful example that permeates throughout the organization. This creates a ripple effect, encouraging every employee to act with integrity, which in turn strengthens the organization's ethical framework. Such leadership fosters an atmosphere of accountability and transparency, essential for building a trustworthy reputation.

Cultivating an environment where ethical practices are the norm rather than the exception requires continuous effort and commitment. It involves not just setting clear ethical guidelines but also providing ongoing education and support to ensure these principles are understood and lived by everyone within the organization. This proactive approach to ethics serves as a protective barrier against potential pitfalls and challenges, ensuring the company remains on a path of integrity.

The commitment to ethical business practices is a testament to an organization's dedication to doing what is right, not just what is profitable. This dedication to ethics not only benefits the company in terms of reputation and financial success but also contributes to a larger societal good. By leading with integrity, businesses can inspire change, promoting a more ethical and equitable world for future generations.

Transparency and Accountability

Businesses that place a high value on transparency and accountability are setting the stage for a culture rooted in trust and integrity. By embracing open communication and being honest, they build meaningful connections with all their stakeholders, ensuring everyone has access to the information they need. This openness to share, combined with a readiness to own their decisions and actions, and quickly correct any missteps, establishes them as trustworthy and responsible entities.

These organizations, by steadfastly adhering to principles of accountability, earn the admiration and loyalty of customers, employees, and the community at large. Their unwavering commitment to ethical practices and their agility in addressing issues as they arise builds a foundation of confidence among all their stakeholders. It is this enduring trust that cultivates lasting relationships, underpinned by mutual respect and shared values.

Moreover, the cycle of transparency and accountability does more than just bolster the company's image; it has a ripple effect, enhancing societal values. Through their actions, these businesses showcase the critical role of integrity in the corporate world, setting a benchmark for others to follow. This not only elevates their own standing but also serves as a beacon, guiding the way towards more ethical and responsible business conduct across the board.

In fostering an environment where accountability is not just expected but integrated into the very fabric of their operations, these companies lead by example. They prove that doing business ethically and transparently is not only possible but also beneficial, paving the way for a future where corporate responsibility is the norm, not the exception. This approach to business not only secures their success but also contributes to a healthier, more equitable society.

The commitment to transparency and accountability is a testament to the power of ethical leadership and the positive change it can engender. It speaks volumes about the potential for businesses to not only achieve their goals but to do so in a way that uplifts and inspires all those they touch. In embracing these values, businesses can transcend the ordinary, becoming pillars of integrity and beacons of trust in the community, inspiring others to follow in their footsteps.

Fair Treatment and Diversity

In the heart of an ethical business lies the unwavering commitment to fairness and equality, pillars that illuminate every decision and action. This principle demands that every person be treated with the utmost dignity and respect, regardless of their background, beliefs, or identity. It is a recognition that diversity is not just a box to check in compliance with laws but a treasure trove of varied perspectives that enrich the organization.

Creating an inclusive environment is a powerful way for companies to unlock the full potential of their teams, enabling each member to contribute their best. This dedication to inclusivity ensures that every voice is not only heard but also valued, paving the way for groundbreaking innovation and collaboration. The result is a workplace that not only boosts employee morale and retention but also shines as a beacon of integrity and social responsibility in the community.

By valuing every individual's contribution, businesses can offer services and products that resonate more deeply with a diverse clientele. This approach goes beyond the confines of the office to impact the wider community positively, fostering a culture of inclusivity and respect. Such a commitment to ethical practices in business is a testament to the power of fairness and equality in driving sustainable growth and creating a positive ripple effect in society.

In this journey, the focus on ethics transforms challenges into opportunities for growth, learning, and improvement. It's about building bridges between different cultures, perspectives, and experiences to create a richer, more vibrant tapestry. The ethical business becomes a lighthouse, guiding the way for others in the industry, demonstrating that success and integrity can go hand in hand.

The path of ethics, fairness, and equality is not just the right thing to do; it's a strategic imperative for any forward-thinking business. It nurtures an environment where creativity flourishes, relationships deepen, and sustainable success is built on the foundation of social responsibility. Through these commitments, businesses can not only achieve their goals but also contribute to a more just and equitable world.

Social Responsibility

Ethical businesses understand that their role extends beyond just making profits; they see the value in contributing positively to society and the environment. By engaging in philanthropy, volunteer work, and sustainable practices, they aim to make a significant impact that goes beyond monetary achievements. These organizations show a deep respect for the well-being of local communities and the planet, committing to actions that help ensure a brighter future for everyone.

Such businesses stand out for their unwavering commitment to social and environmental responsibility, marking a shift from the traditional profit-driven business models. They foster a culture where corporate citizenship is integral, measuring success not just in financial terms but also by the positive changes they bring to society and the environment. This approach sets a powerful example, demonstrating that business can be a force for good, leading the way in responsible and sustainable practices.

By choosing to operate ethically, these companies contribute to a more sustainable and equitable world. They recognize that their business decisions have far-reaching effects, not only for today's society but for future generations as well. Their actions reflect a deep understanding of the interconnectedness of all aspects of society, and by prioritizing ethical practices, they inspire others to follow suit.

The impact of ethical businesses is profound, as they contribute to the creation of a more just and sustainable world. Through their commitment to doing what's right, not just what's profitable, they challenge the status quo and inspire a new wave of business leaders. This transformative approach encourages other companies to reconsider their own practices and align more closely with values of sustainability and social responsibility.

Ethical businesses are beacons of hope and innovation in the business world. By valuing both profit and purpose, they illustrate that success encompasses more than just the bottom line. Their legacy is defined by the positive impact they have on the world, proving that ethical business practices are not only viable but essential for the future of our planet and society.

Continuous Improvement

In the ever-evolving landscape of business, ethical practices stand as a beacon of adaptability and responsiveness to societal shifts and environmental changes. Companies at the forefront of this dynamic environment acknowledge the critical need to stay updated with ethical norms, dedicating themselves to a path of perpetual learning and refinement. By embracing feedback, instituting comprehensive training, and seeking insights from ethics professionals, they exemplify a deep-rooted commitment to maintaining exemplary standards of behavior. This approach not only highlights their dedication to ethical values but also builds a foundation of trust and respect with all their stakeholders.

Organizations that prioritize ongoing enhancement in their ethical frameworks do more than just comply with standards; they foster an ethos of integrity and responsibility that permeates every layer of their operations. Such unwavering focus ensures that ethical considerations are seamlessly woven into the fabric of their decision-making and everyday activities, paving the way for enduring prosperity and achievement. It's this relentless pursuit of ethical superiority that positions these entities as pioneers, inspiring a ripple effect of positive transformation across their sectors and the wider business world.

By setting an example of ethical leadership, these companies illuminate the path for others, proving that success and moral conduct can go hand in hand. Their journey towards ethical excellence is a testament to the belief that doing the right thing is not just good practice but a strategic advantage that propels them forward. In doing so, they not only achieve their own goals but also contribute significantly to elevating industry standards, encouraging a universal stride towards ethical business practices.

The commitment to ethical excellence is a continuous journey, marked by an unyielding dedication to progress and improvement. For these organizations, it's a strategic choice that influences their legacy and defines their identity in the marketplace. As they navigate through challenges and opportunities, their ethical compass guides them, ensuring that they remain steadfast in their principles while adapting to the changing business landscape.

The pursuit of ethical business practices is about more than just adhering to rules; it's about shaping a culture that values transparency, accountability, and respect. Through their actions, these organizations inspire a broader movement towards ethical business conduct, demonstrating that true success is measured not just by financial achievements but by the positive impact on society and the environment. As they lead by example, they pave the way for a future where business and ethics are inextricably linked, creating a world where companies thrive by doing good.

Conclusion

In the journey towards ethical business practices, companies are guided by core values like integrity, transparency, and social responsibility. These values serve as the compass for making decisions that favor the well-being of all, over the allure of immediate profits. Such commitment not only minimizes risks but also cements a bond of trust with stakeholders, paving the path for sustainable success and a meaningful impact on society.

Adopting ethical practices isn't just about following a trend; it's about embedding these principles into the very fabric of an organization's culture. When businesses operate with unwavering integrity and transparency, they not only foster a positive internal environment but also set a benchmark in the industry. This approach ensures that ethical considerations are at the forefront of every decision, demonstrating a commitment to the greater good.

The collective effort to prioritize ethics in business goes beyond just enhancing a company's reputation. It's about creating a ripple effect that encourages other organizations to follow suit, leading to widespread positive change. Through collaboration and a steadfast commitment to these values, businesses can drive innovation and progress that benefits society as a whole.

Envisioning a future where ethical standards are seamlessly integrated into all business operations is not just a dream but a tangible goal. This vision requires dedication from every member within an organization, from leadership to employees, to embrace and act upon these principles daily. Such a united effort can transform the business landscape, making ethical business practices a universal norm rather than an exception.

The pursuit of ethical business practices is a journey that offers far-reaching benefits. It enhances the quality of life for communities, promotes environmental sustainability, and drives economic progress on a global scale. By steadfastly adhering to these ethical principles, businesses can forge a legacy of responsibility and trust, contributing to a better world for future generations.

CASE STUDIES: Embracing Ethical Business Practices

Case Study 1: The Organic Clothing Company

Background:

A small startup, GreenThreads, was founded with a mission to produce environmentally friendly and ethically made clothing. The company used sustainable materials, such as organic cotton and recycled polyester, and ensured fair labor practices by partnering with factories that provided safe working conditions and fair wages.

Challenge:

As GreenThreads grew in popularity, they faced pressure to increase production to meet demand. However, sourcing sustainable materials and maintaining ethical labor practices became increasingly challenging. Competitors were offering cheaper alternatives made with non-organic materials and produced in factories with questionable labor practices.

Solution:

Rather than compromising their values for profit, GreenThreads chose to double down on their commitment to ethical business practices. They invested in building long-term relationships with their suppliers, working closely with them to improve efficiency and find innovative solutions to sustainability challenges. Additionally, the company focused on educating consumers about the importance of ethical fashion and the impact of their purchasing decisions.

Outcome:

Despite facing challenges and experiencing slower growth compared to some competitors, GreenThreads gained a loyal customer base who appreciated their commitment to sustainability and ethics. Over time, the company's reputation as a leader in ethical fashion grew, attracting customers who were willing to pay a premium for their products. GreenThreads' success demonstrated that embracing ethical business practices could be not only morally right but also financially rewarding in the long run.

Case Study 2: The Sustainable Tech Company

Background:

TechTech was a medium-sized technology company specializing in consumer electronics. Concerned about the environmental impact of their products, the company embarked on a journey to adopt sustainable practices throughout their operations. They focused on reducing energy consumption, minimizing waste, and using recyclable materials in their products.

Challenge:

In an industry known for its fast-paced innovation and planned obsolescence, TechTech faced skepticism from investors and shareholders about the feasibility of their sustainable business model. Some argued that prioritizing environmental concerns would hinder the company's ability to compete with larger, less environmentally conscious competitors who could produce cheaper products at a faster pace.

Solution:

TechTech recognized that embracing sustainability was not just a moral imperative but also a strategic advantage. They invested in research and development to create innovative, eco-friendly products that appealed to environmentally conscious consumers. Additionally, the company worked to streamline their supply chain and production processes to reduce waste and energy consumption.

Outcome:

Despite initial doubts, TechTech's commitment to sustainability paid off in the long run. Their eco-friendly products resonated with consumers who were increasingly concerned about the environmental impact of their purchases. As awareness of climate change grew, TechTech's reputation as a sustainable tech company attracted new customers and investors who valued their ethical business practices. Ultimately, the company's success demonstrated that embracing sustainability could drive innovation and competitive advantage in the tech industry.

Examples

1. **Patagonia:** Patagonia, a renowned outdoor clothing and gear company, is dedicated to sustainability and environmental activism, often leading campaigns to protect natural resources and promote ethical business practices. With a commitment to quality and innovation, Patagonia continuously strives to create products that not only meet the needs of outdoor enthusiasts but also minimize their environmental footprint.

2. **Ben & Jerry's:** Ben & Jerry's, a beloved ice cream brand, is not only known for its delicious flavors but also for its social and environmental activism. From supporting fair trade ingredients to advocating for social justice issues, Ben & Jerry's integrates its values into every aspect of its business, inspiring others to make a positive impact through their consumer choices.

3. **The Body Shop:** The Body Shop, a global beauty brand, stands out for its commitment to cruelty-free products and activism for human rights and environmental sustainability. Through its ethical sourcing practices and community trade initiatives, The Body Shop empowers marginalized communities while offering customers ethically produced skincare, makeup, and body care products.

4. **TOMS Shoes:** TOMS Shoes, recognized for its one-for-one giving model, not only produces stylish footwear but also addresses global issues such as poverty and lack of access to education and healthcare. For every pair of shoes purchased, TOMS donates a pair to a person in need, exemplifying its mission to create positive social change through business.

5. **Salesforce:** Salesforce, a leading customer relationship management platform, distinguishes itself not only for its innovative technology but also for its philanthropic efforts and commitment to corporate social responsibility. Through its 1-1-1 model, Salesforce donates 1% of its equity, 1% of its employees' time, and 1% of its products to support nonprofit organizations and communities worldwide, demonstrating its dedication to making a meaningful impact beyond profits.

Top Five Takeaways

1. **Integrity serves as the cornerstone** of ethical business practices, guiding organizations to uphold honesty, accountability, and moral principles in all interactions. By prioritizing integrity, businesses establish a culture of trust and credibility, fostering stronger relationships with customers, employees, and partners.

2. **Transparency plays a pivotal role** in cultivating trust among stakeholders by providing openness and clarity in communication and decision-making processes. When organizations are transparent about their actions, policies, and performance, stakeholders feel empowered and engaged, leading to stronger partnerships and mutual respect.

3. **Fair treatment and embracing diversity** not only foster a culture of inclusivity and equity but also fuel innovation and collaboration within organizations. By recognizing and valuing the unique perspectives and contributions of individuals from diverse backgrounds, businesses can tap into a wealth of creativity and ideas, driving sustainable growth and success.

4. **Social responsibility** goes beyond philanthropy and compliance, encompassing a commitment to ethical conduct and positive impact on society and the environment. By integrating social responsibility into their core business strategies, organizations can contribute to long-term sustainability by addressing pressing societal challenges and creating shared value for all stakeholders.

5. **Continuous improvement** is essential for ensuring that ethical standards evolve and adapt to changing circumstances and emerging ethical dilemmas. By regularly reviewing and enhancing ethical frameworks, policies, and practices, organizations can stay ahead of ethical challenges, maintain relevance, and uphold their commitment to integrity and responsible business conduct.

Actions to Take

1. **Lead by example and prioritize integrity in all decisions:** We believe in setting a standard of integrity through our actions, ensuring that ethical principles guide every decision we make. By consistently demonstrating integrity in our conduct, we inspire trust and accountability among our team members, clients, and partners.

2. **Foster a culture of transparency and open communication:** Our commitment to fostering transparency means we actively share information, encourage honest dialogue, and value diverse perspectives within our organization. By creating an environment where open communication is championed, we empower our team to collaborate effectively and address challenges with clarity and understanding.

3. **Invest in diversity and inclusion initiatives:** We recognize the importance of embracing diversity and inclusion as core values, and we invest in initiatives that promote equitable opportunities for all individuals. Through intentional efforts to foster diversity in our workforce and create an inclusive environment, we enrich

our organization with varied perspectives, experiences, and talents, driving innovation and success.

4. **Implement sustainable business practices:** Sustainability is integral to our business strategy, and we are committed to implementing practices that minimize environmental impact while maximizing long-term value. By integrating sustainable solutions into our operations, supply chain, and product development, we strive to contribute positively to the planet and future generations.

5. **Regularly evaluate and improve ethical policies and procedures:** We understand the importance of regularly assessing our ethical policies and procedures to ensure alignment with evolving standards and best practices. Through continuous evaluation and improvement, we demonstrate our dedication to upholding the highest ethical standards, fostering trust, and meeting the expectations of our stakeholders.

Actions Not to Take

1. **Compromising ethical principles** for short-term gains can lead to long-term consequences, eroding trust and integrity within the organization. It's essential to prioritize ethical considerations even when facing pressure for immediate results, as maintaining integrity fosters sustainable success and positive relationships with stakeholders.

2. **Ignoring feedback or concerns** from stakeholders can result in missed opportunities for improvement and damage to relationships built on trust. Actively engaging with feedback demonstrates a commitment to collaboration and continuous improvement, leading to better outcomes and stronger partnerships in the long run.

3. **Tolerating discrimination or inequality** in the workplace not only violates fundamental human rights but also undermines morale and productivity. By fostering an inclusive and equitable environment, organizations can unlock the full potential of their diverse workforce and cultivate a culture of respect and innovation.

4. **Neglecting social and environmental responsibilities** can lead to reputational damage and regulatory scrutiny, jeopardizing long-term viability and stakeholder trust. Embracing corporate social responsibility practices not only mitigates risks but also creates opportunities for positive impact and sustainable growth within the community and the environment.

5. **Becoming complacent in ethical standards** and practices poses a significant risk to organizational integrity and credibility. Continuously challenging and improving ethical standards ensures alignment with evolving societal expectations and reinforces a culture of accountability and ethical leadership.

Part Two: Strategy and Planning

Strategy and planning are key to long-term success, involving a deep analysis of the present, setting future goals, and creating a roadmap to achieve them. Planning details the steps and resources needed, addressing potential challenges. Together, they enable clear, adaptable progress, fostering sustainable growth and a competitive advantage.

Chapter 6: Developing a Business Strategy

Creating a business strategy is akin to embarking on an exciting voyage into unknown territories. It requires not just the vision to foresee upcoming trends and hurdles but also the strength to overcome challenges that appear without warning. Being flexible and ready to adapt is key in this ever-evolving business landscape, where change is the only constant.

Every step taken in formulating your strategy is pivotal, serving as a cornerstone on which the future of your organization is built. These decisions shape the trajectory and expansion of your business, guiding it towards its aspirations. It's a journey that demands careful planning and a clear focus on where you want to go, ensuring that every move is aligned with your ultimate objectives.

Drawing lessons from both the triumphs and setbacks of the past is invaluable as we chart our course forward. The experiences of those who have navigated similar paths before us light the way, offering wisdom and a framework for tackling upcoming obstacles. This journey highlights the need for unwavering commitment and passion as we venture through the unpredictable waters of the business realm.

Embracing a well-crafted strategy, fueled by a deep dedication to our vision, allows us to navigate with confidence. It's about holding steadfast to our goals, even when faced with the unknown, and pushing forward with determination. This resolve enables us to transform challenges into stepping stones towards success, propelling our ventures to new heights.

The importance of a strategic approach cannot be overstated. It's a blueprint for success that requires both imagination and resilience, enabling us to anticipate changes and respond effectively. With a strong strategy in place and a relentless pursuit of our goals, the path to prosperity is not just a dream but a journey we can confidently embark on, ready to achieve greatness.

Inspirational Quote

"Success is not final, failure is not fatal: It is the courage to continue that counts." - Winston Churchill

Vision and Mission

At the heart of every successful business lies a clearly articulated vision and a compelling mission, essential for steering the organization towards greatness. These foundational elements not only provide a strategic roadmap but also inspire and motivate everyone involved, from employees to stakeholders. By establishing a vision, businesses illuminate the path forward, offering clear guidance on the aspirations and long-term ambitions that define their purpose.

Conversely, the mission is the engine that drives the organization's day-to-day activities, embedding each action with deep significance and intention. It clearly communicates the essence of the company's existence and sets forth the key aims that guide its operations. This focus ensures that every choice and action is in harmony with the business's broader objectives, promoting a cohesive effort towards achieving remarkable outcomes.

The synergy between a distinct vision and a powerful mission is crucial for guiding a company towards its ultimate goals, making every action intentional and goal-directed. This combination acts as a beacon, guiding the organization through challenges and opportunities alike, ensuring that the journey towards success is both deliberate and meaningful. It's this strategic alignment that empowers businesses to transcend ordinary expectations, setting a course for extraordinary achievements.

Moreover, these guiding principles serve as a source of inspiration and motivation, fostering an environment where innovation and progress thrive. They provide a framework within which individuals can align their personal goals with those of the organization, cultivating a culture of shared purpose and collective success. This alignment not only enhances operational efficiency but also strengthens the bond between the company and its stakeholders, driving sustained growth and success.

The essence of a thriving business model lies in its ability to blend a visionary outlook with a mission-driven approach, crafting a narrative that resonates with all those it touches. This strategic foundation not only directs the organization's journey but also enriches it, ensuring that every step taken is infused with meaning and geared towards a common, aspirational future. It is this profound connection between vision and mission that lights the path to innovation, unity, and unparalleled success in the competitive business landscape.

Understanding Your Market

In today's ever-changing business landscape, mastering market dynamics is crucial for achieving success. Understanding the shifting needs and desires of customers is key to crafting products and services that truly connect with your audience. Moreover, the ability to foresee upcoming trends and disruptions sets the foundation for proactive adaptation and innovation, allowing businesses to thrive in a fluid market.

To position your business as a market leader, it's vital to go beyond merely meeting the present demands. Anticipating future developments enables strategic planning and ensures your business remains relevant and ahead of its competitors. This forward-looking mindset not only garners a competitive advantage but also cements your reputation as an innovator in your field.

Being ahead of the curve in predicting market shifts allows for the agile evolution of business strategies. This agility enables companies to introduce groundbreaking products and services, setting new industry standards. As a result, businesses that are quick to adapt and innovate often lead the pack, enjoying sustained growth and increased profitability.

Embracing a visionary approach to business is about fostering a culture of continuous learning and improvement. It involves regularly scanning the horizon for emerging opportunities and challenges. By doing so, businesses can harness the potential of new technologies and methodologies, staying at the forefront of their industry.

The path to sustained business success and growth lies in an unwavering commitment to understanding and anticipating market dynamics. By embracing change, fostering innovation, and always planning for the future, businesses can secure their position as industry leaders. This proactive stance not only ensures long-term profitability but also defines the legacy of the business in the evolving market landscape.

Competitive Analysis

In the ever-evolving world of business, encountering competition is inevitable. Success hinges not on the mere existence of rivals but on how one responds to them. Delving deep into a competitor analysis illuminates their strengths and weaknesses, revealing both the challenges and opportunities they bring. This process is key to understanding the competitive landscape, paving the way for strategic improvements and innovation.

Armed with insights from a detailed competitor analysis, a business can craft its position to spotlight its unique offerings. Identifying what sets it apart allows for tailored strategies that build on strengths and address weaknesses. This forward-thinking stance not only carves a distinct place in the market but also secures a lasting competitive edge.

Understanding the competitive arena empowers a company to innovate and improve continually. It's this cycle of learning and adapting that fosters resilience and growth. By staying attuned to the external environment, a business can anticipate changes and pivot accordingly, ensuring it remains a step ahead.

Adopting a strategic approach to competition transforms challenges into stepping stones for success. It encourages a culture of constant learning, adaptability, and innovation. This mindset turns potential threats into opportunities, guiding a business toward sustained success and leadership in its field.

Thriving in a competitive landscape requires more than just recognition of the competition. It demands a proactive, strategic response that leverages unique strengths and addresses vulnerabilities. Through a commitment to continuous improvement and strategic positioning, a business can not only survive but flourish, setting new standards of excellence in its industry.

Setting Goals and Objectives

Setting goals and objectives is the cornerstone of achieving success, serving as a guiding light towards the fulfillment of your aspirations. Establishing clear targets provides a strong base from which you can develop strategies and make decisions that steer you closer to your ambitions. Embracing the SMART framework—making goals specific, measurable, achievable, relevant, and time-bound—offers a structured and effective approach to goal setting. This method not only simplifies tracking your progress but also bolsters accountability, allowing for adjustments along the way to ensure alignment with your ultimate aims.

Embarking on the path to realize your dreams involves more than just wishful thinking; it necessitates unwavering discipline and a deep-seated commitment to your objectives. By adopting a methodical approach to setting and pursuing your goals, you're able to accurately gauge your advancement and stay concentrated on your end goals. It's important to acknowledge that the road to success is often paved with hurdles and setbacks. Yet, with a meticulously crafted plan and the determination to push through adversity, you arm yourself with the key ingredients for surmounting challenges and reaching your goals.

The essence of goal setting lies in its ability to transform vision into reality, turning abstract dreams into achievable milestones. By breaking down your overarching aims into smaller, more manageable tasks, you create a roadmap that guides your every step. This incremental approach not only keeps motivation high but also fosters a sense of accomplishment as you tick off each milestone, propelling you forward towards your larger objectives.

Success is not just about reaching a destination; it's about the growth and learning that occur along the journey. Each goal achieved is a testament to your hard work, discipline, and resilience, serving as a building block for future endeavors. This journey of continuous improvement and the pursuit of excellence is what shapes character and defines true achievement.

The power of goal setting lies in its capacity to inspire action and drive change. By setting clear, attainable objectives and dedicating yourself to their pursuit, you unlock your potential to achieve greatness. Remember, the most successful individuals and organizations are those that consistently set high standards, pursue their goals with passion, and are not afraid to recalibrate their direction in the face of new challenges.

Execution and Adaptation

In the world of business, it's understood that no strategy is immune to flaws, and it's rare for any plan to unfold without deviation from its original course. This inherent uncertainty underscores the vital role of agility in the corporate realm. The hallmark of a successful business lies in its ability to quickly pivot and adapt to unexpected challenges and obstacles, demonstrating resilience and strategic flexibility.

The ability to reassess and adjust strategies in light of new information or market changes is of paramount importance. It's this flexibility that allows businesses to remain competitive and innovative in a landscape that is constantly evolving. Successful enterprises are those that view adaptation not as a challenge but as an opportunity to evolve and strengthen their market position.

In the fast-paced and unpredictable arena of entrepreneurship, flexibility and resilience are more than just advantageous traits; they are fundamental to survival and prosperity. The businesses that endure over time are not the ones that avoid setbacks but those that navigate through challenges by making timely and effective adjustments. This ability to adapt to changing conditions signifies a proactive approach to growth and success.

Adopting a mindset that welcomes change as a catalyst for improvement is crucial for anyone aspiring to succeed in the dynamic business environment. This perspective encourages continuous learning and the pursuit of innovation, ensuring that a business remains relevant and forward-thinking. It's through embracing change that businesses can uncover new opportunities and pathways to success.

Building resilience and cultivating flexibility are essential strategies for thriving in today's ever-changing business landscape. These qualities enable businesses to respond effectively to uncertainties and capitalize on new opportunities, laying the groundwork for sustained growth and success. In embracing these principles, entrepreneurs and business leaders can steer their ventures toward a prosperous future with confidence and strategic insight.

Conclusion

Creating a business strategy is not just about planning; it's about aligning our every step with the grand visions and aspirations that guide us. This vision, when fueled by our unwavering commitment to our mission, lays a robust foundation for growth and achievement. Moreover, leveraging the wisdom and experiences of those who have tread this path before us brings a depth of insight that significantly enriches our strategic planning. This fusion of motivation and practical knowledge empowers us to confidently and flexibly navigate the ever-evolving business terrain.

As we venture forward, it is our perseverance that will illuminate the path, keeping us anchored even amidst the stormiest of seas. Innovation, our relentless driving force, encourages us to constantly seek out new territories and seize the myriad opportunities that await. This journey, underscored by an unyielding pursuit of excellence and a zeal for exploration, is set to be a voyage of substantial growth and profound discoveries.

Our commitment to dreaming big and the relentless pursuit of turning those dreams into reality opens the door to unparalleled achievements and thrilling ventures. It is this boldness to envision and execute that sets the stage for us to reach unprecedented heights and truly make a mark. In doing so, we not only achieve our own goals but also inspire those around us to embark on their own journeys of success and innovation.

Embracing the journey with an open heart and a clear vision, we find that every challenge faced is an opportunity for learning and every failure a stepping stone to success. This mindset transforms obstacles into pathways and skepticism into the fuel for our journey. It is in the dedication to our vision, the courage to innovate, and the resilience to persevere that our true potential unfolds.

Our journey in crafting and executing a business strategy is an exhilarating adventure that demands passion, insight, and resilience. By drawing upon the collective wisdom of the past and harnessing the power of innovation, we navigate the complexities of the business world. This approach not only ensures our growth and success but also inspires a legacy of excellence and innovation for generations to come.

CASE STUDIES: Developing a Business Strategy

Case Study 1: Diversification Strategy for a Consumer Goods Company

Background:

ABC Corporation, a leading consumer goods company known for its household cleaning products, sought to diversify its business to mitigate risks and capitalize on new growth opportunities. With increasing competition and market saturation in the cleaning products industry, ABC Corporation recognized the need to expand into adjacent markets to sustain long-term growth.

Challenge:

The challenge for ABC Corporation was to identify viable diversification opportunities that aligned with its core competencies and strategic objectives. Additionally, the company needed to develop a comprehensive business strategy to enter new markets while minimizing risks and maximizing returns on investment.

Solution:

To address these challenges, ABC Corporation conducted extensive market research and analysis to identify potential growth areas and assess market dynamics. They evaluated various options for diversification, including expanding their product portfolio, entering new geographic markets, and exploring partnerships or acquisitions.

After careful consideration, ABC Corporation decided to diversify into the personal care products market, leveraging its expertise in consumer goods manufacturing and distribution. They identified a growing demand for natural and eco-friendly personal care products and developed a range of new offerings, including shampoo, body wash, and skincare products.

To support their diversification strategy, ABC Corporation invested in product development, marketing, and distribution infrastructure. They also pursued strategic partnerships with retailers and online platforms to expand their reach and gain access to new customer segments.

Outcome:

By executing their diversification strategy effectively, ABC Corporation successfully entered the personal care products market and achieved significant revenue growth. Their new product offerings resonated with consumers seeking natural and eco-friendly alternatives, driving sales and market share gains. Additionally, diversifying into the personal care segment helped ABC Corporation reduce its reliance on the cleaning products market and mitigate risks associated with industry-specific challenges. Overall, the company's strategic approach to diversification enabled it to strengthen its competitive position and position itself for long-term success.

Case Study 2: Digital Transformation Strategy for a Financial Services Firm

Background:

XYZ Bank, a traditional financial services firm with a large network of branches and a legacy IT infrastructure, recognized the need to embrace digital transformation to remain competitive in an increasingly digital world. With the rise of fintech startups and changing customer preferences, XYZ Bank sought to modernize its operations and enhance its digital capabilities.

Challenge:

The challenge for XYZ Bank was to navigate the complexities of digital transformation while ensuring regulatory compliance, safeguarding customer data, and maintaining trust and confidence in its brand. Additionally, the company needed to overcome internal resistance to change and foster a culture of innovation and collaboration among its employees.

Solution:

To address these challenges, XYZ Bank developed a comprehensive digital transformation strategy focused on customer experience, operational efficiency, and innovation. They invested in upgrading their IT infrastructure, implementing cloud-based technologies, and developing digital banking platforms to improve accessibility and convenience for customers.

Additionally, XYZ Bank leveraged data analytics and artificial intelligence to gain insights into customer behavior, personalize services, and identify opportunities for cross-selling and upselling. They also launched initiatives to enhance cybersecurity measures, protect customer data, and comply with regulatory requirements.

To drive employee engagement and foster a culture of innovation, XYZ Bank invested in training and development programs, established cross-functional teams to collaborate on digital initiatives, and incentivized employees to embrace digital tools and technologies.

Outcome:

By executing their digital transformation strategy effectively, XYZ Bank transformed its operations and enhanced its competitiveness in the financial services industry. The company's digital banking platforms and personalized services resonated with customers, driving customer acquisition and retention. Additionally, improvements in operational efficiency and cost savings resulting from digital initiatives helped XYZ Bank improve profitability and maintain a competitive edge in a rapidly evolving market. Overall, the company's strategic approach to digital transformation enabled it to position itself as a leader in innovation and technology adoption within the financial services sector.

Examples

1. **Apple Inc.:** Apple Inc. has established itself as a pioneer in the technology industry, offering a wide range of products including iPhones, iPads, and Mac computers. The company is renowned for its innovation and design, consistently setting trends in consumer electronics.

2. **Amazon.com:** Amazon.com is a global e-commerce giant that revolutionized online shopping by offering a vast selection of products with convenient delivery options. Beyond retail, Amazon has expanded into cloud computing with Amazon Web Services (AWS), becoming a dominant player in the tech industry.

3. **Tesla, Inc.:** Tesla, Inc. is at the forefront of the electric vehicle market, committed to sustainable energy solutions through its range of electric cars and energy storage products. Founded by Elon Musk, Tesla is also pioneering in autonomous driving technology, aiming to revolutionize transportation.

4. **Coca-Cola Company:** The Coca-Cola Company is a global beverage leader, offering a wide variety of soft drinks, waters, and juices in over 200 countries. Known for its flagship product, Coca-Cola, the company has a rich history of over 130 years and continues to be a symbol of refreshment and happiness around the world.

5. **Procter & Gamble:** Procter & Gamble, often known as P&G, is a multinational corporation that provides a wide array of consumer goods, from personal care to household cleaning products. With its commitment to quality and innovation,

P&G has become a household name, building trust with consumers worldwide for over 180 years.

Top Five Takeaways

1. **Define a clear vision and mission** for your business. Establishing a clear vision and mission is crucial as they serve as the foundation for all strategic decisions and actions your company will take. These elements help in aligning the team's efforts towards common goals.

2. **Understand your market** and anticipate future trends. Gaining a deep understanding of your market, including current demands and potential future trends, is essential for staying ahead of competitors. This knowledge allows for proactive strategy adjustments and innovation.

3. **Conduct thorough competitive analysis** to identify opportunities and threats. A detailed analysis of your competitors can uncover valuable insights about their strengths and weaknesses, providing opportunities for your business to capitalize on and threats to mitigate.

4. **Set SMART goals and objectives** to guide your efforts. Setting Specific, Measurable, Achievable, Relevant, and Time-bound (SMART) goals ensures that your business objectives are clear and attainable, guiding your team's efforts towards meaningful outcomes.

5. **Embrace agility and resilience** in the face of challenges. The ability to quickly adapt to changes and recover from setbacks is critical for long-term success. Embracing agility and resilience allows your business to navigate through challenges more effectively.

Actions to Take

1. **Develop a compelling vision and mission statement.** Crafting a compelling vision and mission statement can inspire your team and provide a clear direction for your company. It acts as a guiding star for decision-making and strategy development.

2. **Stay informed about market trends and customer preferences.** Keeping abreast of the latest market trends and understanding customer preferences are

key to developing products and services that meet their needs. This proactive approach can lead to greater innovation and customer satisfaction.

3. **Analyze your competitors' strategies and offerings.** By carefully analyzing the strategies and offerings of your competitors, you can identify gaps in the market and areas for improvement in your own business. This insight is invaluable for staying competitive and innovative.

4. **Set specific, measurable goals with realistic timelines.** Establishing specific and measurable goals within realistic timelines helps ensure that your team is focused and motivated to achieve them. This clarity in goal setting aids in tracking progress and adjusting strategies as necessary.

5. **Remain flexible and adapt your strategy as needed.** The business environment is constantly changing, so it's important to remain flexible and ready to adapt your strategy in response to new challenges and opportunities. This flexibility can be the difference between thriving and merely surviving.

Actions Not to Take

1. **Neglect to define a clear vision and mission.** Failing to define a clear vision and mission for your business can lead to confusion and misaligned efforts within your team, ultimately hindering your company's potential for success.

2. **Ignore changes in the market landscape.** Ignoring shifts in the market landscape can result in missed opportunities and an inability to respond effectively to new challenges, putting your business at a disadvantage.

3. **Underestimate the importance of competitive analysis.** Underestimating the value of competitive analysis can leave your business vulnerable to threats and blind to opportunities, limiting your ability to compete effectively.

4. **Set vague or unrealistic goals.** Setting goals that are either too vague or unrealistic can demotivate your team and lead to a lack of clear direction, making it difficult to measure success and make necessary adjustments.

5. **Resist adapting to changing circumstances.** Resisting the need to adapt to changing circumstances can stifle innovation and growth, leaving your business unable to respond effectively to new challenges and market demands.

Chapter 7: Conducting Market Research and Analysis

Market research and analysis stand as the cornerstone of successful business strategies, offering the insights necessary for making informed decisions. These tools enable a deep dive into consumer behaviors, industry shifts, and the competitive arena, arming businesses with the knowledge to steer their courses with confidence. Armed with these insights, companies can chart a path through market complexities, seizing opportunities to innovate and expand.

This chapter unfolds the transformative power of market research and analysis, underscoring their crucial role in equipping businesses for competition in a constantly changing market. It highlights how these practices empower companies to stay ahead, by identifying trends and leveraging opportunities for growth. Through this exploration, businesses are shown how to maintain their edge and thrive amidst market fluctuations.

The value of market research and analysis lies in their ability to offer a predictive view, enabling businesses to anticipate and adapt to market dynamics. By meticulously gathering and analyzing data, businesses can spot trends indicating shifts in consumer preferences, technological advancements, and emerging competitive challenges. This foresight encourages proactive strategy adjustments, product development, and marketing innovations, ensuring businesses remain relevant and competitive.

In recognizing the importance of market research and analysis, companies are better positioned to pioneer innovation, cultivate sustainable growth, and achieve a dominant market presence. These practices are not just about responding to the current market conditions but shaping the future of the business landscape. They provide the blueprint for building resilient, forward-thinking companies that are prepared for whatever lies ahead.

As we delve deeper into the subject, it becomes clear that market research and analysis are not optional but essential for any business aiming for longevity and success. They offer a clear advantage in a fast-paced world, allowing businesses to not just survive but flourish. This chapter serves as a testament to the power of informed decision-making in setting the stage for achievement and excellence in the business world.

Inspirational Quote

"Success is not final, failure is not fatal: It is the courage to continue that counts." — Winston Churchill

Understanding Your Audience

Understanding the needs and desires of your target audience is crucial in developing products and services that resonate and fulfill their expectations. Conducting thorough market research gives businesses the chance to discover essential demographic information, preferences, and the unique challenges their potential customers face. This knowledge enables the tailoring of products and services to make them exceptionally appealing and pertinent to the intended market.

Empathy is key in this endeavor, as it allows companies to see their offerings through their customers' eyes. Adopting an empathetic stance fosters a deeper, more meaningful connection with the audience, pivotal for nurturing trust and loyalty. When customers feel genuinely understood and appreciated, they're more inclined to champion the brand, spreading word of their positive experiences.

This approach transcends mere transactions, transforming them into opportunities for adding substantial value to people's lives. It's not just about selling a product or service; it's about offering a solution that genuinely enhances the customer's world. This perspective is vital for creating offerings that don't just meet needs but exceed expectations, elevating the customer's experience.

By prioritizing empathy and understanding in business strategies, companies can build a solid foundation of trust and loyalty among their customers. This not only boosts the brand's reputation but also secures a dedicated customer base that is essential for sustained success. It's a testament to the power of truly understanding and valuing the customer's perspective.

The journey towards creating products and services that deeply connect with an audience begins with a profound understanding of their needs, desires, and challenges. Through empathy and dedicated market research, businesses can tailor their offerings to meet and exceed expectations, fostering a loyal community of customers who feel valued and understood. This approach is the cornerstone of long-term success, proving that genuine connection and understanding are indispensable in today's competitive marketplace.

Identifying Market Trends

Understanding market trends is pivotal for businesses aiming to navigate the complex landscape of today's economy. These trends serve as beacons, guiding companies toward opportunities for growth and alerting them to potential obstacles. By analyzing and adapting to these shifts, businesses can ensure their strategies are in harmony with current consumer demands and technological advancements, positioning themselves as leaders in their fields.

Staying ahead of the curve is crucial for any business that aspires to lead and innovate. Viewing changes and challenges as opportunities allows companies to transform potential threats into engines of innovation. This forward-thinking approach not only sets the stage for the creation of revolutionary products and services but also solidifies a company's standing as a trailblazer in its industry.

The ability to adapt and evolve with the market is what distinguishes successful companies from the rest. Through constant vigilance and a willingness to embrace new opportunities, businesses can drive their growth and secure a dominant position in their sectors. It's this agility and foresight that empower companies to not just survive but thrive in the face of change.

Innovation is at the heart of business growth and sustainability. By fostering a culture that embraces change and seeks out innovation, companies can break new ground and redefine industry standards. This commitment to innovation not only delivers unique value to customers but also establishes a company as a leader in its market, admired for its creativity and forward-thinking.

Businesses that excel in identifying and leveraging market trends set themselves apart. These are the organizations that lead their industries, driven by a relentless pursuit of excellence and a deep understanding of the ever-changing business landscape. Their success lies not just in what they do, but in how they adapt and respond to the world around them, always with an eye towards the future.

Analyzing Competitors

Analyzing your competition is not just about copying what they do; it's about finding your own path to success in a crowded marketplace. By diving deep into what your rivals are doing right and where they're falling short, you can discover untapped opportunities and innovate in ways they haven't imagined. This approach helps you pinpoint what makes your business special and how to leverage those strengths to rise above the rest.

With a clear understanding of your competitors, you're in a powerful position to craft a brand identity that truly resonates with your audience. It's about fine-tuning your message to spotlight how your brand delivers unique value, setting you apart from the crowd. This focus on what makes you different not only attracts attention but also cements your status as the go-to choice for your customers.

By strategically using insights from competitor analysis, you can shape a brand that speaks directly to the heart of your target market. This means sharpening your value proposition to clearly showcase the superior benefits of choosing your products or services over others. Such differentiation is key to not just catching the eye of potential customers but also winning their loyalty.

This process of strategic positioning is crucial for drawing in new customers and keeping them engaged over time. It's about consistently proving that your brand is the best option available, enhancing consumer preference and loyalty. As a result, your brand's presence in the market grows stronger, setting you up for long-term success and a significant competitive edge.

Understanding your competition is about much more than just staying a step ahead; it's about creating a unique space for your brand that attracts and retains a loyal customer base. Through careful analysis and strategic differentiation, you can highlight what makes your brand special and why consumers should choose you. This not only strengthens your market presence but also secures your competitive advantage, paving the way for sustained growth and success.

Leveraging Data Analytics

Data analytics stands as the backbone of contemporary business success, offering a lens to peer into vast data landscapes to reveal crucial insights and trends. By harnessing advanced analytics tools and methodologies, companies can convert untapped data into valuable knowledge. This knowledge serves as the foundation for informed strategic planning, enabling organizations to refine their operations and boost productivity.

Incorporating data-driven practices is key for companies looking to excel in the dynamic environment of today's economy. The strategic application of data analytics empowers firms to navigate toward their goals with precision. It illuminates paths to discovering emerging market trends and consumer behaviors, as well as forecasting future developments, positioning businesses to adapt swiftly and stay ahead of the curve.

A commitment to data-driven decision-making propels organizations forward, ensuring they are equipped to meet the challenges and opportunities of the digital age. It fosters a culture of innovation and continuous improvement, where data becomes a strategic asset in crafting cutting-edge solutions and services. Through this approach, businesses can distinguish themselves, enhancing their competitive advantage and securing a dominant place in their sectors.

The transformative power of data analytics is a game-changer for businesses intent on carving out a leadership position in their industries. It provides a clear roadmap for growth, operational excellence, and customer satisfaction. By prioritizing data analytics, companies unlock the potential to not only survive but thrive in the market, adapting with agility to the ever-changing business landscape.

Embracing a data-centric strategy is a wise move for any organization aspiring to be at the forefront of innovation. Data analytics is more than a tool; it's a strategic partner in driving growth, efficiency, and sustainability. In the quest for market leadership, leveraging data analytics is not just an option; it's an imperative for success in the modern business world.

Adapting to Change

In today's ever-evolving business world, being adaptable is not just an asset; it's a necessity for achieving lasting success and sustainability. Companies that embrace change as an opportunity for growth and innovation set themselves apart from those who see it as a threat. This willingness to evolve ensures they remain nimble, quickly adapting to market changes and consumer needs, which is crucial for thriving in today's unpredictable environment.

Adopting a mindset geared towards adaptability fosters a culture of perpetual learning and improvement within an organization. It encourages the exploration of new technologies, methodologies, and strategies, nurturing an environment where creativity and innovation can flourish. As organizations become proficient in adjusting to change, they carve out a unique competitive advantage that's hard for others to match.

By facing changes head-on, companies become stronger, more resilient entities. This resilience equips them to navigate future uncertainties with greater confidence and strategic acumen, turning potential challenges into opportunities for growth. In doing so, they not only ensure their survival but also lay the foundation for long-term prosperity.

Moreover, adaptability leads to the development of a more dynamic and responsive business model. This agility allows companies to capitalize on emerging trends and opportunities, positioning them at the forefront of their industries. It's a strategy that not only secures a company's current standing but also ensures its relevance and leadership in the future.

Adaptability is the key to unlocking a business's full potential in today's fast-paced market. It's about fostering a culture that values continuous learning, embraces innovation, and is always prepared to pivot in response to the changing business landscape. Companies that master the art of adaptability not only stand the test of time but also lead the charge in shaping the future of their respective industries.

Conclusion

In the ever-evolving landscape of business, the timeless truth that "knowledge is power" takes on a pivotal role, especially when it comes to market research and analysis. These essential processes grant businesses a deeper insight into their target audience, enabling them to customize their offerings to meet the unique desires and needs of their customers. Furthermore, the ability to identify and act on emerging market trends places companies at the forefront of innovation, ensuring their products and services remain both relevant and competitive.

The practice of analyzing competitors is not just a task; it's a strategic opportunity to distinguish your business in the crowded marketplace. This critical analysis reveals gaps in the market that can be transformed into unique selling propositions, helping your brand to stand out. By doing so, businesses not only find their niche but also establish a strong, differentiated presence that resonates with customers.

In today's data-rich world, leveraging data analytics emerges as a cornerstone for businesses keen on crafting a path to success. This approach unlocks a treasure trove of insights regarding customer behaviors, preferences, and feedback, which are instrumental in guiding strategic decisions and fostering innovation. It is the clarity gained from these insights that empowers businesses to make informed, strategic decisions that drive growth.

Adapting to change is another non-negotiable for businesses striving for longevity and relevance in the fast-paced market. This adaptability cultivates a culture of agility and responsiveness within organizations, allowing them to pivot quickly in response to market changes or disruptions. It's this proactive stance that enables businesses to navigate market complexities with finesse, keeping them steps ahead of challenges and competitors alike.

Armed with a thorough understanding of market dynamics, customer insights, and an unwavering willingness to embrace change, businesses position themselves for unparalleled growth and success. It's this strategic combination of knowledge, analysis, and adaptability that sets the stage for achieving long-term objectives and securing a competitive edge. In doing so, businesses not only thrive but also contribute to a dynamic, ever-evolving marketplace where innovation and customer satisfaction lead the way.

CASE STUDIES: Conducting Market Research and Analysis

Case Study 1: Launching a New Mobile App in the Fitness Industry

Background:

FitLife, a startup company specializing in fitness and wellness, developed a new mobile app aimed at providing personalized workout plans and nutrition guidance to users. Before launching the app, FitLife needed to conduct market research to understand consumer preferences, identify competitors, and assess market trends in the fitness and health app industry.

Challenge:

The fitness app market was highly competitive, with numerous established players offering a wide range of features and services to users. FitLife faced the challenge of differentiating their app from competitors and identifying a target market segment with unmet needs or underserved preferences.

Solution:

FitLife employed a multi-faceted approach to market research and analysis to address these challenges. They conducted surveys, interviews, and focus groups with fitness enthusiasts and potential users to gather insights into their preferences, habits, and pain points regarding fitness apps. Additionally, FitLife analyzed industry reports, app store reviews, and competitor offerings to identify trends and opportunities in the market.

Based on their research findings, FitLife identified a niche market segment of busy professionals seeking convenient and customizable fitness solutions that could fit into their hectic schedules. They tailored their app features and user interface to meet the needs of this target audience, emphasizing flexibility, convenience, and personalization.

Outcome:

Armed with insights from their market research, FitLife successfully launched their mobile app targeted at busy professionals looking for personalized fitness solutions. Their app quickly gained traction in the market, attracting a loyal user base and positive reviews. FitLife's emphasis on convenience and personalization resonated with users, enabling the company to differentiate itself from competitors and establish a strong presence in the fitness app industry.

Case Study 2: Entering a New Geographic Market for a Fashion Retailer

Background:

FashionForward, a fashion retailer known for its trendy and affordable clothing, sought to expand its operations into a new geographic market to capitalize on opportunities for growth and diversification. Before entering the new market, FashionForward needed to conduct market research to understand local consumer preferences, identify competitors, and assess market dynamics.

Challenge:

Expanding into a new geographic market presented several challenges for FashionForward, including cultural differences, regulatory requirements, and competition from local and global retailers. Additionally, the company needed to adapt its product offerings, pricing strategies, and marketing campaigns to resonate with the preferences and lifestyles of consumers in the new market.

Solution:

FashionForward employed a comprehensive approach to market research and analysis to address these challenges. They conducted surveys, focus groups, and interviews with local consumers to gain insights into fashion trends, purchasing behaviors, and brand perceptions in the target market. Additionally, FashionForward analyzed demographic data, economic indicators, and competitor strategies to assess market potential and identify strategic entry points.

Based on their research findings, FashionForward developed a localized marketing strategy, adapted their product assortment to suit local tastes and preferences, and established partnerships with local influencers and fashion bloggers to enhance brand visibility and credibility in the new market.

Outcome:

By leveraging market research to inform their entry strategy, FashionForward successfully launched its operations in the new geographic market and achieved significant revenue growth. Their localized approach to product offerings and marketing resonated with consumers, driving sales and market share gains. Additionally, FashionForward's strategic partnerships and community engagement efforts helped the company build brand loyalty and establish itself as a trusted fashion retailer in the new market. Overall, the company's strategic approach to market research and analysis enabled it to overcome entry barriers and capitalize on opportunities for growth and expansion.

Examples

1. **Nielsen Holdings** is a global data and measurement firm that specializes in understanding consumer behavior. They provide critical insights that companies need to understand their audience and market trends.

2. **McKinsey & Company** stands as a premier management consulting firm, advising businesses, governments, and institutions on strategic and operational issues. Their expertise helps organizations navigate complex challenges and transform their operations for better performance.

3. **Amazon** has revolutionized the retail landscape by offering an extensive array of products through its online platform. Beyond retail, it has expanded into cloud computing, digital streaming, and artificial intelligence, becoming a tech giant with a vast influence on global markets.

4. **Apple Inc.** is renowned for its innovation in consumer electronics, software, and online services. With iconic products like the iPhone, iPad, and MacBook, Apple has set new standards in design, usability, and performance.

5. **Procter & Gamble,** a multinational corporation, is a leader in the consumer goods industry, offering a wide range of products in beauty, health care, and home care segments. Their brands, known for quality and reliability, have become household names worldwide, fostering trust and loyalty among consumers.

Top Five Takeaways

1. **Delve into understanding who your audience is**, exploring their needs, preferences, and behaviors to tailor your approach effectively. This deep comprehension allows for more targeted and impactful strategies.

2. **Keep a pulse on the latest market trends**, ensuring your strategies remain relevant and proactive. Being informed helps in anticipating shifts and capitalizing on opportunities swiftly.

3. **Conduct thorough analyses of your competitors** to uncover unique selling propositions and areas for improvement. This insight is crucial for carving out a distinct market position and staying ahead.

4. **Leverage data analytics to gain strategic insights**, guiding decision-making with evidence-based conclusions. Utilizing data not only enhances efficiency but also drives smarter, more informed strategies.

5. **Cultivate flexibility and agility** within your organization to navigate changes successfully. An adaptable approach is key to overcoming challenges and seizing new opportunities in a dynamic environment.

Actions to Take

1. **Prioritize comprehensive market research** to gather detailed insights about your target audience and the overall market landscape. This foundational step is critical for informed strategy development and execution.

2. **Implement advanced analytics tools** to decipher complex data, enabling more precise and strategic business decisions. These tools offer the capability to uncover patterns and trends that may not be immediately obvious.

3. **Make it a habit to stay abreast of industry** news and trends, ensuring your business remains competitive and forward-thinking. Regular updates can provide a strategic edge and foster innovation.

4. **Consistently review and adjust your strategies** in response to new data, market feedback, and emerging trends. This ongoing evaluation ensures your approach remains effective and aligned with your objectives.

5. **Encourage a workplace ethos that values innovation** and continuous learning, fostering an environment where new ideas and knowledge sharing flourish. This culture is essential for sustained growth and adaptability.

Actions Not to Take

1. **Avoid making strategic decisions based solely on intuition**, without the support of data analysis. Relying on gut feelings without empirical evidence can lead to missed opportunities and flawed strategies.

2. **Do not ignore feedback from customers** or insights from competitors, as they are valuable sources of information for improvement and innovation. This feedback is vital for staying relevant and competitive.

3. **Refrain from overlooking emerging market trends**, which could signal important shifts in consumer behavior or technology advancements. Staying informed is critical for adapting and thriving in a constantly evolving market.

4. **Resist becoming too comfortable with past successes**, which can lead to stagnation. Continuous improvement and striving for excellence are essential for long-term success and resilience.

5. **Do not fear or resist change**; instead, embrace it as an opportunity for growth and learning. Viewing change positively can transform challenges into valuable opportunities for development and innovation.

Chapter 8: Creating a Comprehensive Business Plan

A well-crafted business plan is the cornerstone of success for every aspiring entrepreneur. It transcends being merely a collection of ideas, evolving into a strategic guide that navigates the turbulent waters of the business landscape. It empowers entrepreneurs to tackle challenges head-on and seize opportunities, illuminating the route to their ambitions with clarity and precision.

This plan is not just a document; it is the foundation upon which informed decisions are made and effective management practices are built. It encompasses goals, strategies, market insights, and financial projections, laying a solid framework for steering the business forward. By meticulously detailing these elements, the business plan becomes an invaluable tool for shaping a prosperous future.

In the journey of creating a business plan, we delve into the essence of conveying a compelling business vision that secures the confidence and support of investors, partners, and stakeholders. This endeavor demands a profound comprehension of the market, a crisp articulation of your unique value, and an exhaustive evaluation of your financial sustainability. Such a plan signals to all stakeholders the existence of a clear and achievable roadmap to profitability and expansion.

A meticulously assembled business plan is a testament to an entrepreneur's commitment to their vision and their capability to navigate the competitive terrain. It assures stakeholders of the entrepreneur's dedication and strategic acumen, offering a blueprint for growth and success. Through this rigorous planning and analysis process, entrepreneurs craft a beacon that guides their venture, ensuring they remain on course towards triumph.

The act of drafting a business plan is, therefore, not merely a procedural step, but a strategic endeavor that sets the stage for a venture's journey. It is an assertion of vision, a declaration of strategy, and a pledge of growth. Entrepreneurs who invest their time and effort into developing a robust business plan are laying the groundwork for success, setting a course for a journey that is as rewarding as the destination itself.

Inspirational Quote

"Success is not the key to happiness. Happiness is the key to success. If you love what you are doing, you will be successful." - Albert Schweitzer

Vision and Mission

At the core of every triumphant business plan lies a clear and compelling vision statement. This vision not only outlines your long-term goals and aspirations but also acts as the guiding star for your entire business journey. It ensures that despite the daily complexities and operational challenges, your team remains focused and aligned towards a shared objective, thus fostering a culture of motivation and dedication towards the enterprise's success.

The vision statement is essentially the dream you are working tirelessly to turn into reality. It encapsulates the future you envision for your business, making it an indispensable part of your strategic planning. This visionary blueprint is critical not just for maintaining direction but also for inspiring your team, stakeholders, and customers by sharing a glimpse of the promising future you aim to create.

On the flip side, the mission statement holds equal importance by defining the core purpose of your business. It clearly outlines how your business intends to make a positive impact on the world, explaining why your company exists and the unique value it offers to customers, stakeholders, and the community. This mission is the driving force behind every action and decision in the organization, ensuring that every step taken is in harmony with the business's core values and objectives.

Together, the vision and mission statements are the heart and soul of your business strategy. They do more than just guide; they inspire. They fuel passion among your team and stakeholders, turning the daily grind into meaningful strides towards achieving the lofty goals you've set. These statements serve as a constant reminder of what you're fighting for, energizing and rallying everyone towards a common purpose.

These foundational elements of your business plan are not just statements but a call to action. They articulate a future filled with purpose and promise, set the stage for strategic alignment, and inspire everyone involved to push beyond their limits. By defining where you want to go and why you want to get there, they lay the groundwork for a journey that is not only successful but also profoundly impactful.

Market Analysis

Grasping the essence of your market is fundamental to crafting a powerful business strategy. Engaging in comprehensive market research helps you understand prevailing trends, scrutinize the competition, and pinpoint opportunities for growth. This journey into the heart of consumer behavior and market fluctuations allows companies to tailor their offerings, ensuring they resonate deeply with the desires of their audience. By aligning products or services with market demands, businesses not only boost customer satisfaction but also lay the groundwork for enduring expansion.

In the business world, the value of knowledge is immeasurable, serving as the lifeblood of strategic decision-making. Armed with insights into the latest market trends and a deep understanding of consumer preferences, companies can foresee shifts and adjust their tactics proactively. This forward-thinking stance on market intelligence positions businesses to navigate the complexities of a dynamic commercial environment confidently.

The cultivation of market knowledge enables organizations to carve out a competitive advantage, keeping them steps ahead of their rivals. It's about more than just staying in the race; it's about leading the pack through innovation and adaptability. As the marketplace evolves, so too must the strategies that drive business success, ensuring that companies remain relevant and responsive to consumer needs.

Investing in market research is not merely a task; it's a strategic imperative that informs every aspect of business planning and execution. From product development to marketing strategies, understanding the market landscape shapes how businesses approach their goals. It's a continuous cycle of learning and application, where each insight contributes to stronger, more effective business strategies.

The pursuit of market knowledge is a journey towards achieving business excellence. It's about harnessing the power of information to steer your company towards its long-term objectives with confidence and precision. In the relentless pursuit of success, staying informed and adaptable is the key to overcoming obstacles and seizing opportunities in the ever-changing world of business.

Unique Value Proposition

In the vibrant tapestry of the business world, our enterprise shines brightly, anchored by a Unique Value Proposition (UVP) that defines our essence and sets us apart in a crowded marketplace. Our UVP is the beacon that guides customers to us, offering something extraordinary—be it unparalleled quality, unbeatable prices, or exemplary customer service. This distinctive edge not only draws customers in but also carves a significant niche for us among our rivals, showcasing our unparalleled commitment to excellence.

At the heart of our mission lies a steadfast dedication to not only meet but surpass the expectations of our customers. This dedication ensures that the hallmarks of our identity are woven into every aspect of our business operations. By relentlessly pursuing excellence and making our unique qualities palpably evident, we demonstrate an unwavering commitment to the value and satisfaction of our customers.

Our strategy to distinguish ourselves in the market is a comprehensive one, seamlessly integrating our UVP into all facets of our business model. From innovative marketing tactics to the development of cutting-edge products and personalized customer service, our approach ensures that our core values and strengths are consistently communicated. This strategic integration helps potential customers grasp the essence of what makes us different and better.

Emphasizing our UVP is more than a business strategy; it's a commitment to understanding and addressing the unique needs of our customers. By highlighting what makes us special, we not only solidify our place in the market but also build a deep connection with our audience. This connection fosters a sense of trust and loyalty, which is essential for sustaining long-term relationships with our customers.

Our focus on delivering and exceeding our UVP is the key to not just attracting new patrons but also nurturing a loyal customer base. This dedication to our unique value not only enhances our competitive stance but also elevates our market presence. Through this focused approach, we ensure that our business not only thrives but also serves as a testament to the power of understanding and fulfilling the needs of those we serve.

Marketing and Sales Strategy

Creating a dynamic marketing and sales strategy is key to driving business growth and increasing revenue. This approach integrates a mix of digital and traditional marketing efforts to reach and engage your target audience effectively, turning potential leads into dedicated customers. Embracing a variety of channels, including social media, email marketing, and strategic partnerships, can significantly expand your reach and amplify your marketing impact.

Utilizing these diverse platforms enables businesses to share their message broadly and connect with a wider audience. At the core of successful sales is the ability to communicate effectively, adapting your sales pitch to meet the unique needs and dreams of your audience. Authentic engagement with potential customers is vital, as it establishes a real connection and trust, paving the way for turning leads into loyal supporters.

Understanding the specific preferences and expectations of your target market allows you to customize your communication strategies to align with their desires. This tailored approach ensures your messaging resonates deeply, fostering a stronger bond with your audience. By focusing on clear, persuasive, and passionate communication, businesses can significantly improve their sales results and cultivate enduring customer relationships.

Investing time in refining your marketing and sales strategies not only boosts your business's visibility but also enhances its reputation and customer loyalty. It's about crafting messages that speak directly to the hearts and minds of your audience, making every interaction meaningful and impactful. This strategic focus on effective communication and targeted marketing efforts is a powerful driver of business success, ensuring that your brand stands out in a crowded marketplace.

The development of a comprehensive marketing and sales strategy is a transformative process that requires dedication, creativity, and a deep understanding of your audience. By leveraging a mix of marketing channels and focusing on genuine, engaging communication, businesses can achieve remarkable growth and build a loyal customer base. This approach not only elevates your brand's presence but also sets the foundation for sustained success and profitability.

Financial Projections and Funding

Creating a solid business plan is anchored in meticulous financial analysis and forward-looking projections. It's essential to clearly outline your startup costs, expected revenue streams, and profit margins with precision and attention to detail. This financial blueprint is crucial not only for guiding internal decision-making and strategy but also for attracting investment or supporting a self-funded growth strategy.

Understanding your financial situation deeply enables strategic planning and informed decision-making, setting the stage for long-term success. Accurate and detailed financial projections are key to navigating the path toward sustainable profitability. This clarity and foresight are fundamental for both managing your business effectively and communicating its potential to investors.

It's important to find the right balance between optimism and realism in your financial projections. Overestimating your potential without realistic bases can lead to strategic errors, while too much caution might not fully capture your business's growth possibilities. Striking this balance is crucial for presenting a compelling and achievable business case.

Seeking expert financial advice is invaluable in refining your financial strategy to ensure it's both solid and feasible. Experts can offer insights that fine-tune your projections, making them more credible and aligned with industry standards. This step can significantly enhance your business plan's attractiveness to investors and increase your chances of success.

Utilizing financial consultants or advanced modeling tools can further bolster the reliability of your financial forecasts. These resources add a layer of professionalism and precision to your projections, making your business plan stand out in a competitive landscape. By investing in these tools and expertise, you position your business for a brighter and more profitable future.

Conclusion

Creating a comprehensive business plan is not just a procedural step; it's an act of envisioning the future and laying the foundation for your business's dreams to become reality. It demands a profound comprehension of your vision, an exhaustive examination of the market, and a crystal-clear presentation of what sets your business apart. This meticulous process is key to setting your business's strategic compass and unifying all stakeholders towards a shared ambition.

Effectively sharing this vision and strategy is a powerful way to win the trust and backing of investors, employees, and customers. It marks the beginning of a journey toward achieving remarkable success. A thoughtfully designed business plan acts as a beacon, guiding your venture through the business world's intricacies with confidence and clarity.

A well-structured business plan is akin to a navigator, identifying potential hurdles and formulating strategies to vault over them. This ensures that your business is not only resilient but also adaptable to the ever-evolving market dynamics. It's about planning meticulously, understanding the business ecosystem deeply, and being prepared to manage risks while capturing opportunities.

This thorough preparation and strategic foresight are instrumental in building confidence among your stakeholders. It shows them that the business is not just prepared for the present but is strategically poised for future challenges and opportunities. This level of readiness is essential for inspiring confidence and securing a robust foundation for the long-term triumph and sustainability of the business.

A comprehensive business plan is your business's roadmap to navigating the complexities of the market with agility and precision. It's about anticipating challenges, embracing opportunities, and moving forward with a clear vision. This not only sets the stage for immediate success but also ensures enduring growth and stability, marking the path toward achieving your business aspirations.

CASE STUDIES: Creating a Comprehensive Business Plan

Case Study 1: Launching a Sustainable Food Delivery Service

Background:

GreenEats, a startup company passionate about sustainability and healthy eating, aimed to launch a sustainable food delivery service offering organic, locally sourced meals. Before starting operations, GreenEats needed to create a comprehensive business plan to outline their vision, market opportunity, operational strategy, and financial projections.

Challenge:

The challenge for GreenEats was to develop a business plan that not only articulated their mission and values but also demonstrated the viability and scalability of their business model. Additionally, the company needed to address potential challenges such as sourcing sustainable ingredients, managing delivery logistics, and attracting customers in a competitive market.

Solution:

To address these challenges, GreenEats conducted extensive market research to identify consumer preferences, market trends, and competitor offerings in the food delivery industry. They surveyed potential customers to gauge interest in sustainable and organic meal options and conducted interviews with local farmers and suppliers to establish partnerships for sourcing ingredients.

Based on their research findings, GreenEats developed a comprehensive business plan outlining their value proposition, target market segments, marketing strategy, operational processes, and financial projections. They emphasized their commitment to sustainability and transparency in sourcing ingredients, as well as their focus on providing healthy, nutritious meals that catered to various dietary preferences and restrictions.

Outcome:

Armed with a comprehensive business plan, GreenEats successfully launched their sustainable food delivery service and gained traction in the market. Their emphasis on sustainability and health resonated with environmentally conscious consumers, driving customer acquisition and loyalty. Additionally, GreenEats' strategic partnerships with local farmers and suppliers helped differentiate them from competitors and ensure a consistent supply of high-quality ingredients. Overall, the company's comprehensive business plan provided a roadmap for success and enabled them to establish themselves as a leader in sustainable food delivery.

Case Study 2: Establishing a Boutique Fitness Studio

Background:

FitFusion, a group of fitness enthusiasts passionate about helping others achieve their health and wellness goals, sought to establish a boutique fitness studio offering personalized training programs and group classes. Before launching the studio, FitFusion needed to create a comprehensive business plan to outline their concept, target market, operational strategy, and financial projections.

Challenge:

The challenge for FitFusion was to develop a business plan that not only captured their vision and unique value proposition but also demonstrated the demand and profitability of their business model. Additionally, the company needed to address considerations such as location selection, equipment procurement, staffing requirements, and marketing strategies to attract clients in a competitive fitness market.

Solution:

To address these challenges, FitFusion conducted market research to assess demand for boutique fitness services, identify target customer demographics, and evaluate competitor offerings in the local market. They surveyed potential clients to understand their fitness goals, preferences, and willingness to pay for personalized training programs and group classes.

Based on their research findings, FitFusion developed a comprehensive business plan outlining their studio concept, target market segments, pricing strategy, class offerings, staffing plan, and financial projections. They emphasized their commitment to providing personalized, results-driven fitness experiences in a supportive and welcoming environment.

Outcome:

Armed with a comprehensive business plan, FitFusion successfully launched their boutique fitness studio and attracted a loyal clientele. Their focus on personalized training programs and small group classes resonated with individuals seeking individualized attention and community support in their fitness journey. Additionally, FitFusion's strategic location selection, effective marketing strategies, and investment in high-quality equipment and experienced instructors helped differentiate them from competitors and establish a strong brand presence in the local fitness market. Overall, the company's comprehensive business plan provided a roadmap for success and enabled them to achieve their vision of helping clients lead healthier, happier lives through fitness.

Examples

1. **Apple Inc.** is renowned for its innovation in the technology sector, leading the market with products like the iPhone, iPad, and Mac computers. The company's emphasis on design and functionality has solidified its status as a global leader in consumer electronics.

2. **Tesla, Inc.** has revolutionized the automotive industry by prioritizing electric vehicles (EVs) and sustainable energy solutions. Their commitment to innovation extends beyond cars to energy storage and solar technology, aiming to reduce the world's reliance on fossil fuels.

3. **Airbnb** has transformed the travel and hospitality industry by enabling people to list, discover, and book accommodations around the world through its online platform. This approach has not only made travel more accessible but also allows hosts to earn income from their available space.

4. **Starbucks Corporation** is a global coffeehouse chain recognized for its specialty coffee and warm, inviting store environments. Beyond coffee, Starbucks is committed to sustainability and ethical sourcing, striving to positively impact the communities where it operates.

5. **SpaceX** is at the forefront of space exploration and transportation, aiming to make space travel more accessible and ultimately colonize Mars. Their groundbreaking work includes the development of reusable rockets, significantly reducing the cost of space missions.

Top Five Takeaways

1. **Clearly define your vision and mission.** It's crucial to establish a clear vision and mission for your business, as they will guide all your strategic decisions and actions. A well-defined vision and mission provide direction and inspire your team and stakeholders.

2. **Conduct thorough market research.** Understanding the market is essential before launching your business. Thorough market research helps identify your target audience, competition, and market trends, enabling informed decision-making.

3. **Articulate your unique value proposition.** Clearly communicate what makes your product or service unique and why customers should choose it over competitors. A compelling unique value proposition distinguishes your business in a crowded market.

4. **Develop a robust marketing and sales strategy.** Creating a comprehensive marketing and sales strategy is vital for reaching your target audience and driving sales. This strategy should outline how you plan to attract, engage, and retain customers.

5. **Create realistic financial projections.** Developing realistic financial projections is critical for understanding your business's financial health and potential. These projections help in planning for growth, securing investments, and managing cash flow.

Actions to Take

1. **Invest time in market research.** Dedicating time to market research is fundamental for understanding your industry, customers, and competitors. This insight is invaluable for making strategic business decisions.

2. **Seek feedback from mentors and industry experts.** Gaining insights from mentors and industry experts can provide valuable perspectives and advice. Their feedback can help refine your strategies and avoid common pitfalls.

3. **Continuously refine and update your business plan.** The business landscape is constantly changing, so it's important to regularly update your business plan. This ensures your strategies remain relevant and aligned with your goals.

4. **Network with potential investors and partners.** Building relationships with potential investors and partners is crucial for business growth. Networking can open up new opportunities and provide access to resources and expertise.

5. **Stay adaptable and agile in the face of challenges.** The ability to adapt and be agile is essential in today's fast-paced business environment. Being flexible allows you to navigate challenges and seize new opportunities effectively.

Actions Not to Take

1. **Rush through the planning process.** Rushing the planning process can lead to overlooked details and flawed strategies. Take the time to thoroughly plan to set a solid foundation for your business.

2. **Overlook the importance of financial projections.** Ignoring the importance of financial projections can jeopardize your business's financial stability. Accurate projections are crucial for effective financial planning and attracting investors.

3. **Neglect to update your business plan regularly.** Failing to regularly update your business plan can lead to missed opportunities and strategic misalignments. Keeping your plan current ensures it reflects the latest market conditions and business objectives.

4. **Ignore feedback from stakeholders.** Ignoring feedback from customers, employees, and other stakeholders can hinder your business's growth. Feedback is a valuable resource for improving your products, services, and overall strategy.

5. **Stray from your core values and mission.** Deviating from your core values and mission can erode trust with your stakeholders and dilute your brand. Staying true to your founding principles is key to building a strong, cohesive brand identity.

Chapter 9: Setting SMART Goals for Success

Setting SMART goals is a cornerstone of success in both personal and professional realms, providing a structured blueprint for growth and achievement. These goals are designed to be Specific, giving clarity and focus; Measurable, to track progress effectively; Achievable, ensuring they are within reach; Relevant, aligning with overall ambitions; and Time-bound, with a clear deadline. This methodical approach focuses efforts and guides every action towards the ultimate goal, enhancing the journey towards success.

Adhering to the SMART framework significantly boosts the chances of accomplishing your objectives, unlocking your full potential in the process. It offers a detailed roadmap, transforming ambitious visions into achievable milestones. By setting goals that meet these criteria, you equip yourself with a focused strategy to navigate the path to success, ensuring that every effort is purposeful and aligned with your broader goals.

The power of SMART goal-setting lies in its ability to break down lofty dreams into manageable, concrete steps. It instills a sense of personal accountability and encourages consistent progress through regular milestone achievements. This not only keeps motivation high but also builds a structured path towards realizing your dreams, making the journey as rewarding as the destination.

Incorporating SMART goals into your strategy is transformative, acting as a catalyst for growth and success. It allows for a clear visualization of your path, making it easier to identify and celebrate each step forward. This clarity and structure bring a sense of control and purpose to your endeavors, elevating your potential to not just meet, but exceed your aspirations.

Ultimately, mastering the art of SMART goal-setting is a vital skill for anyone looking to excel and achieve their dreams. It's a powerful tool that provides direction, enhances motivation, and ensures a focused approach to personal and professional development. Embracing this technique can dramatically increase your ability to achieve success, making your aspirations not just a possibility, but a reality.

Inspirational Quote

"Inspiration is the wind beneath the wings of achievement."

Setting Goals

Embarking on the journey to turn dreams into reality begins with setting goals. This essential step transforms our deepest aspirations into actionable plans, serving as the blueprint for our success. By clearly defining our objectives, we create a path that leads directly to our desired outcomes, anchoring our dreams in the realm of possibility.

Each goal we establish is akin to planting a seed in the fertile soil of our ambitions. These seeds hold the promise of growth and transformation, waiting patiently to burst into life. With careful nurturing and unwavering focus, these goals can blossom into achievements that mirror our initial visions, showcasing the power of intent and purpose.

The path to realizing our dreams is paved with the goals we set and achieve along the way. Every milestone reached signifies progress, a step forward in the garden of our aspirations that we diligently tend to. This journey demands persistence and resilience, as we navigate the challenges that arise, always keeping our eyes on the prize.

Commitment to our goals goes beyond mere planning; it involves a relentless pursuit of the end result, despite the hurdles that may come our way. This steadfast dedication not only cultivates personal growth but also steers us towards success. It teaches us that through perseverance and clarity of vision, even the loftiest of dreams can be within our reach.

Setting and pursuing goals is a testament to the human spirit's capacity to dream and achieve. It reinforces the belief that with a clear plan, determination, and a heart full of ambition, there is no limit to what we can accomplish. This journey, rich with purpose and passion, leads us to not just meet, but exceed our own expectations, turning the once intangible into tangible triumphs.

Clarity in Vision

The journey to success begins with setting SMART goals, which starts by precisely defining what you aspire to achieve. Defining your goals with the utmost clarity is crucial, as it allows you to visualize the outcome you're striving for. This act of visualization is more than just a planning step; it's a powerful motivator, painting a vivid picture of your desired future and setting the stage for your journey towards achievement.

Having a crystal-clear vision of your goals is the foundation upon which your pathway to success is built. The next step is to outline a strategic plan to reach these objectives, transforming your ultimate aim into a series of manageable steps. This approach not only makes the journey less daunting but also ensures that every effort you make is a step closer to your ultimate destination.

Breaking down your goals into smaller, achievable tasks is a vital strategy for maintaining focus and momentum. It offers a clear roadmap for your journey, ensuring that each action you take is purposeful and aligned with your broader aspirations. This structured approach not only keeps you on track but also instills a sense of accomplishment as you progress, making your goals seem increasingly attainable.

Methodical planning is the key to transforming your dreams into reality. It involves not just envisioning the end result but also meticulously mapping out the route to get there. This detailed planning turns the path to success from a concept into a practical, navigable route, bringing your envisioned future within reach.

By embracing this strategic and structured approach to goal setting, you're not just dreaming; you're actively constructing the future you desire. Each step, guided by clarity and purpose, moves you closer to turning your aspirations into achievements. In this way, the process of setting and pursuing SMART goals is not just about reaching a destination but about embarking on a transformative journey that leads to personal and professional growth.

Specificity in Goals

Transforming vague dreams into specific goals marks the first step on the path to success. By detailing your ambitions, you provide yourself with a clear target. This clarity paves the way for a focused strategy, ensuring every step taken is in the right direction toward your aspirations.

Setting specific goals lays the foundation for measurable progress, essential for maintaining motivation and evaluating advancement. The precision of your objectives simplifies the creation of a strategic plan, guiding you through the complexities of your journey. With these clear benchmarks, you're equipped to track your progress meticulously, keeping your motivation alive and your actions aligned with your ultimate purpose.

A well-defined goal enables efficient resource management and anticipates potential challenges, ensuring a smoother journey toward your objectives. This foresight allows for the pre-emptive addressing of obstacles, streamlining the path to achievement. It's this strategic planning that turns aspirations into tangible successes.

Measuring your progress becomes straightforward with specific goals, allowing for adjustments along the way to stay aligned with your targets. This adaptability is crucial in navigating the unpredictable nature of any journey toward success. It ensures that you remain resilient, responsive, and on track, regardless of the challenges that arise.

Specificity in goal setting not only increases the likelihood of success but also enriches the journey itself. It transforms the process into an organized, rewarding experience, where each step is a calculated move towards realizing your dreams. Through this meticulous approach, achieving your goals becomes not just a possibility, but an inevitable outcome of your dedication and strategic planning.

Measurability for Progress

Setting measurable goals is the cornerstone of any successful journey. This strategy allows you to keep a vigilant eye on your progress, ensuring that you remain motivated and focused throughout your endeavors. Establishing clear benchmarks and milestones serves as a roadmap, guiding you step by step toward your aspirations with clarity and purpose.

By celebrating each accomplishment, no matter the size, you affirm your dedication to your objectives and uplift your spirits. These moments of recognition highlight the distance traveled and the growth achieved along the way. They become the wind beneath your wings, propelling you forward when the path seems long and the peaks too high.

Each small victory is a testament to your perseverance and hard work. Acknowledging these successes injects a burst of energy into your journey, illuminating the way forward. It's these celebrations that often provide the much-needed encouragement to press on, even when obstacles loom large on the horizon.

Incorporating this approach into your strategy for success not only keeps you aligned with your goals but also sharpens your focus on areas needing attention or improvement. It's a dynamic process of assessment and realignment that ensures every step taken is a step closer to your ultimate aim. This methodical progression cultivates a sense of achievement and satisfaction that is unparalleled.

The journey toward achieving your goals is enriched by each milestone celebrated and every challenge overcome. This journey molds you into a more resilient and determined individual, ready to seize your dreams with both hands. Remember, the key to unlocking your potential lies in setting clear, measurable goals and taking the time to honor every victory along the way.

Achievability through Action

Setting realistic goals is the cornerstone of achieving success, acting as a beacon that guides your efforts towards tangible achievements. By carefully assessing your resources, skills, and capabilities, you can craft a strategy that bridges the gap between your dreams and the actions required to realize them. This pragmatic approach ensures that your aspirations are not just castles in the air, but achievable milestones rooted in your current reality and the resources at your disposal.

Dividing grand ambitions into smaller, more manageable tasks is a powerful method to keep motivation high and progress continuous. This strategy provides a structured pathway to your larger goals, transforming an overwhelming journey into a series of achievable steps. Celebrating each small victory not only boosts morale but also helps to stave off the feeling of being overwhelmed, making the journey towards your goals a more enjoyable and fulfilling experience.

By adopting a step-by-step approach, you ensure that each task is focused and purposeful, keeping you on track towards your ultimate objective. This methodical progression fosters a sense of accomplishment, as every small task completed is a building block in the foundation of your larger goal. It's a way to maintain momentum, making the process of achieving your dreams less intimidating and more achievable.

Incorporating this mindset into your goal-setting strategy not only enhances your ability to reach your goals but also enriches the journey. It teaches resilience, patience, and the importance of celebrating every step of progress, no matter how small. This philosophy turns the path to achievement into a series of lessons in perseverance and dedication, which are invaluable traits for success in any endeavor.

Setting realistic goals and breaking them down into manageable tasks is about more than just achieving objectives; it's about creating a sustainable approach to success. This approach allows you to adapt to challenges, learn from setbacks, and continue moving forward with confidence. Embracing this strategy not only brings your dreams within reach but also builds a foundation of habits and attitudes that will support your success in all areas of life.

Relevance to Your Purpose

Aligning your goals with your core values, passions, and long-term ambitions is crucial for a fulfilling journey. This harmony ensures your objectives are not merely checkpoints but bridges to a life rich in purpose and joy. When your goals mirror what's truly important to you, they transform into potent forces that awaken your zeal and drive.

This profound connection with your goals strengthens your dedication and perseverance, making the path to achievement both meaningful and gratifying. Goals that resonate deeply with your personal mission act as a guiding light, helping you navigate through tough times and setbacks. Such alignment ensures that every step you take is a step closer to your grand vision, making each success feel incredibly rewarding.

Having goals aligned with your personal purpose also cultivates resilience, empowering you to overcome challenges with unwavering determination. This sense of purpose turns obstacles into opportunities for growth, driving you forward with confidence. In essence, when your goals reflect your values and dreams, you are not merely pursuing success; you are living it, one goal at a time.

Moreover, goals that are in sync with your inner values serve as a compass during times of uncertainty. They keep you grounded and focused, ensuring that your efforts are directed towards what truly matters. This alignment transforms every challenge into a milestone, pushing you closer to your ultimate aspirations.

Achieving goals that resonate with your core identity is the essence of true success. It's about realizing a version of success that is uniquely yours, rather than conforming to external definitions. By pursuing goals that align with your personal values and aspirations, you are crafting a life that is not only successful but deeply satisfying and meaningful.

Time-Bound Commitment

Incorporating deadlines into your goals transforms them into beacons of urgency, lighting the path to proactive achievement. This approach combats procrastination effectively, imbuing each task with a deep sense of purpose and dedication. By adopting this strategy, you not only expedite your journey towards your objectives but also create a structured environment that fosters success.

It's crucial to strike a balance between ambition and realism when setting these deadlines. Ensuring that your goals are challenging yet achievable encourages personal growth while keeping them realistic prevents discouragement. This careful calibration of expectations sets the stage for a rewarding journey towards your aspirations.

Setting realistic deadlines is an art that requires a keen understanding of your abilities and resources. It encourages you to push your boundaries thoughtfully, avoiding the pitfalls of impractical ambitions. This approach keeps motivation alive, as each achieved milestone fuels the belief in your capacity to overcome challenges.

A well-balanced strategy in goal-setting accommodates the unexpected, allowing for flexibility without compromising the ultimate objective. This adaptability is crucial in navigating the journey towards your goals, providing a safety net that enables you to adjust plans without losing sight of the end goal. It's about moving forward, regardless of the hurdles, with resilience and adaptability.

Finding the sweet spot where ambition and realism converge is the cornerstone of effective goal-setting. This balance maximizes personal growth and achievement, turning aspirations into attainable targets. Embracing this approach not only leads to success but also enriches the journey with valuable lessons and personal development.

Persistence in Pursuit

Facing challenges and overcoming setbacks are key components of the road to success. This journey often pushes us to our limits, requiring a deep commitment to our aspirations, regardless of the obstacles we face. It is essential to stay resilient, viewing each challenge as an opportunity to grow and strengthen our determination. Moving forward, even when the journey is tough, is crucial for achieving our goals.

Every hurdle we encounter should be seen not as a blockade but as a chance for personal and professional development. These challenges teach us valuable lessons in resilience, enhance our problem-solving abilities, and underscore the significance of steadfastness. By embracing each setback as a learning opportunity, we can approach our objectives with increased enthusiasm. This perspective helps turn potential roadblocks into milestones on our path to success.

Persistence in the face of adversity is not just about enduring; it's about thriving. Each challenge presents a unique opportunity to test our resolve and push our boundaries. By adopting a positive outlook towards difficulties, we can discover our true potential and unlock new levels of achievement.

In this journey, it's important to remember that success is not a destination but a continuous process of growth and improvement. The obstacles we overcome add to our experience, making us wiser and more equipped to handle future challenges. This ongoing cycle of learning and advancing propels us closer to our ultimate goals, enriching our personal and professional lives.

The essence of perseverance lies in not just surviving challenges but in using them as catalysts for growth and success. By maintaining our focus and dedication, even in the face of difficulty, we can transform obstacles into opportunities for advancement. This approach not only leads us to our desired outcomes but also builds a foundation of resilience and determination that benefits all areas of our lives.

Consistent Action

Consistency is the cornerstone of turning dreams into reality. When individuals commit to daily progress towards their goals, no matter how small, they lay down the foundation for success. This principle of unwavering action serves as a powerful catalyst for growth, ensuring that each small step taken today adds up over time.

Through consistent effort, the journey toward achieving our aspirations becomes a testament to the power of perseverance and commitment. This dedication not only instills discipline but also builds the resilience necessary to face and overcome obstacles. With every step forward, the path to our goals becomes more defined and achievable, highlighting the importance of persistence in the pursuit of excellence.

The magic of consistency lies in the compound effect of daily efforts. As these efforts accumulate, they lead to significant achievements that underscore the value of steadfast dedication. This process showcases the transformative power of sticking to one's path, turning gradual progress into monumental success.

Achieving one's dreams is inherently linked to the commitment to make regular progress. Embracing this consistency nurtures a strong sense of discipline and resilience, essential qualities for navigating the challenges that arise along the way. Each day's progress, building on the previous one, illuminates the path to our ambitions, making them more attainable than ever before.

The essence of realizing significant milestones resides in the relentless pursuit of consistent action. This unwavering dedication is the key to unlocking one's potential and transforming aspirations into tangible achievements. It is a testament to the fact that persistence, above all, is the gateway to achieving our dreams and fulfilling our true potential.

Adaptability to Change

Pursuing your dreams demands a commitment to flexibility and an open mind. Being open to revising your approach as you receive new information and feedback is crucial. This adaptability enables you to overcome obstacles and refine your strategies, leading to improved results.

The journey toward achievement is often marked by uncertainty and change. Recognizing that change is a constant companion on this journey allows you to welcome it, opening the door to more effective solutions and strategies. By embracing the possibility of altering your course, you position yourself to navigate challenges with greater ease and closer to success.

Adapting to change is not just about adjusting your strategies; it's about evolving with the landscape of your goals. This evolution is essential for continuous improvement and growth, ensuring that you are always moving forward, even in the face of adversity. Such a mindset turns challenges into stepping stones towards your aspirations.

In every endeavor, the ability to remain flexible in the face of unforeseen circumstances is invaluable. It equips you to manage the unpredictable nature of any pursuit with grace and resilience. This adaptability is a powerful tool, enhancing your journey and paving the way for success in ways you might not have imagined.

Ultimately, embracing change and maintaining adaptability are foundational to not just achieving your goals but also to personal and professional development. By staying open to new ideas and ready to pivot when necessary, you foster an environment of continuous learning and growth. This approach not only propels you towards your objectives but also enriches your journey with invaluable experiences and lessons learned.

Conclusion

Embracing SMART goals lays the foundation for success across the many facets of life, from personal growth and career milestones to academic pursuits. This powerful acronym stands for Specific, Measurable, Achievable, Relevant, and Time-bound, providing a blueprint for setting goals that are clear and within reach. This approach not only charts a path forward but also ignites motivation by establishing attainable benchmarks, making the journey towards achievement both directed and rewarding.

The essence of setting SMART goals lies in the precision and purpose they bring to the goal-setting process. Each goal is crafted with careful thought, ensuring it's tailored to personal ambitions or professional aspirations. This methodical approach fosters a sense of accountability and progress, as each step taken is a measured stride towards the realization of one's objectives. By aligning goals with the SMART criteria, individuals gain the insight needed to evaluate their journey, adapt strategies, and stay aligned with their ultimate ambitions.

Embarking on the journey of SMART goal-setting is an exercise in clarity, resolve, and persistent effort. Clarity sharpens the focus on the desired outcome, cutting through the fog of ambiguity. Resolve acts as the engine of perseverance, powering through obstacles and setbacks. Meanwhile, persistent effort ensures that small, steady steps are taken towards the summit of achievement. Together, these qualities create a resilient mindset that, when harnessed within the SMART framework, paves the way for turning aspirations into achieved goals.

The synergy of clarity, determination, and consistent action within the SMART framework is transformative. It turns the art of goal setting into a strategic endeavor, where dreams are not just envisioned but methodically pursued. This alignment of purpose and action empowers individuals to explore their capabilities, push boundaries, and realize their full potential. It's a journey that demands dedication but offers the profound reward of personal and professional fulfillment.

SMART goals are the compass by which individuals navigate the seas of ambition towards the shores of success. This disciplined approach ensures that every goal is a beacon, guiding efforts and measuring progress with precision. It's a testament to the power of strategic planning and the relentless pursuit of excellence. By embracing the principles of SMART goal-setting, individuals unlock a world of possibilities, setting the stage for achievements that resonate both now and in the future.

CASE STUDIES: Setting SMART Goals for Success

Case Study 1: Enhancing Sales Performance Through SMART Goals

Background:

XYZ Corporation, a leading provider of IT solutions, faced stagnating sales numbers in the competitive market. The sales team struggled to meet their quarterly targets, leading to decreased morale and motivation.

Objective:

To rejuvenate the sales team's performance and significantly increase sales numbers within the next quarter.

Action Plan:

The management decided to implement SMART goals to address this challenge. The new strategy was outlined as follows:

1. **Specific:** Increase sales numbers by targeting new industries such as healthcare and education, which were identified as growth areas through market research.

2. **Measurable:** Aim for a 20% increase in sales revenue compared to the previous quarter.

3. **Achievable:** Provide the sales team with additional training on the latest IT solutions tailored to the healthcare and education sectors, coupled with enhanced marketing support.

4. **Relevant:** Focus on sectors less affected by economic downturns, ensuring the sales targets are practical and aligned with current market demands.

5. **Time-bound:** Set a clear deadline for the end of the next quarter to achieve this goal.

Outcome:

By the end of the quarter, XYZ Corporation reported a 25% increase in sales revenue, surpassing their initial goal. The focused approach allowed the sales team to develop expertise in high-demand areas, thereby increasing their success rate in closing deals. The SMART goal-setting process not only led to improved sales performance but also boosted the team's confidence and morale.

Case Study 2: Improving Employee Retention Through SMART Goals

Background:

ABC Tech, a startup specializing in mobile applications, noticed a high employee turnover rate, particularly among its software development team. This turnover not only increased recruitment and training costs but also impacted project timelines and team morale.

Objective:

To reduce the annual employee turnover rate by creating a more engaging and satisfying work environment.

Action Plan:

Management implemented SMART goals to tackle employee retention issues with the following plan:

1. **Specific:** Improve employee satisfaction through enhanced career development opportunities and work-life balance initiatives.

2. **Measurable:** Reduce the employee turnover rate by 15% within one year.

3. **Achievable:** Offer professional development programs, including workshops and certifications, and introduce flexible working hours and remote work options.

4. **Relevant:** Ensuring that the initiatives align with employee needs, as identified through surveys and feedback sessions, to make the workplace more appealing.

5. **Time-bound:** Achieve the set goals within a 12-month period, with quarterly reviews to monitor progress and make necessary adjustments.

Outcome:

After a year, ABC Tech observed a 10% reduction in the turnover rate, slightly below the target but still a significant improvement. Employee surveys indicated higher job satisfaction, particularly valuing the professional development opportunities and the flexibility in work arrangements. The company plans to continue refining its strategies based on ongoing feedback, demonstrating the importance of setting SMART goals that are flexible and responsive to real-world outcomes.

Both case studies exemplify how setting SMART goals can lead to tangible success in different organizational challenges, from boosting sales to improving employee retention. By being specific, measurable, achievable, relevant, and time-bound, goals become clear and actionable pathways to success.

Examples

1. **Elon Musk** is known globally as the CEO of SpaceX, a pioneering company in private space exploration. He is also at the helm of Tesla, leading the charge in electric vehicle innovation.

2. **Oprah Winfrey,** a media powerhouse, has made significant contributions to entertainment and publishing. Her philanthropic efforts are widespread, supporting various causes and empowering communities.

3. **Michael Jordan,** often hailed as the greatest basketball player of all time, has left an indelible mark on the sport. His legacy extends off the court, with successful ventures in branding and team ownership.

4. **Sheryl Sandberg** has played a crucial role as the Chief Operating Officer of Facebook, steering the company through periods of exponential growth. She is also celebrated for her advocacy for women in the workplace, authoring influential books on the subject.

5. **NASA,** the National Aeronautics and Space Administration, has been at the forefront of space exploration and scientific discovery for decades. This agency is responsible for groundbreaking missions that have expanded our understanding of the universe.

Top Five Takeaways

1. For a successful vision, it's crucial to have **clear and well-defined objectives**. Clear articulation of your vision ensures everyone understands the direction and goals.

2. **Goals that are detailed and precise** tend to be more directly actionable, making it easier to plan steps towards achieving them. Specific goals provide a roadmap, guiding you and your team on what needs to be accomplished.

3. **When goals are measurable,** it becomes possible to observe and evaluate the extent of your progress. This allows for adjustments and improvements, ensuring you stay on track towards your objectives.

4. **Aligning your goals** with your core purpose not only brings about deeper motivation but also ensures that your efforts are meaningful and fulfilling. This alignment acts as a powerful driver, propelling you forward with a clear sense of why you're doing what you're doing.

5. **Goals with a set timeline** foster a sense of urgency and responsibility, prompting you to act decisively. Time-bound objectives encourage you to prioritize tasks and manage your time effectively, leading to better outcomes.

Actions to Take

1. **Clearly define what you envision** for the future to ensure you and your team have a shared understanding of the destination. A well-articulated vision serves as a guiding light for all your actions and decisions.

2. **Transform your overarching goals** into specific, measurable steps to streamline the path towards achievement. This breakdown makes it easier to monitor progress and maintain momentum.

3. **Implement deadlines for your goals** to instill a sense of urgency and foster accountability within your team or for yourself. Deadlines help to prioritize tasks and maintain focus on the most critical objectives.

4. **Maintain a strong commitment** to your goals and engage in consistent actions towards achieving them. Persistence and regular effort are key to overcoming obstacles and realizing your ambitions.

5. **Be open to modifying your strategies** based on results and feedback. An adaptable approach allows for continuous improvement and increases the likelihood of success.

Actions Not to Take

1. **Avoid setting goals that are too vague** or unrealistic, as they can lead to confusion and demotivation. Clear, achievable goals are essential for progress and motivation.

2. **Do not fall into the trap of procrastination** or postponing necessary actions. Delaying tasks only hinders progress and can lead to missed opportunities.

3. **Ignoring constructive feedback** or refusing to adjust your approach can stall your progress. Adaptability is crucial for overcoming challenges and achieving long-term success.

4. **Do not let the fear of failure deter you** from pursuing your goals. Embrace challenges as opportunities for growth and learning, rather than obstacles.

5. **Never lose sight of your core purpose and values**. They are your compass in navigating decisions and actions, ensuring that your journey is both meaningful and aligned with your true self.

Chapter 10: Implementing Effective Change Management

Change is not just a part of life and the corporate world; it is the backbone of success and growth. The mastery of navigating through change is what separates the leaders from the followers in the dynamic world of business. Being adept at managing change means more than just coping with the new; it involves leading with purpose, embodying resilience, and encouraging a culture of flexibility and innovation among all team members.

This section delves into the core principles and actionable strategies that are key to mastering change management. It's designed to provide individuals and organizations with the necessary tools to thrive in periods of uncertainty and change. Embracing change as a catalyst for growth and innovation transforms potential hurdles into opportunities. By dissecting effective change management techniques, this section sheds light on ways to empower employees, align organizational objectives with change efforts, and cultivate a culture that celebrates adaptability and steadfastness.

Understanding and implementing the fundamentals of change management equips businesses to confidently approach the complexities of transformation. It's about fostering a strategic perspective that not only navigates through change but leverages it for organizational advancement. This proactive approach ensures that businesses remain relevant and competitive, turning potential challenges into victories.

The journey through change management is about more than survival; it's about thriving. It offers a roadmap for businesses to not just anticipate change but to mold it into an asset. This transformational journey ensures that companies don't just endure but excel, making change a powerful ally in the quest for enduring success and market leadership.

The art of change management is a critical skill set for anyone looking to excel in today's ever-changing business environment. It's about seeing change not as an impediment but as an invaluable opportunity for innovation and growth. With the right mindset and strategies, change becomes a stepping stone towards achieving unparalleled success and securing a competitive edge in the marketplace.

Inspirational Quote

"The art of life is a constant readjustment to our surroundings."

— Kakuzo Okakura

Embrace Change Wholeheartedly

Change, while often perceived as daunting, is actually a gateway to unparalleled growth and innovation. When we approach change with an open heart and eagerness to learn, every new challenge becomes a valuable lesson leading us towards progress. Viewing change through this positive lens transforms it from a hindrance into a powerful catalyst for advancement, empowering both individuals and teams to approach transitions with confidence and enthusiasm.

Recognizing change as a driver of progress is key to building a resilient and adaptable culture. This perspective fosters a constructive approach to facing the unknown, simplifying the process of spotting and grabbing opportunities for betterment and innovation. By welcoming change as a crucial component of growth, we set the stage for ongoing creativity and the refinement of our methods and strategies, enhancing not just personal capabilities but also bolstering the collective strength of teams.

Adopting an attitude that embraces change as an opportunity rather than a threat encourages a mindset of resilience and adaptability. This approach makes navigating the uncertainties of change more manageable and allows for the identification of potential improvements and innovative solutions. When we see change as a natural part of our development, it becomes a catalyst for creative thinking and the continuous improvement of both our personal abilities and our collaborative efforts.

By perceiving change as an ally in our journey, we enable ourselves and our teams to approach challenges with a proactive and positive outlook. This shift in perspective enhances our capacity to adapt to new situations with optimism, fostering a culture that thrives on transformation and growth. It is in this environment that individuals and teams can truly flourish, turning the challenges of change into stepping stones for success.

Embracing change with an open mind and a positive spirit is essential for fostering innovation and progress. This attitude not only empowers individuals to face transitions with confidence but also strengthens teams, making them more resilient and adaptable in the face of change. As we continue to view change as a valuable opportunity for growth, we pave the way for a future marked by creativity, resilience, and continuous advancement.

Communicate Transparently

In the journey toward impactful change management, clear and effective communication stands as the cornerstone of success. Establishing an environment of transparency fosters a deep sense of trust, significantly reducing uncertainties that team members and stakeholders may face. By ensuring everyone is on the same page about why changes are necessary, the expected outcomes, and how these changes will affect their roles, we lay the groundwork for a unified approach to transformation.

Creating a culture that promotes open dialogue further enhances the change management process. When people have access to various platforms to share their thoughts and concerns, it makes them feel valued and a crucial part of the decision-making process. This inclusivity helps in identifying and addressing any issues early on, and cultivates a sense of community and consensus, making the transition smoother for everyone involved.

The importance of keeping all stakeholders informed cannot be overstated. By doing so, we not only align our teams but also increase the likelihood of successful change adoption across the organization. This strategic alignment ensures that everyone moves forward together, with a clear understanding of their role in the change process.

Prioritizing effective communication and active engagement with stakeholders throughout the change management journey paves the way for more favorable outcomes. It transforms potential challenges into opportunities for growth and strengthens the organization's adaptability and resilience. This proactive approach to communication builds a solid foundation for enduring success and a culture that embraces change with confidence.

The art of mastering change management lies in the power of communication. Through transparency, open dialogue, and stakeholder engagement, we can navigate the complexities of change with ease. By embracing these principles, we not only achieve our organizational goals but also foster an environment that is agile, responsive, and prepared for the future.

Cultivate a Culture of Resilience

Resilience is the remarkable ability of individuals to bounce back swiftly from challenges, showcasing their inherent strength and flexibility in the face of adversity. It plays a pivotal role in both our personal lives and professional journeys, allowing us to handle setbacks with poise and grow stronger from them. Cultivating a resilient mindset involves facing challenges head-on, interpreting them not as unbeatable obstacles but as chances to evolve and learn. This mindset shift enables us to adopt a more adaptable and sturdy approach to navigating life's unpredictable twists and turns.

To build resilience, it's important to embrace challenges with an open heart, seeing them as opportunities to strengthen our character and enhance our problem-solving skills. This proactive stance helps in developing a durable spirit, capable of withstanding life's trials and tribulations. Embracing such challenges not only fosters personal growth but also equips us with the resilience needed to thrive in various aspects of life.

Promoting a culture that values resilience is crucial in creating environments where individuals feel encouraged and supported to confront difficulties with determination. Celebrating every small victory and learning from setbacks instills a sense of progress and appreciation for the journey, not just the destination. Recognizing the lessons in failures shifts our perspective, making us see change as an avenue for personal and professional enrichment.

This culture of resilience not only bolsters an individual's capacity to flourish in challenging situations but also strengthens the fabric of communities and organizations. It transforms obstacles into stepping stones, paving the way for innovation and growth. By viewing challenges as catalysts for development, individuals contribute to building a more resilient, dynamic, and forward-thinking community or organization.

Resilience is about more than just surviving; it's about thriving. It empowers us to face the future with confidence, knowing that we have the strength to overcome whatever comes our way. By fostering resilience, we unlock our full potential, setting the stage for a life of achievement, fulfillment, and continuous learning. This journey of resilience not only shapes us into more adaptable and robust individuals but also inspires those around us to embrace life's challenges with optimism and courage.

Empower and Support Your Team

In the face of change, it's natural for a team to encounter feelings of uncertainty and resistance. Leadership plays a pivotal role in navigating these waters with empathy and careful planning. By providing the team with essential resources, training, and support, leaders can ease the transition and set the stage for a successful adaptation.

Encouraging team members to embrace their roles with initiative and independence not only aids in adjusting to new circumstances but also cultivates a culture of innovation and adaptability. This approach not only assists in the immediate transition but also instills a sense of ownership and responsibility among team members. Celebrating and rewarding their contributions further solidifies a positive mindset towards change, enhancing the team's resilience and flexibility for whatever lies ahead.

The investment in team development and well-being is crucial for fostering a supportive and encouraging work atmosphere. Recognizing and supporting team members' contributions leads to increased dedication to the organization and a greater willingness to deliver their best work. This nurturing environment not only helps the team through current transitions but also equips them for future obstacles, laying a solid foundation of trust and teamwork.

Creating a focus on team development and well-being results in a more engaged, efficient, and vibrant team. Such a team is better prepared to tackle challenges and achieve outstanding outcomes, even during periods of significant change. This approach demonstrates a commitment to not just the immediate goals but the long-term success and growth of both individuals and the team as a whole.

Navigating change with a focus on team support and development leads to a stronger, more adaptable organization. It's about transforming challenges into opportunities for growth and innovation. By fostering a culture that values flexibility, collaboration, and continuous improvement, leaders can guide their teams through any change, achieving remarkable results and setting a standard for excellence in their industry.

Lead by Example

True leadership transcends the mere act of issuing commands or setting benchmarks. It involves embodying the very traits you wish to inspire within your team, such as adaptability and resilience. When a leader demonstrates an unwavering commitment to embracing change and navigating new terrains, they set a profound example for their team to emulate. This, in turn, fosters a workplace culture that values flexibility and readiness, qualities that are indispensable in the dynamic landscape of today's world.

A leader who is open to change and actively seeks out opportunities to adapt not only showcases their own growth mindset but also encourages their team to view challenges through a lens of optimism. This approach instills a collective belief in the power of positive change, motivating team members to approach new situations with enthusiasm rather than apprehension. It's a strategy that prepares the team not just to face the present with confidence but also to anticipate the future with excitement.

Empathy is the cornerstone of effective leadership, especially during times of change. A leader who genuinely understands and addresses the apprehensions of their team members about the unknown demonstrates a deep commitment to their overall well-being. This empathetic stance ensures that every individual feels valued and supported, creating a solid foundation for a resilient and adaptive team culture.

By exemplifying resilience and maintaining a hopeful outlook in the face of challenges, a leader can create an environment where support and motivation thrive. This positive atmosphere enables team members to quickly adapt to changes, fostering a collective spirit of perseverance and determination. As a result, the team does not just survive transitions but thrives through them, emerging stronger and more united in the face of adversity.

Cultivating a team that champions change requires a leader to not only be a model of adaptability and empathy but also to actively encourage these qualities within their team. This approach builds a cadre of individuals who are not only equipped to tackle current challenges but are also enthusiastic about facing future opportunities. Such a team, led by a visionary and empathetic leader, becomes an unstoppable force, ready to navigate the complexities of the modern world with grace and agility.

Conclusion

Change management is not just about implementing new processes; it's about cultivating an attitude that sees change as an opportunity for growth and innovation. This mindset shifts the way organizations approach challenges, viewing them not as barriers but as opportunities to enhance creativity and drive improvements. By fostering a culture that emphasizes transparency, resilience, and empowerment, leaders are better positioned to guide their teams through transitions, enhancing overall morale and strengthening commitment to the organization's goals.

Creating an environment that supports adaptation and growth requires intentional leadership and a focused strategy. Leaders need to prioritize open communication, ensuring every team member is aligned with the organization's vision, understands the rationale behind changes, and knows their specific role in the journey. This strategy builds a foundation of trust and inclusion, where employees feel valued and actively engaged in the change process, not just passive participants.

Such a proactive approach to change management not only makes transitions smoother but also reinforces the collective spirit and dedication to the organization's vision. It demonstrates the power of viewing change not as a hurdle but as a stepping stone towards achieving greater things together. By valuing each team member's contribution and fostering an environment of mutual respect and collaboration, organizations can navigate change more effectively.

In this context, leadership is not just about directing; it's about inspiring and empowering others to embrace change with a positive outlook. This involves creating a space where feedback is encouraged, and every voice is heard, further strengthening the bonds within the team. It's through these collective efforts that organizations can turn the challenges of change into opportunities for innovation and growth.

The success of change management lies in recognizing that it's as much about the people as it is about the processes. By embracing these principles, organizations set themselves on a path to sustained success, proving that with the right mindset and leadership, change can be a powerful catalyst for improvement and innovation. This approach not only achieves immediate goals but also prepares the organization for future challenges, ready to adapt and thrive in an ever-changing world.

CASE STUDIES: Implementing Effective Change Management

Case Study 1: A Global Retail Chain's Technology Upgrade

Background:

A leading global retail chain faced challenges with its outdated inventory and sales tracking system, leading to inefficiencies, lost sales, and a decline in customer satisfaction. The company decided to implement a new, state-of-the-art software system to enhance operational efficiency and customer experience.

Challenge:

The main challenge was the resistance from employees accustomed to the old system. There was a fear of the unknown, concerns about the complexity of the new system, and anxiety about job security.

Change Management Strategy:

- **Communication**: The company launched a communication strategy that included workshops, detailed presentations, and Q&A sessions to explain the reasons for the change, its benefits, and how it would improve both customer service and employee workflow.

- **Training:** Comprehensive training sessions were organized for all employees. The training was customized to different departments, ensuring relevance and addressing specific concerns.

- **Support Structures:** The company established a support system, including a help desk and peer champions, to provide ongoing assistance and encourage the use of the new system.

Outcome:

The transition to the new software was smoother than anticipated, with significant improvements in inventory management, a reduction in checkout times, and enhanced customer satisfaction. Employee feedback eventually turned positive, acknowledging the benefits of the new system for their daily tasks.

Case Study 2: Healthcare Provider's Shift to Digital Records

Background:

A mid-sized healthcare provider aimed to transition from paper-based patient records to a digital system. The goal was to improve the efficiency of patient care, reduce errors, and comply with new healthcare regulations.

Challenge:

The primary challenge was the staff's reluctance to change due to unfamiliarity with digital systems and concerns about data security and patient privacy.

Change Management Strategy:

- **Leadership Involvement:** The initiative was led by a change management team, including senior doctors and administration staff, who championed the project and engaged with employees at all levels.

- **Customized Training Programs:** Training programs were developed to cater to the varying levels of digital literacy among staff members. These included hands-on sessions, demonstrations, and simulations.

- **Feedback and Adaptation:** The change management team implemented a feedback loop, allowing staff to voice concerns and suggest improvements. This feedback was used to make iterative adjustments to the training and support provided.

Outcome:

The transition to digital records was successful, leading to a significant reduction in administrative errors, faster access to patient information, and an overall improvement in patient care. Staff members who were initially resistant to the change became some of its strongest advocates, recognizing the benefits of the digital system.

These case studies demonstrate that effective change management requires careful planning, clear communication, tailored training, and ongoing support. By addressing employee concerns and involving them in the process, organizations can navigate the challenges of change and achieve their desired outcomes.

Examples

1. **Apple Inc.** has consistently demonstrated a knack for innovation, staying ahead in technology trends and consumer preferences. Its adaptability has allowed it to remain a leader in the ever-evolving tech industry.

2. **Procter & Gamble** stands out for its systematic change management strategies, ensuring resilience and growth in the competitive consumer goods sector. This approach has enabled the company to navigate through market shifts and maintain its market dominance.

3. **Toyota** is celebrated for fostering a culture of continuous improvement, which empowers its workforce to enhance efficiency and adaptability. This philosophy has been instrumental in Toyota's agile response to changes in the automotive market.

4. **Netflix** has revolutionized the entertainment industry with its disruptive business model, challenging traditional media outlets. Its quick adaptation to new technologies and consumer behaviors has cemented its position as a streaming giant.

5. **NASA** showcases unparalleled change management skills, tackling the complexities of space exploration with innovative solutions. Its ability to manage and adapt to the challenges of each mission underscores its role as a pioneer in space advancements.

Top Five Takeaways

1. **Viewing change as a catalyst**, embrace it as a chance to evolve and bring about innovative solutions. This perspective not only drives progress but also positions us to stay ahead in a dynamic environment.

2. **To build a foundation of trust** and ensure everyone is moving in the same direction, it's essential to practice open and clear communication. Transparent sharing of information removes uncertainties and strengthens team cohesion.

3. **Develop an environment where resilience is not just encouraged** but celebrated, highlighting the importance of being adaptable and eager to learn

from various situations. Such a culture not only helps in navigating challenges but also in turning them into opportunities for personal and professional growth.

4. **Supporting your team during times of change** is crucial; provide them with the necessary resources and training to navigate transitions smoothly. This empowerment enables them to approach change confidently and contributes to the overall resilience of the organization.

5. **Leading by example**, show a consistently positive and proactive attitude towards change. This approach not only motivates your team but also sets a powerful precedent for how challenges and new opportunities are addressed within the organization.

Actions to Take

1. **Establish and maintain transparent communication** pathways that allow for continuous feedback and open dialogue. This ensures that all team members feel heard and valued, fostering a culture of trust and collaboration.

2. **Offer comprehensive training programs** and allocate sufficient resources to assist employees in navigating through periods of transition. By doing so, you empower your workforce to adapt to new challenges and enhance their skill sets effectively.

3. **Recognize and commemorate achievements** and significant progress within the team, big or small. Celebrating these moments boosts morale and encourages individuals to maintain their efforts and strive for excellence.

4. **Promote a culture that values** the pursuit of knowledge and personal development, encouraging employees to adopt a mindset geared towards ongoing learning and self-improvement. This approach nurtures an environment where innovation and creativity flourish.

5. **Lead with integrity** by consistently displaying resilience and flexibility in the face of adversity. Your example sets a powerful precedent for your team, inspiring them to approach challenges with determination and a positive attitude.

Actions Not to Take

1. **Overlooking or minimizing the concerns** and feedback of stakeholders can lead to missed opportunities for improvement and innovation. It's essential to actively listen and engage with stakeholders to foster a collaborative and inclusive environment.

2. When changes are made **without clear communication** or gaining the support of employees, it can lead to confusion, frustration, and a lack of trust in leadership. Transparent communication and involving employees in the decision-making process can enhance buy-in and commitment to change.

3. **Micromanaging employees** or maintaining tight control during periods of transition can stifle creativity and hinder the ability of teams to adapt effectively. It's important for leaders to trust their teams, providing guidance and support without overbearing oversight.

4. **Failing to provide adequate support** and resources for employees during change can leave them feeling overwhelmed and ill-equipped to succeed. Providing training, guidance, and the necessary tools is crucial for employees to confidently navigate and thrive in new circumstances.

5. **Allowing resistance to change** to persist without addressing it can damage team morale and decrease productivity. Proactively identifying and addressing concerns, through open dialogue and support, can mitigate resistance and foster a positive transition experience.

Part Three: Marketing and Sales

Marketing and sales are vital to a business, working together to drive growth and revenue. Marketing identifies and attracts prospects, while sales converts these leads into customers through personalized engagement and negotiation. Their combined efforts are key to achieving business goals and securing a market edge.

Chapter 11: Identifying Target Markets and Customers

Understanding and identifying your target markets and customers is the cornerstone of business success. It acts as the foundation upon which effective strategies are built, unlocking doors to growth and fostering lasting bonds with those you serve. With a clear grasp of who your audience is, you can tailor your offerings to perfectly match their needs and desires, creating a synergy that is crucial for sustained success and a competitive edge.

In this chapter, we explore the intricate blend of art and science involved in pinpointing and comprehending your target market. Our goal is to illuminate the varied needs and wishes of potential customers, revealing how businesses can craft solutions that not only meet but surpass these expectations. By zeroing in on creating products and services that truly resonate with your audience, you lay the groundwork for cultivating a devoted customer base.

This strategic focus on alignment between what you offer and what your customers seek is the key to unlocking long-term success. It ensures that every product or service is designed with the customer in mind, leading to higher satisfaction rates and fostering a sense of loyalty. In turn, this loyalty translates into sustainable growth and profitability for your business, as satisfied customers are more likely to return and spread the word.

Moreover, by consistently delivering on promises and exceeding expectations, businesses establish themselves as leaders in their markets. This leadership is not just about being at the forefront; it's about setting the pace and direction for the industry, inspiring innovation, and raising standards. Such positioning not only attracts more customers but also sets a business apart from its competitors.

The journey of identifying and understanding your target market is a continuous one, filled with learning and adaptation. It requires a commitment to listening, learning, and evolving alongside your customers. By staying attuned to their changing needs and preferences, you ensure that your business remains relevant, competitive, and on a path of growth and success. This is the essence of building a brand that lasts and making a difference in the lives of those you serve.

Inspirational Quote

> "Your customers are the lifeblood of your business. Understand them, serve them, and watch your dreams flourish."

Embrace Empathy

Empathy sits at the heart of truly grasping the essence of our target markets and customers. By immersing ourselves in their experiences, we gain invaluable insights into their lives, allowing us to view the world through their eyes. This profound comprehension cultivates a sincere bond between brands and their communities, facilitating interactions that are rich with meaning.

Such connections transcend mere transactional relationships, elevating customer satisfaction to new heights and nurturing a sense of loyalty. It is this loyalty that lays the groundwork for enduring partnerships, heralding a future where businesses and customers grow together in harmony. Empathy, therefore, isn't just beneficial; it's transformative, enriching both the consumer experience and the brand's reputation.

In the realm of business innovation, empathy acts as a powerful force for change. It equips organizations with the ability to create solutions that truly resonate with their audience, born from a deep understanding of their needs and aspirations. This empathetic approach ignites a spark of creativity, leading to the development of products and services that are not only relevant but also visionary.

Empathy does more than just foster understanding—it's the cornerstone of innovation, customer loyalty, and lasting relationships. It inspires companies to look beyond the present, to innovate with foresight and compassion. Through empathy, businesses have the potential to transform their connections with customers into meaningful partnerships that stand the test of time.

Empathy is an indispensable tool in the modern business landscape. It enriches interactions, strengthens bonds, and drives innovation, proving itself to be much more than a mere emotional response. By embracing empathy, we pave the way for a future where businesses and customers are united in their journey, achieving mutual success and satisfaction.

Listen Intently

Listening is a multifaceted skill that transcends merely hearing words. It requires engaging not only with your ears but with empathy and attention, making a conscious effort to comprehend the deeper messages conveyed by your customers. This means focusing intently on their words, observing their behavior, and appreciating their input, thus turning listening into an art of understanding beyond the surface.

Such attentive listening to your customers uncovers invaluable insights, akin to discovering hidden treasures. These revelations provide a rich source of knowledge, enabling you to tailor your products or services more effectively to their needs. By harnessing these insights, you can refine your business strategies to align more closely with customer expectations, enhancing their overall experience with your brand.

Incorporating this deep understanding into your business operations transforms your approach into one that is highly customer-centric. This adaptation not only improves customer satisfaction but also builds a strong foundation of loyalty. Customers feel valued and understood, which in turn fosters a positive perception of your brand in the marketplace.

Moreover, this practice of active listening and integrating feedback cultivates an environment of continuous improvement within your organization. It encourages openness to change and adaptability, key qualities for staying relevant and competitive in today's fast-paced market. Your business becomes more agile, able to respond swiftly to shifts in customer preferences and market dynamics.

The act of listening with intent and empathy is a powerful tool for any professional seeking to make a meaningful impact. It bridges the gap between businesses and their customers, creating a dialogue that enriches both parties. By prioritizing this level of engagement, you not only enhance your service or product but also contribute to building a more connected and responsive business landscape.

Deep into Data

In today's dynamic market environment, data acts as the guiding light for businesses navigating through the complexities of consumer behavior and market trends. By engaging deeply with analytics, businesses uncover patterns and opportunities that are not immediately obvious. This exploration empowers them to craft strategies with precision, securing a competitive advantage in their industries.

Leveraging data through market research and customer feedback, companies illuminate their path forward, making every step informed and strategic. This approach not only demystifies consumer preferences but also charts a course towards innovation and growth. Data, thus, becomes more than just numbers; it transforms into a strategic asset that drives decision-making and business success.

The power of data lies in its ability to forecast market changes and to cater to consumer desires proactively. By understanding the nuances of their audience, businesses can offer tailored experiences that resonate deeply. This not only enhances customer engagement but also cements long-term loyalty, paving the way for sustained growth.

Embracing data-driven strategies allows companies to sail smoothly through the vast and sometimes turbulent seas of the global market. With data as their compass, businesses can navigate challenges with agility, making well-informed decisions that propel them forward. This journey, guided by insights and analytics, is both efficient and rewarding, leading to destinations of success and innovation.

Letting data lead the way is not just about keeping pace with market dynamics; it's about setting the pace, defining trends, and delivering value that distinguishes a business from its competitors. Data, when harnessed effectively, is the cornerstone of building a resilient, customer-centric, and forward-thinking business. It is the key to unlocking potential, driving innovation, and achieving lasting success in today's ever-evolving market landscape.

Cultivate Connection

Creating a strong connection with your audience is akin to tending to a garden that blooms and thrives with consistent care, dedication, and genuine affection. When you engage in real conversations, tailor experiences to individual needs, and provide steadfast support, you show that you truly understand and care for your audience. This method builds a bridge of trust and loyalty, laying the groundwork for a relationship that stands the test of time.

In an era where impersonal dealings are often the standard, adding a personal touch can elevate you above your competitors. It's a powerful way to stand out, showing your audience that you see them as more than just transactions. This personal investment in their experience can become your trademark, distinguishing you in a crowded market.

Caring for your audience's needs with sincerity transcends ordinary business interactions, creating a vibrant community where people feel appreciated and listened to. This community not only boosts satisfaction among your audience but also fosters organic growth through positive recommendations. Amidst a sea of shallow connections, your genuine efforts shine brightly, drawing people toward your brand.

Your commitment to real connections signals a shift from prioritizing profit to valuing human relationships. This approach not only sets a new standard for how businesses operate but also builds a foundation of loyal supporters. Your audience, feeling respected and valued, becomes more engaged and actively participates in your community.

By focusing on authentic interactions, you position yourself as a leader who puts people first. This leadership style attracts a devoted following, ensuring your audience is not just satisfied but also feels a part of something greater. Such a community, built on trust and genuine care, supports not just your business goals but also fosters a sense of belonging among its members.

Adapt and Evolve

In the ever-evolving world of business, change stands as the only constant, challenging professionals at every turn. Embracing this dynamic landscape, adapting strategies with agility, and evolving to meet the needs of the audience are fundamental for achieving lasting success. It's essential to stay abreast of market trends, technological innovations, and shifts in consumer preferences to stay ahead.

Knowledge of the latest developments arms businesses with the power to foresee and adapt to changes, ensuring they remain relevant and competitive. This proactive approach not only maintains a company's relevance but also strengthens its position in the market. Being informed and ready to pivot strategies as needed is a hallmark of a resilient and forward-thinking business.

Agility and flexibility are more than just buzzwords in the relentless quest for business excellence; they are the cornerstones of success in our fast-paced world. These attributes allow organizations to respond quickly to changes, capture emerging opportunities, and avoid potential pitfalls. Cultivating a culture that welcomes change and promotes adaptability is key to staying ahead of the curve.

Encouraging a mindset that sees change as an opportunity rather than a threat can transform challenges into stepping stones for growth. This philosophy helps businesses not only to survive but to thrive, setting them apart from the competition. It's this adaptive capability that marks the difference between leaders and followers in any industry.

Navigating the complex waters of change with dexterity and vision is what defines successful businesses. The journey is continuous, requiring an unwavering commitment to learning, adapting, and innovating. Those who master the art of change are the ones who write their own futures, leading their industries toward new horizons with confidence and expertise.

Conclusion

Identifying target markets and customers is not just a part of business strategy; it is a deep and meaningful journey that allows us to connect with people on a human level. It challenges us to look beyond the numbers and see our customers as individuals with unique dreams, hopes, and desires. When we approach our business with this level of empathy and understanding, we not only meet their needs more effectively but also build lasting relationships that go beyond the typical transactional nature of buying and selling.

Deeply understanding our customers, serving them with dedication, and continuously adapting to meet their changing needs are essential for creating a sustainable and successful business. This commitment ensures that we remain relevant in a dynamic marketplace while making a significant impact on the lives of those we serve. It's this focus on the customer's wellbeing and success that lays the foundation for our own long-term achievements and helps us leave a positive mark on the world.

By placing the customer at the heart of everything we do, we foster a culture of care and commitment that resonates through every aspect of our business. This approach not only enhances our service offering but also strengthens our brand, making us a preferred choice for many. Our dedication to understanding and fulfilling the needs of our customers ensures we grow together, building a future where both our clients and our business thrive.

Embracing the evolving needs of our customers as opportunities for growth and innovation, we remain agile and forward-thinking in our strategies. This mindset allows us to anticipate market trends and adapt our offerings to stay ahead of the curve, ensuring we always provide value and relevance. By being proactive and responsive, we build trust and loyalty with our customers, which are invaluable assets in today's competitive landscape.

The journey of identifying and connecting with our customers is an enriching experience that benefits both the business and the individuals we serve. It is a continuous process of learning, adapting, and growing that requires patience, insight, and genuine care. By committing to this journey, we not only achieve business success but also contribute to creating a more connected and empathetic world.

CASE STUDIES: Identifying Target Markets and Customers

Case Study 1: Eco-Friendly Home Goods Store

Background:

A new startup focused on eco-friendly home goods wanted to establish a strong market presence. Their product range included sustainable kitchenware, biodegradable cleaning supplies, and recycled home decor.

Challenge:

The primary challenge was identifying a customer base that valued sustainability and was willing to pay a premium for eco-friendly products. The company needed to ensure that its marketing efforts reached and resonated with this specific demographic.

Strategy:

The company conducted market research to identify potential customers who prioritize environmental sustainability in their purchasing decisions. They used online surveys, social media analytics, and trend analysis to gather data on consumer behavior and preferences related to eco-friendly products.

Implementation:

Based on the research findings, the company targeted urban millennials and Gen Z consumers who were active on social media and showed a strong preference for sustainable living. The marketing strategy included:

- **Collaborations** with eco-conscious influencers to showcase products.

- **Engaging content** on social media platforms highlighting the environmental impact of using their products.

- **Email marketing campaigns** focused on the benefits of sustainable living and how their products contribute to that lifestyle.

Results:

The targeted approach led to a significant increase in brand awareness within the identified customer segments. The company saw a 40% increase in website traffic from the targeted demographics and a 25% increase in sales within the first six months of implementing the strategy.

Case Study 2: Fitness App for Busy Professionals

Background:

A tech startup developed a fitness app designed for busy professionals. The app offers quick, effective workout routines, nutritional guidance, and stress management techniques.

Challenge:

The startup faced the challenge of standing out in a crowded fitness app market and needed to identify a target customer segment that would benefit most from their product.

Strategy:

To pinpoint their target market, the company analyzed employment trends, lifestyle habits, and health goals of various demographics. They used data analytics tools to assess social media behavior and online forums where busy professionals discussed their challenges with maintaining a healthy lifestyle.

Implementation:

The findings led the company to focus on professionals aged 25-45 who valued efficiency and personal well-being but had limited time. The marketing strategy included:

- **LinkedIn advertising campaigns** showcasing testimonials from professionals who achieved their fitness goals with the app.

- **Partnerships with corporations** to offer the app as part of employee wellness programs.

- **Content marketing** on their platforms that provided tips for integrating fitness and healthy eating into a busy schedule.

Results:

This targeted approach helped the company achieve a 30% increase in app downloads and subscriptions from the identified customer segment within the first quarter of launching the marketing strategy. The partnerships with corporations also opened new revenue streams and increased brand visibility among professionals.

These case studies illustrate the importance of identifying and understanding target markets and customers for developing effective marketing strategies. By conducting thorough market research and tailoring their approaches to meet the specific needs and preferences of their target demographics, both companies were able to achieve significant growth and establish a strong presence in their respective markets.

Examples

1. **Apple Inc.** has developed an unparalleled understanding of its target market, enabling it to design products that closely align with consumer desires and expectations. This keen insight into consumer behavior has allowed Apple to create a lineup of products that not only meet but often exceed the expectations of its users.

2. **Nike** excels in understanding the aspirations of its target audience, skillfully forging emotional connections through its marketing campaigns and product designs. By tapping into the passions and aspirations of its consumers, Nike has consistently driven sales and built a loyal customer base.

3. **Amazon** leverages advanced data analytics to tailor its recommendations, offering a personalized shopping experience that keeps customers coming back. This strategic use of data not only enhances the overall customer experience but also significantly increases the likelihood of repeat purchases.

4. **Starbucks** has mastered the art of creating a welcoming environment that fosters a sense of community among its customers. By offering a wide range of customized options, Starbucks caters to the diverse tastes and preferences of its global customer base, making each visit a unique experience.

5. **Airbnb** revolutionized the hospitality industry by focusing on the desires of travelers looking for more personal and authentic lodging experiences. This innovative approach to accommodations has enabled Airbnb to meet the evolving needs of modern travelers, setting new standards in the industry.

Top Five Takeaways

1. **Empathy plays a crucial role** in truly grasping the needs and feelings of your audience. It allows you to connect on a deeper level, ensuring your messages resonate more effectively.

2. By **actively engaging with and listening to customer feedback**, you can make informed adjustments to your products or services. This ongoing dialogue helps tailor your offerings to better meet customer needs.

3. **Utilizing data-driven insights** can significantly inform your decision-making process. These insights offer a concrete basis for strategic choices, enhancing the effectiveness of your plans.

4. **Building genuine relationships** with your customers can significantly enhance their loyalty to your brand. Authentic interactions and connections are fundamental in creating a loyal customer base.

5. **The ability to adapt and evolve** with the market is crucial for long-term success. Staying flexible ensures your business remains competitive and relevant, even as trends and consumer preferences shift.

Five Actions to Take

1. **Carry out comprehensive market research** to gain a deep understanding of who your target audience is and what they need. This will enable you to tailor your products and marketing strategies more effectively to their preferences.

2. **Create detailed buyer personas** that represent your ideal customers. By doing so, you can make your marketing efforts more personalized and relevant, increasing the chances of engagement and conversion.

3. **Put in place robust systems** that enable the consistent collection and analysis of customer feedback. This ongoing process will help you understand your customers' experiences and how you can improve them.

4. **Provide outstanding customer service** at every opportunity to foster a sense of trust and loyalty among your customer base. Satisfied customers are more likely to become repeat buyers and recommend your business to others.

5. **Constantly seek ways to innovate and update** your product or service offerings in response to evolving customer needs and market trends. Staying ahead in this way ensures your business remains competitive and relevant.

Five Actions Not to Take

1. **Failing to pay attention to customer feedback** or considering it trivial can lead to missed opportunities for improvement. This oversight can alienate customers, making them feel undervalued and ignored.

2. **Believing that a single solution can meet the needs** of every customer overlooks the diversity within your target market. Such an assumption can result in products or services that fail to resonate with or meet the specific needs of different customer segments.

3. **Underestimating the value of establishing authentic relationships** with customers can hinder the development of loyalty and trust. Genuine engagement goes beyond transactions, fostering a sense of community and belonging among your customer base.

4. **Ignoring the latest developments** in your industry and shifts in consumer preferences can put your business at a competitive disadvantage. Staying informed enables you to adapt and innovate, ensuring your offerings remain relevant and appealing.

5. **Maintaining a rigid business strategy** without openness to adaptation can stifle growth and innovation. Flexibility in responding to new challenges and opportunities is crucial for long-term success and sustainability.

Chapter 12: Developing a Brand Identity and Positioning

In the vast and dynamic realm of business, standing out amidst a sea of competitors is not just beneficial but essential. Crafting a brand identity that resonates uniquely with consumers requires more than just being different; it's about forming meaningful connections and nurturing lasting relationships. This endeavor is a complex tapestry of decisions and interactions, each meticulously woven to tell your brand's unique story. It's an artful journey that combines creativity with strategic insight, grounded in the genuine essence of your brand.

The journey toward redefining your brand is an exploration into its core, uncovering the unique value it offers and the deep connections it can forge with your audience. It's a balance of innovative thinking and strategic planning, designed to ensure every facet of your brand echoes with your intended audience. This journey paves the way for a brand to not just capture attention but to cultivate enduring loyalty, establishing a presence that's felt deeply in the market.

To embark on this transformative path, it's crucial to possess a profound understanding of your brand's essence and its capacity to engage with people on a personal level. This process is where vision meets creativity, allowing each element of your brand to resonate profoundly with those you aim to reach. By embracing this journey, your brand can evolve into a beacon of loyalty, its presence not just seen but felt across the marketplace.

Navigating the intricate process of brand development is akin to charting a course through uncharted waters—it requires both courage and insight. It's about harmonizing the innovative with the strategic, ensuring that your brand not only stands out but also connects on a deeper level. This path, while challenging, opens up endless possibilities for growth and connection, establishing a legacy that transcends fleeting market trends.

Let's journey together through this process, harnessing creativity and authenticity to etch your brand's mark on the hearts and minds of your audience. It's a collaborative endeavor that promises not just to redefine your brand's identity but to forge a path toward lasting recognition and success. This is more than just brand development; it's the crafting of a legacy that resonates with every heartbeat of your target demographic.

Inspirational Quote

> *"Your brand is not just a logo or a tagline; it's the sum total of every experience, emotion, and perception your audience associates with you."*

Embrace Authenticity

At the heart of a truly impactful brand lies the principle of authenticity, which paves the way for deep and meaningful connections with its audience. By remaining true to its core principles, mission, and vision, a brand can align its essence with the values of its customers, fostering a relationship based on mutual understanding and respect. This steadfast dedication to authenticity enables a brand to openly share its unique journey and beliefs, cultivating a strong bond of trust and loyalty among its followers.

Authenticity in branding transcends the mere presentation of an idealized facade; it emphasizes the significance of genuine representation and transparency, particularly during challenging times. It challenges the pursuit of flawlessness, advocating for a brand that is relatable and grounded in reality. Embracing its flaws and being candid about its trials, a brand showcases its commitment to honesty and integrity, enhancing its appeal and credibility.

This honest approach not only bolsters the brand's reputation but also nurtures a more profound, authentic connection with its audience. Such a connection lays the groundwork for a supportive and loyal community, united by shared values and a mutual sense of respect. It's through these genuine interactions that a brand can truly resonate, leaving a lasting impression on the hearts and minds of its consumers.

In this era of constant information and choices, authenticity stands out as a beacon of trust and reliability for consumers seeking to connect with a brand that shares their values. A brand's commitment to authenticity fosters an environment where open communication and sincerity thrive, further enriching the relationship with its audience. This not only sets the brand apart in a crowded market but also ensures its long-term success and relevance.

The pursuit of authenticity is a journey that rewards both the brand and its community with an unbreakable bond, rooted in honesty and shared purpose. It's a testament to the power of staying true to oneself, proving that authenticity is not just a strategy, but a core value that shapes every aspect of a brand's identity. This approach not only wins the hearts of consumers but also paves the way for a legacy of integrity and trust.

Define Your Purpose

At the heart of every successful brand lies a purpose that transcends the mere pursuit of profit. This purpose, your brand's reason for being, goes beyond financial gains to articulate a deeper, more meaningful raison d'être. This foundational purpose serves as a guiding light for strategic decisions, ensuring that every action taken is in harmony with the company's broader vision.

A brand infused with a clear and compelling purpose ignites a sense of passion and commitment among its team members. They become part of a mission that has a significant impact, fostering a culture where everyone is united by a common goal. This unity not only enhances team morale but also drives the brand forward with a collective energy that is both powerful and inspiring.

When a brand's purpose resonates on a personal level with its audience, it fosters a connection that goes beyond the superficiality of mere transactions. This resonance taps into the dreams, values, and desires of the audience, making the brand an inspirational figure in their lives. By aligning its purpose with the aspirations of its audience, a brand becomes more than just a provider of goods or services; it becomes a source of inspiration and a catalyst for change.

This deep connection between a brand and its audience builds a bridge of shared values and ideals. It transforms the relationship into one that is rooted in mutual understanding and shared aspirations. As a result, the brand not only elevates its own image but also secures a loyal following of consumers who see a reflection of their own values and beliefs within the brand.

A well-defined and authentic purpose acts as the cornerstone of a brand's identity. It not only guides the brand towards strategic growth but also fosters a lasting bond with its audience. Through this bond, the brand achieves not just temporary success, but a legacy of impact and inspiration that resonates through generations.

Know Your Audience Intimately

Unlocking the secrets to your audience's heart is an art form that transcends mere numbers and figures. It's about embarking on a journey to understand their dreams, fears, and desires, capturing the very soul of what they seek. Through active listening, heartfelt engagement, and unwavering empathy, you forge a bond that transcends transactional relationships, allowing for a genuine connection that resonates deeply.

This profound connection is the key to customizing your brand's narrative and experiences in a way that truly speaks to your audience. It's not just about making noise; it's about crafting symphonies of relevance that echo their innermost thoughts and feelings. By tuning into their unique frequencies, your brand becomes a mirror reflecting their own aspirations, ensuring your message not only reaches them but touches them at their core.

When you align your brand's essence with the heartbeats of your audience, you create more than just engagements; you create emotional landmarks. Tailoring your communication to match the depth of your understanding transforms each interaction into a memorable experience. This approach doesn't just capture attention; it captivates hearts, building a bridge of loyalty and trust that is both rare and precious.

The magic lies in transforming insights into actions that resonate with your audience on a personal level. By weaving their aspirations and concerns into the very fabric of your brand, you not only make them feel seen and understood but also valued and cherished. This is the cornerstone of building a lasting relationship where loyalty is not asked for but naturally given.

In this dance of connection and understanding, every step taken in sync with your audience's rhythm amplifies the impact of your brand. It's about creating a legacy of meaningful interactions that leave a lasting imprint on their hearts. By dedicating yourself to truly understanding and valuing your audience, you don't just reach out to them; you reach deep within them, igniting a spark of connection that fuels enduring engagement and loyalty.

Craft a Compelling Narrative

Storytelling is a luminous beacon in the journey of brand development, illuminating the path to genuine connections with audiences. It crafts a bridge built on compelling narratives, transporting a brand's essence and values directly into the hearts of its audience. This technique transcends mere storytelling; it weaves an emotional tapestry that binds the audience to the brand, making every narrative a conduit of inspiration and connection.

At the heart of every memorable brand is a story that echoes its identity and core values, serving as a foundation for a distinct and relatable market presence. This narrative is the brand's signature, a distinguishing mark in the bustling marketplace. By infusing emotion and relatability into their stories, brands do more than just capture attention; they cultivate loyalty and nurture a community of passionate followers, embedding themselves deeply in the collective consciousness of their audience.

A masterfully told brand story is not just a recount of events; it is an artful expression that engages the audience on a profound level. It is through this art of storytelling that brands can truly differentiate themselves, turning ordinary interactions into memorable experiences. This emotional engagement is the key to not only attracting but also retaining a dedicated following, turning casual observers into lifelong advocates.

In crafting these narratives, brands unlock the power to not only communicate but to connect, transforming their message into a resonant echo that lingers long after the story has been told. It is this resonance that fosters a deep, enduring bond between brand and audience, a bond that thrives on shared values and aspirations. Through storytelling, brands have the unique opportunity to not just be heard, but to be felt, understood, and remembered.

Storytelling emerges not merely as a strategy but as a vital essence of brand building, a journey that intertwines brand and audience in a shared narrative. It is through these stories that brands can illuminate their uniqueness, sparking an emotional alchemy that transforms interest into loyalty. In the end, it's the stories that we remember, the stories that inspire us, and the stories that make brands a beloved part of our lives.

Consistency is Key

Consistency serves as the foundation upon which trust and recognition are built, essential for forging a lasting connection with your audience. By presenting a cohesive brand identity across all channels, from your digital footprint on the web and social media to every customer interaction, you craft an unmistakable and reliable presence. This harmony in your brand's messaging, aesthetic, and overall experience is pivotal in strengthening your position within the competitive market landscape. When individuals come across your brand, the goal is for them to immediately identify and connect with it, regardless of the platform or context.

A consistent brand representation ensures a smooth and intuitive experience for your audience, effectively removing any potential for confusion. This strategic coherence fosters a deep emotional bond, elevating your brand's memorability. More than just replicating visuals like logos or color palettes, true consistency lies in the uniformity of values, tone, and character conveyed at every point of contact. Such meticulous attention to consistency cements your brand in the consciousness of your customers, simplifying their decision to prefer your offerings over others.

This approach not only aids in distinguishing your brand but also in manifesting a sense of reliability and professionalism that customers value. The consistent delivery of your brand's message and values reassures customers of your commitment to quality and excellence. As a result, your brand becomes a symbol of trustworthiness and credibility, key attributes that consumers seek in today's saturated markets.

Adopting a holistic strategy for brand consistency goes beyond mere aesthetics; it's about crafting a narrative that resonates deeply with your audience. Each interaction is an opportunity to reinforce your brand's core message and values, creating a cohesive story that spans across all customer touchpoints. This narrative becomes a powerful tool in building a strong, enduring brand identity that not only attracts but retains customer loyalty.

The pursuit of brand consistency is a strategic endeavor that demands meticulous planning and execution. It's a commitment to maintaining a unified brand identity that resonates with your audience at every touchpoint. By achieving this level of consistency, you not only enhance your brand's market position but also forge a powerful, emotional connection with your audience. This connection is the ultimate catalyst for building a memorable brand that stands the test of time, ensuring your place at the forefront of your industry.

Conclusion

Agility and a well-defined brand identity have become essential. A robust brand acts as a beacon, guiding companies through the fluctuating tides of market trends and consumer behaviors. It demands a dedication to being genuine, a clear articulation of the brand's mission, and a deep insight into the needs and desires of the target audience. By adhering to these principles, companies can weave a story that not only engages but also forms meaningful connections with their customers.

Creating a narrative that resonates deeply with your audience is key to establishing a brand that endures and thrives over time. This narrative transcends mere transactions, embodying the brand's core values and aspirations. Such a strategic approach ensures the brand's appeal remains strong, navigating through changes in consumer tastes and market dynamics with grace. The essence of this journey is not just in being noticed but in becoming a significant part of your customers' lives, fostering a relationship that is both sincere and lasting.

In the heart of building a memorable brand lies the art of storytelling, where consistency in messaging plays a pivotal role. This storytelling is not just about the products or services offered but reflects the brand's underlying ethos and vision. By consistently communicating this narrative, brands can maintain their relevance and charm, even as the business landscape evolves. This endeavor transforms the brand into an experience, deeply embedding it in the emotional landscape of its audience.

The journey of brand building is both an art and a science, requiring a harmonious blend of authenticity, purpose, and understanding of the consumer. This blend enables brands to craft stories that are not only captivating but also deeply relatable. As these stories unfold, they pave the way for a brand that not only exists in the marketplace but also lives in the hearts and minds of its audience, achieving a timeless connection.

The goal of establishing a strong brand identity is to create a legacy that transcends the ebbs and flows of market trends. It's about forging a bond that is not merely based on transactions but on shared values and experiences. This vision for brand identity and positioning is what sets apart successful businesses, allowing them to shine brightly as beacons of innovation, trust, and connection in the ever-evolving tapestry of the business world.

CASE STUDIES: Developing a Brand Identity and Positioning

Case Study 1: Revitalizing a Heritage Brand

Background:

A well-established clothing brand, known for its quality and durability, faced stagnation in a rapidly evolving fashion industry. Their target demographic had aged, and younger audiences perceived the brand as outdated.

Challenge:

The brand needed to rejuvenate its identity to appeal to a younger demographic without alienating its existing customer base. The challenge was to modernize the brand while retaining its heritage and core values.

Strategy:

1. **Research and Insights**: Conducted market research to understand the preferences and values of younger audiences. Insights revealed a growing demand for sustainable and ethically produced clothing.

2. **Brand Redefinition:** The brand redefined its identity to focus on sustainability and ethical production, aligning with the values of the target demographic. The new brand identity emphasized the brand's commitment to quality and durability, positioning these as forms of sustainability.

3. **Visual Identity Overhaul:** Introduced a modern logo and visual aesthetic that maintained elements of the brand's heritage. The new design was applied across all branding materials, including packaging, in-store displays, and online presence.

4. **Strategic Marketing Campaigns:** Launched marketing campaigns that highlighted the brand's new focus. Collaborations with eco-conscious influencers and the use of social media platforms were key strategies to engage with younger audiences.

5. **Product Innovation:** Developed a new product line featuring sustainable materials and ethical production processes, directly addressing the interests of the target audience.

Outcome:

The rebranding effort was a success. The brand saw a significant increase in engagement from younger demographics, with social media metrics indicating a positive reception to the new brand identity and positioning. Sales figures rose, particularly in the sustainable product line, demonstrating the effective alignment of brand identity with consumer values.

Case Study 2: Launching a Tech Startup's Brand

Background:

A tech startup developed an innovative app designed to simplify personal finance management for millennials. The app combined AI-driven insights with user-friendly design but struggled to stand out in a crowded market.

Challenge:

The startup needed to establish a strong brand identity and position itself uniquely in the competitive personal finance space. The goal was to communicate the app's unique value proposition clearly and attract early adopters.

Strategy:

1. **Market Analysis:** Conducted an analysis of competitors to identify gaps in the market. This analysis revealed an opportunity to position the app as not only a finance tool but also a lifestyle enhancer for millennials.

2. **Defining the Brand:** Developed a brand identity that resonated with the target audience's desire for simplicity, efficiency, and personal growth. The messaging focused on empowering users to take control of their finances with ease.

3. **Visual and Verbal Identity:** Created a vibrant and modern visual identity that stood out from traditional finance apps, using a bright color scheme and a conversational tone in all communications to make finance feel accessible and engaging.

4. **Launch Campaign:** Implemented a targeted launch campaign using social media platforms, influencer partnerships, and content marketing to generate

buzz. The campaign highlighted user stories and the tangible benefits of using the app.

5. **Community Engagement:** Established a community around the brand by offering financial literacy resources, workshops, and interactive Q&A sessions. This approach helped build trust and loyalty among the target audience.

Outcome:

The startup successfully carved out its niche in the personal finance market. The brand's unique positioning as a lifestyle and personal growth tool, rather than just a finance app, resonated well with millennials. Downloads and active users increased significantly in the months following the launch, with positive feedback on the app's ease of use and impact on users' financial literacy and management skills.

Examples

1. **Nike** is celebrated for its motivational brand message that inspires athletes around the world. Its iconic swoosh logo is universally recognized, symbolizing excellence and innovation in sportswear.

2. **Apple** sets the standard for innovation in technology, offering products that blend cutting-edge functionality with sleek, minimalist design. This brand has become a cultural icon, representing a lifestyle of elegance and forward-thinking.

3. **Coca-Cola** stands as a beacon of timeless appeal, with its brand being synonymous with refreshment and joy across generations. Its logo and products are universally recognized, embodying a sense of global community and shared experiences.

4. **Airbnb** has revolutionized the way people think about travel accommodations, offering unique homes and experiences that connect travelers with local communities. This company is praised for its innovative platform that promotes a sense of belonging anywhere in the world.

5. **Patagonia** is a pioneer in environmental sustainability, dedicating its business practices to preserving the natural world. It is also known for its ethical approach to business, ensuring that products are made responsibly and with the least harm to the planet.

Top Five Takeaways

1. **Being authentic** is essential and cannot be compromised; it's crucial to remain faithful to the core values and essence of your brand. This authenticity helps in building trust and a genuine connection with your audience.

2. **It's important to establish a purpose** for your brand that goes beyond just making profits; a purpose that ignites passion and fosters a deep sense of commitment among your team and your customers. This deeper mission can drive motivation and loyalty in ways that financial goals alone cannot.

3. **Gaining a deep understanding of your audience** is key to crafting messages that truly resonate with them. By knowing their needs, preferences, and challenges, you can tailor your brand messaging in a way that speaks directly to their hearts and minds, making your communications more effective and impactful.

4. **Creating a narrative that touches the emotions** of your audience can significantly enhance engagement and connection. A story that encapsulates the values and mission of your brand, and is presented in an emotionally compelling way, can leave a lasting impression on your audience and strengthen their relationship with your brand.

5. **Ensuring consistency in how your brand presents itself** across all platforms and touchpoints is critical for reinforcing your brand's identity and its positioning in the market. This uniformity helps in creating a cohesive and reliable brand experience for your customers, which can greatly enhance brand recognition and loyalty.

Actions to Take

1. To effectively reach and engage your target audience, it's essential to **conduct comprehensive market research**. This process involves gathering and analyzing data about your potential customers to understand their needs, preferences, and behaviors.

2. **Clearly articulating your brand's mission, vision, and values** is crucial for establishing a strong identity. These elements serve as the foundation of your brand, guiding your business strategies and helping to connect with your audience on a deeper level.

3. **Leveraging compelling storytelling across different media channels** can significantly enhance your brand's appeal. By sharing engaging stories that resonate with your audience, you can create emotional connections and foster loyalty.

4. **Creating brand guidelines** is vital for maintaining consistency in your messaging and visual identity across all platforms. These guidelines ensure that every piece of content you produce aligns with your brand's ethos, enhancing recognition and trust among your audience.

5. **Actively seeking feedback** from your audience is a key strategy for refining your brand positioning. By listening to their opinions and insights, you can make informed adjustments to better meet their needs and strengthen your brand's market presence.

Actions Not to Take

1. **Making sacrifices in the authenticity of your brand** for the sake of quick profits can be detrimental. It risks alienating loyal customers who value genuine connections with the brands they support.

2. **Failing to establish a brand purpose** that extends beyond just making money can limit the depth of connections with consumers. A meaningful mission resonates more and fosters a stronger community around the brand.

3. **Not maintaining a unified branding approach** across various platforms can lead to confusion and dilute the brand's message. Consistency is key to building trust and recognition among your audience.

4. **Disregarding the opinions and critiques** of your audience can be a significant oversight. Engaging with and learning from feedback is crucial for growth and improvement.

5. **Mimicking the strategies of competitors** without tailoring them to fit your unique brand identity can backfire. It's important to differentiate your brand and offer something unique to your audience.

Chapter 13: Leveraging Digital Marketing Channels

Embracing digital marketing is not just an advantage; it's a necessity for businesses aiming to thrive amidst fierce competition. The evolution of technology coupled with the widespread use of the internet has revolutionized the way businesses connect with their customers, offering them a vast digital landscape to explore. By strategically navigating through digital marketing channels, businesses can amplify their visibility, drawing in and maintaining customer interest with unmatched precision and effectiveness. This pivotal approach not only cultivates a robust brand presence but also deepens connections with their audience, setting the foundation for lasting relationships.

The digital era offers an extraordinary opportunity for businesses to transcend traditional boundaries and reach a global audience. With an array of digital tools and platforms at their disposal, businesses can effortlessly bridge the gap between them and potential customers, irrespective of geographical constraints. This global reach fosters a more inclusive market, where personalization of marketing efforts becomes not just possible but highly effective, allowing businesses to craft messages that deeply resonate with their target demographic. The power of digital marketing lies in its ability to tailor experiences to individual needs and preferences, thus enhancing the relevance and impact of marketing campaigns.

Harnessing digital marketing strategies paves the way for businesses to achieve remarkable growth and establish themselves as leaders in their respective industries. The versatility of digital marketing means companies can engage with their audience through multiple channels and formats, from social media to email campaigns, each offering unique ways to tell their story and showcase their value proposition. This multi-channel approach ensures businesses can reach their audience wherever they are, making every interaction count. The result is a more cohesive and compelling brand narrative that captivates and retains customer interest.

The shift towards digital marketing is more than a trend; it's a strategic imperative that enables businesses to stay relevant and responsive in an ever-changing market landscape. By leveraging digital channels, companies can gain valuable insights into customer behavior and preferences, allowing them to adapt and evolve their strategies in real-time. This agility is crucial for staying ahead of the curve and meeting the demands of a digitally savvy consumer base. The ability to quickly pivot and respond to market trends underscores the importance of digital marketing in sustaining business growth and resilience.

Ultimately, mastering digital marketing is synonymous with mastering the art of engaging and retaining customers in the digital age. Businesses that excel in digital marketing not only see a boost in customer engagement and loyalty but also in their overall performance and profitability. This success stems from the ability to create more personalized, meaningful, and memorable customer experiences, powered by insights derived from digital interactions. As businesses continue to navigate the digital landscape, those that can effectively leverage digital marketing will find themselves not just surviving but thriving, setting new benchmarks for success in their industries.

Inspirational Quote

> *"Success in digital marketing is not about finding the right strategy; it's about creating the right mindset to adapt, innovate, and persevere in the face of constant change."*

Embrace Innovation

Embracing innovation is not just a strategy but a necessity. It acts as the driving force for companies striving to lead their industries and eclipse their rivals. When companies commit to seeking out fresh ideas, leveraging the latest technologies, and adopting innovative strategies, they break free from conventional bounds and redefine what's possible.

This relentless quest for innovation does more than just introduce new concepts; it fundamentally enhances the way businesses connect with their audiences. It opens the door to crafting campaigns that are not only memorable but also profoundly influential. Through a steadfast dedication to innovation, businesses can forge deeper relationships with their customers, setting the stage for unforgettable experiences that resonate long after the initial interaction.

Moreover, innovation in digital marketing goes beyond the thrill of pioneering breakthroughs; it underscores the vital role of continuous evolution and refinement. This ongoing process of improvement ensures that marketing efforts are not just current but also consistently effective, striking a chord with the intended audience every time. It's this commitment to perpetual enhancement that allows businesses to maintain their edge, build enduring loyalty, and solidify their standing in a constantly changing digital landscape.

By nurturing a culture that values continuous innovation, companies are not just staying ahead; they are setting new standards. This philosophy drives them to exceed expectations, pushing boundaries to discover new horizons in digital marketing. It is this visionary approach that empowers businesses to achieve unparalleled success, captivating their audiences in ways that go beyond conventional marketing tactics.

The journey of innovation in digital marketing is an ongoing saga of transformation and growth. It invites businesses to explore uncharted territories, refine their methods, and continually adapt to the ever-shifting digital arena. In doing so, they not only achieve excellence in their campaigns but also inspire a legacy of innovation that propels the entire industry forward. Through innovation, businesses are not just participating in the digital marketing landscape; they are actively shaping its future.

Know Your Audience

The key to unlocking the full potential of any marketing campaign lies in the profound understanding of your target audience. Delving deep into the demographics, behaviors, and preferences of your audience paves the way for a marketing approach that hits the mark with precision. It is through this meticulous analysis that marketers can craft messages and content that not only reach but deeply resonate with their audience, creating a harmonious synergy between brand and consumer.

Adopting a tailored approach to your marketing strategy is not just beneficial; it's essential for forging meaningful connections. By immersing yourself in the needs and desires of your audience, you have the opportunity to create content that speaks volumes. This personalized touch not only elevates the relevance of your message but also captivates the audience, ensuring your brand's voice is heard loud and clear amidst the cacophony of the digital world.

The magic of custom-tailored content lies in its power to transform passive observers into active participants. When your message aligns with what your audience truly values, it sparks an undeniable interest and fosters loyalty that transcends the superficial layers of engagement. This strategic alignment breeds a unique form of engagement that nurtures a bond built on genuine interest and mutual respect.

At the heart of impactful digital marketing lies the commitment to understanding and catering to the unique preferences and behaviors of your target audience. Such a focused approach not only garners higher engagement rates but also carves out a niche of loyal followers. These meaningful interactions are the cornerstone of not just a successful campaign, but a thriving brand that resonates with its audience on a profound level.

The journey to elevating your digital marketing efforts to new heights is grounded in the dedication to truly understanding your audience. This path leads to the creation of compelling content that not only meets the audience where they are but also guides them closer to your brand. By centering your strategies around the preferences and needs of your target audience, you unlock the door to unparalleled engagement and loyalty, marking the success of your digital marketing endeavors.

Focus on Value

In the vibrant tapestry of today's digital world, where the battle for attention spans resembles a crowded marketplace, offering undeniable value to your audience is more than a strategy—it's a necessity. This value can unfold in myriad ways, from delivering content that enlightens and inspires, to crafting personalized experiences that resonate deeply, or providing customer service that truly goes above and beyond. It's essential to ensure that every interaction with your audience is an opportunity to enhance their perception of your brand's value, thereby setting your brand apart in a sea of digital noise and forging a path to meaningful connections.

By consistently infusing value into every aspect of your audience's experience, you lay the groundwork for trust, loyalty, and advocacy—key pillars in the edifice of a successful brand-consumer relationship. These foundational elements foster a sense of community and belonging among your audience, a vital connection in today's digital age. When people feel genuinely valued and understood by a brand, they transform into loyal advocates, championing your brand's cause and ethos with fervor.

This cycle of advocacy and loyalty is not just beneficial; it's transformative, offering your brand a sustainable competitive edge in the bustling digital arena. In a world where consumers are bombarded with choices, standing out for the right reasons—through unwavering commitment to value—can make all the difference. It's this dedication to excellence and authenticity that can elevate your brand from merely being noticed to being remembered and revered.

Such advocacy is the lifeblood of long-term success in the digital domain, creating a virtuous circle of growth, engagement, and loyalty. As your brand becomes a beacon of value and integrity, it naturally attracts more like-minded individuals, expanding your community of advocates and further cementing your brand's position in the marketplace. This isn't just about immediate gains; it's about building a legacy of excellence that resonates with consumers on a profound level.

The journey to capturing and retaining attention in the digital age is paved with the genuine value you offer to your audience. This approach not only distinguishes your brand amidst the cacophony of digital noise but also nurtures a loyal community of advocates who see your brand as an integral part of their lives. In embracing this ethos, you're not just building a brand; you're creating a movement, one that's grounded in value, trust, and mutual respect.

Cultivate Authenticity

In the ever-evolving landscape of digital marketing, authenticity has emerged as the cornerstone of strategies that lead to success. It demands that brands present themselves in a manner that is genuine, transparent, and resonates with the human touch. When brands courageously share their stories, core values, and missions with honesty, they forge a deeper connection with their audience, inviting them to see the real people behind the corporate facade. This practice not only brings brands to life but also significantly elevates their appeal among consumers, making them more relatable and engaging.

The focus on authenticity cultivates a fertile ground for trust to blossom, paving the way for the development of sincere relationships between brands and their audiences. Such relationships are anchored in mutual respect and understanding, pillars that are indispensable in the fiercely competitive arena of today's market. By prioritizing authenticity in their communications, brands can ensure that these bonds withstand the test of time and emerge stronger in the face of adversity.

This strategy of embracing authenticity does more than just benefit the brand in terms of increased loyalty and engagement. It acts as a beacon, guiding the digital marketplace towards a future where interactions are not only more genuine but also more meaningful. In a world saturated with information and options, the ability to stand out by being authentically human is a powerful differentiator.

Moreover, when brands commit to being authentic, they contribute to a digital ecosystem that values transparency and honesty. This not only enhances the quality of interactions within the digital sphere but also sets a new standard for how businesses should communicate with their stakeholders. It encourages a shift from transactional relationships to those that are built on shared values and mutual growth.

The path to creating lasting impressions and building strong connections in the digital age is paved with authenticity. By embracing their true selves, brands not only enrich their own narratives but also play a crucial role in shaping a more authentic, transparent, and relatable digital marketplace. This approach not only fosters loyalty and engagement but also heralds a new era of marketing where genuine connections triumph over superficial engagements.

Embrace Agility

In the fast-paced world of digital marketing, staying agile is more than a necessity—it's a strategy for success. The ability to swiftly adapt to changing market trends and consumer behaviors is what sets leading companies apart, allowing them to seize new opportunities and tackle challenges head-on. By adopting a flexible mindset in strategy development and execution, organizations unlock the potential to swiftly embrace innovative technologies, platforms, and insights, keeping them at the forefront of their industry.

Agility in digital marketing is not just about being reactive; it's about being one step ahead. It involves a proactive approach to foreseeing shifts in the market and understanding customer needs before they become apparent. This forward-thinking mentality enables companies to explore new marketing avenues, experiment with novel tactics, and fine-tune their strategies using up-to-the-minute data and feedback. Such an approach not only meets but anticipates customer demands, fostering a deeper connection and loyalty.

The power of agility lies in its ability to transform challenges into opportunities for growth and innovation. Companies that embrace this agile mindset can quickly pivot their strategies, making the most of emerging trends and technologies. This capacity to adapt and innovate ensures that businesses remain relevant and competitive, even in a crowded marketplace.

Embedding agility into the core of digital marketing strategies is essential for navigating the digital world's complexities with finesse. It empowers businesses to respond dynamically to the ever-changing landscape, ensuring they can thrive in the long term. Through continuous learning and adaptation, companies can maintain their edge, driving sustained growth and success.

The essence of agility in digital marketing transcends mere adaptability—it's about cultivating a culture of innovation, responsiveness, and proactive change. Organizations that champion agility are not just surviving; they're thriving, setting new standards for excellence and redefining what it means to be successful in the digital age. By prioritizing agility, businesses can ensure they not only navigate the present with confidence but are also well-equipped to shape the future.

Conclusion

In the dynamic landscape of digital marketing, embracing the full potential of various channels is not just about adopting the latest strategies or technologies. It's about fostering a culture of innovation, where each step forward is a leap towards establishing new standards in the digital marketplace. This journey requires a deep understanding of the available tools and a steadfast commitment to addressing the ever-changing needs of your audience. Such a mindset empowers marketers to stay adaptable and agile, traits that are crucial for navigating the swift currents of the digital world.

To embody this innovative and empathetic approach, marketers must blend foresight with flexibility, enabling them to foresee market trends and respond with nimble strategies. This synergy converts potential challenges into opportunities for growth, cultivating a resilient mindset that values experimentation and continuous learning. By adopting this philosophy, digital marketers can adeptly manage the intricacies of the online environment, making strategic decisions that foster genuine connections and sustainable development.

The essence of digital marketing success lies in not merely keeping pace with the digital evolution but in setting the pace, leading with visionary insight and imaginative solutions. This requires a proactive stance, where anticipating the future becomes second nature, and creativity in problem-solving is paramount. Such an approach not only enhances engagement with your target audience but also secures a competitive edge in the rapidly evolving digital arena.

In cultivating this environment, it's essential to encourage a spirit of curiosity and openness, where new ideas are welcomed and risks are seen as stepping stones to innovation. This encourages a workplace where breakthroughs are common, and the status quo is continuously challenged. By embracing this mindset, teams can unlock unprecedented levels of creativity and efficiency, propelling their brands to new heights in the digital domain.

The journey through digital marketing is one of constant learning and adaptation, where success is measured by the ability to foresee changes and craft strategies that resonate with audiences on a profound level. It's about building relationships based on trust and value, leveraging every tool and insight to deliver experiences that captivate and convert. With this approach, the possibilities are limitless, inviting marketers to explore uncharted territories with confidence and creativity.

CASE STUDIES: Leveraging Digital Marketing Channels

Case Study 1: Small Business E-commerce Growth Through Social Media Marketing

Background:

A small, artisanal candle-making business aimed to increase its market reach and sales. With a modest budget and limited physical presence, the business sought to leverage digital marketing to expand its customer base and enhance brand recognition.

Strategy:

The business focused on social media marketing, primarily using platforms like Instagram and Facebook. They crafted a content strategy that highlighted the unique aspects of their products, including the handcrafted process, the quality of materials, and the personal stories behind each scent.

Implementation:

1. **Visual Content Creation:** High-quality images and videos showcasing the candles, their production process, and usage scenarios were shared.
2. **Engagement Tactics:** Interactive posts, such as polls about new scents or behind-the-scenes stories, were used to engage the audience.
3. **Influencer Partnerships:** Collaborations with micro-influencers who aligned with the brand's values were initiated to reach a wider audience.
4. **Targeted Ads:** A portion of the budget was allocated to targeted ads on these platforms, aimed at users interested in home decor, artisanal products, and wellness.

Results:

1. The business saw a 60% increase in online sales within the first six months.
2. Social media followers doubled, significantly enhancing brand visibility.
3. Engagement rates soared, with a notable increase in user-generated content, where customers shared their own stories and experiences with the products.
4. The influencer collaborations led to features in popular lifestyle blogs, further increasing brand credibility and reach.

This case demonstrates the power of leveraging social media channels for small businesses. By creating engaging content, fostering community, and utilizing targeted advertising, the business significantly expanded its online presence and sales, proving that strategic use of digital marketing can yield substantial results even with limited resources.

Case Study 2: Tech Startup Drives Lead Generation Through Content Marketing and SEO

Background:

A B2B tech startup, offering innovative cloud-based solutions, sought to establish its presence in a competitive market and generate leads. With a focus on long-term growth, the startup aimed to build its authority and attract potential clients through digital channels.

Strategy:

The company decided to invest in content marketing and search engine optimization (SEO) to increase its visibility and attract quality leads. The goal was to provide valuable content that addressed the pain points of their target audience while improving search engine rankings.

Implementation:

1. **Content Creation:** The startup developed a comprehensive blog, covering topics relevant to potential clients, such as cloud security, industry trends, and best practices.

2. **Keyword Optimization:** SEO research was conducted to identify high-value keywords to incorporate into their content, optimizing for both search engines and user experience.

3. **Lead Magnets:** High-quality resources such as e-books, whitepapers, and case studies were created as lead magnets to capture contact information.

4. **Email Marketing:** An email marketing strategy was implemented to nurture leads through informative and engaging newsletters.

Results:

1. The website's organic traffic increased by 150% within a year, with a significant improvement in search engine rankings for targeted keywords.

2. The lead generation rate saw a remarkable increase, with a 40% rise in lead capture through the website.

3. The quality of leads improved, with a higher conversion rate from initial contact to qualified sales leads.

4. The content pieces were shared widely across industry platforms, enhancing the startup's credibility and authority in the field.

For the tech startup, investing in content marketing and SEO proved to be a highly effective strategy for building brand authority and generating leads. By providing value-driven content and optimizing for search engines, the startup not only improved its online visibility but also established a strong foundation for sustained growth and market penetration.

Examples

1. **Nike** has consistently set the standard for digital marketing innovation, crafting campaigns that deeply connect with audiences worldwide. Their strategic use of social media, influencer partnerships, and cutting-edge technology ensures they remain a beloved brand across the globe.

2. **HubSpot** stands out for its pioneering inbound marketing strategy, emphasizing the creation and distribution of content that genuinely serves and engages its target audience. By focusing on drawing customers through helpful and informative content, they've become a leading name in digital marketing education and resources.

3. **Airbnb's** use of digital marketing channels has been pivotal in transforming the travel sector, creating a platform that emphasizes community and shared experiences. Their campaigns highlight the unique accommodations and local experiences available, appealing to travelers seeking more than just a place to stay.

4. **Glossier** has brilliantly harnessed the power of user-generated content and a vibrant social media presence to build a brand that's perceived as authentic and relatable. Their approach encourages customer engagement and loyalty, making Glossier a cosmetic industry standout for its genuine connection with fans.

5. **Dollar Shave Club** revolutionized the grooming industry with its clever, humorous digital marketing campaigns that struck a chord with the millennial demographic. Their direct-to-consumer model, combined with memorable advertising, has made them a case study in how to appeal to a younger audience with humor and relatability.

Top Five Takeaways

1. To remain competitive and lead in your industry, it's essential to **prioritize innovation and continuously seek ways to advance**. Staying ahead of the curve allows you to anticipate market trends and meet future demands effectively.

2. **Gaining a deep understanding of your audience** is crucial for crafting messages that resonate on a personal level. By tailoring your messaging to meet their specific needs and preferences, you can engage more effectively and create meaningful connections.

3. **Building trust and loyalty with your audience** is foundational, and delivering genuine value is the key to achieving this. When customers see the real benefits in what you offer, they are more likely to stay loyal and advocate for your brand.

4. **Cultivating authenticity** in your brand's voice and actions helps foster genuine connections with your audience. Authenticity resonates with people, encouraging them to engage more deeply with your brand and its message.

5. **Embracing agility in your business operations** and strategy enables you to adapt swiftly to changes in the market. This flexibility can give you a competitive advantage, allowing you to respond to new opportunities and challenges with speed and efficiency.

Actions to Take

1. **Embrace a culture of continuous** learning and experimentation within your organization, encouraging employees to explore new ideas and approaches, which can lead to groundbreaking innovations. By investing in ongoing education and creating an environment that supports risk-taking, you cultivate a dynamic team capable of adapting to evolving market demands and staying ahead of the competition.

2. **Dive deep into audience research**, utilizing a variety of methods such as surveys, interviews, and data analysis to truly understand the needs, preferences, and behaviors of your target demographic. By gaining comprehensive insights into your audience, you can tailor your products, services, and marketing strategies to better resonate with their desires and aspirations, fostering stronger connections and driving business growth.

3. **Craft a comprehensive content strategy** that revolves around providing meaningful value to your audience, whether through informative articles, entertaining videos, or interactive experiences. By aligning your content with the needs and interests of your target market, you can establish your brand as a trusted authority in your industry and nurture long-term relationships with customers.

4. **Infuse your brand with humanity** by sharing genuine stories and experiences that reflect the values and personality of your company. By showcasing the

people behind your brand and highlighting their authentic journeys, you create emotional connections with your audience, fostering loyalty and trust that goes beyond mere transactions.

5. **Maintain agility and adaptability** in the face of ever-evolving digital trends and opportunities, continuously monitoring the landscape for emerging technologies, platforms, and consumer behaviors. By staying nimble and responsive, you can seize new avenues for growth and innovation, positioning your brand as a leader in the digital realm.

Actions Not to Take

1. **Neglecting to adapt to changing market trends** and consumer behaviors can lead to missed opportunities and decreased competitiveness. It's crucial for businesses to stay agile and responsive, continually analyzing market shifts and evolving their strategies to meet evolving consumer needs and preferences.

2. **Relying solely on outdated or ineffective marketing tactics** limits your reach and effectiveness in connecting with your target audience. Embracing modern, data-driven approaches and leveraging emerging technologies can revitalize your marketing efforts and drive better results in today's dynamic landscape.

3. **Sacrificing authenticity for short-term gains** can damage your brand reputation and erode consumer trust in the long run. Building genuine connections with your audience by staying true to your brand values and delivering authentic experiences fosters loyalty and sustainable growth over time.

4. **Overlooking the importance of providing genuine value** to your audience diminishes engagement and loyalty. By focusing on addressing your audience's needs and pain points, you can cultivate stronger relationships and position your brand as a trusted resource in your industry.

5. **Failing to prioritize continuous improvement** and innovation in your digital marketing efforts stagnates growth and leaves you vulnerable to competitors. Embracing a culture of experimentation and learning, and regularly evaluating and refining your strategies, enables you to stay ahead of the curve and drive sustained success in the digital realm.

Chapter 14: Mastering the Art of Selling

The mastery of sales is akin to possessing the keys to a kingdom of success. It goes beyond the simple act of exchanging goods or services for money, highlighting the significance of fostering deep connections, understanding the core needs of customers, and delivering unparalleled value. This mastery involves a profound dive into human psychology, the finesse of effective communication, and the craft of persuasion, marking a journey that requires relentless commitment, steadfast perseverance, and a constant pursuit of excellence.

Embarking on the path to sales mastery is not merely about the pursuit of financial rewards; it represents a journey of personal and professional evolution. It pushes individuals to stretch beyond their comfort zones, encouraging continuous learning and adaptation in a world that never stands still. This journey is more than just mastering the art of sales; it's an opportunity for growth, a deeper understanding of human behavior, and improving the ability to forge meaningful connections with others.

Let us embark on this transformative journey together, recognizing that the true rewards of mastering sales extend far beyond monetary success. This path offers the enriching experience of personal growth, allowing us to develop professionally and personally. It challenges us to rise above the ordinary, to continually learn and adapt, enhancing our capacity to understand and connect with people on a profound level.

The mastery of sales is not just about the art of closing deals but about opening doors to new possibilities and horizons. It invites us to explore the vast landscape of human psychology, to refine our communication skills, and to perfect the art of persuasion. This journey is an invitation to develop a deeper understanding of ourselves and others, paving the way for not only professional success but personal fulfillment as well.

Inspirational Quote

"Success in sales comes down to your willingness to listen, learn, and adapt. Embrace rejection as fuel for your ambition, and let persistence be your guiding light on the path to mastery."

The Power of Mindset

In the dynamic landscape of sales, embracing a positive mindset stands as a cornerstone for success. Cultivating an abundance mentality transforms the way we view the world, opening our eyes to the vast opportunities that lie in wait. By replacing self-doubt and fear of rejection with confidence and openness, we unlock our true potential, making every challenge a stepping stone to greater achievements.

Each interaction in sales, no matter how small, is a chance to learn, grow, and inch closer to our goals. Viewing potential setbacks as learning experiences shifts our perspective, allowing us to approach each situation with curiosity and a drive to improve. This mindset turns the sales journey into an enriching experience, filled with lessons that pave the way to success.

The path of a sales professional is inevitably marked by ups and downs, making resilience not just a trait but a necessity. It is in the face of challenges that our strength and determination are tested, and where true growth occurs. Embracing adversity with a positive attitude enables us to emerge stronger, more skilled, and ready to tackle the next challenge.

Staying positive and resilient in the competitive arena of sales is more than just a strategy; it's a philosophy that enriches our professional journey. This approach fosters not only personal growth but also drives us towards achieving our objectives, setting us apart in the field. It is the resilient who navigate the complexities of sales with grace, turning obstacles into opportunities for advancement.

A positive and resilient mindset is the key to unlocking the full potential of a sales professional. By viewing every challenge as an opportunity for growth and maintaining an optimistic outlook, we set the stage for success. This mindset not only enhances our personal development but also propels us forward in the competitive world of sales, where resilience and positivity are the hallmarks of true achievers.

Understanding Your Audience

Mastering the art of selling requires a deep dive into understanding what truly motivates your audience. By actively listening and engaging in conversations that matter to them, you uncover not just their needs but their deepest aspirations. It is in empathizing with their challenges that we forge connections that transcend mere transactions, highlighting how our offerings can bring real solutions to their lives.

To excel in sales, building a foundation of trust and rapport with your audience is paramount. This is cultivated through a genuine expression of interest in their success and well-being, signaling that your intentions go beyond just making a sale. At its heart, selling is about problem-solving and enriching the customer's experience, turning every interaction into a chance to positively influence their journey.

When we approach selling with the mindset of adding value, we transform the process into a meaningful exchange. This shift in perspective ensures that every discussion is an opportunity to demonstrate how our products or services can make a tangible difference. It's about presenting solutions that resonate with their unique situations, thereby cementing a relationship built on reliability and mutual benefit.

The essence of selling lies in the ability to see beyond the immediate transaction, focusing instead on the lasting impact we can have on someone's life. By aligning our offerings with the real needs and dreams of our customers, we not only achieve success in sales but also contribute to their personal and professional growth. This approach not only elevates our practice of selling but also enriches the lives of those we serve.

The art of selling is much more than the exchange of goods for money; it's about creating relationships that are rooted in understanding, trust, and mutual respect. As we hone our skills in identifying and addressing the needs of our customers, we not only excel in our careers but also play a pivotal role in empowering others to achieve their goals. Through this lens, selling becomes an avenue for making a lasting, positive impact in the world.

Crafting Compelling Stories

In the heart of every successful sales and marketing strategy lies the timeless art of storytelling. It's a profound human connection that when harnessed, transforms simple messages into compelling tales of possibility and promise. Through these narratives, businesses can vividly showcase the unique benefits of their offerings, creating a personal bridge between their products or services and the lives of their audience.

Crafting stories that resonate on a personal level enables companies to illustrate not just what they sell, but the value it adds to the consumer's life. By integrating testimonials and case studies, these stories become more than just narratives; they turn into evidence of success, providing tangible proof of the positive changes customers can experience. This blend of storytelling and factual backing strengthens the trust and credibility in a brand, making its message all the more persuasive.

Emotional engagement is the cornerstone of effective storytelling in sales and marketing. When a story touches the heart, it not only captures attention but also sparks a desire for action. This emotional connection is what sets the stage for a compelling call to action, urging potential customers to take the leap and experience the benefits for themselves.

In a world where consumers are bombarded with countless choices, the ability to stand out rests significantly on how well a brand tells its story. Stories imbue products with meaning, turning ordinary features into extraordinary benefits that people can relate to and desire. This strategic differentiation is what elevates a brand, making its value proposition not just heard, but felt on a deeper level.

The magic of storytelling in sales and marketing lies in its power to convert abstract features into stories of transformation. It's about painting a picture where the audience can see themselves, highlighting not just the functional attributes of a product or service, but how it enhances their lives. In this way, storytelling becomes not just a tool for engagement, but a bridge to a better understanding and appreciation of the value a brand brings to the table.

The Art of Persuasion

Persuasion is a blend of art and science, combining the delicate art of influencing others with the strategic application of proven principles. It requires a deep understanding of key persuasion techniques such as reciprocity, scarcity, and authority, which act as ethical guides in leading others toward making informed decisions. These foundational principles, deeply rooted in psychological research, provide a clear path through the intricate web of human behavior and decision-making, offering a powerful toolkit for those looking to shape outcomes, whether in business dealings or personal relationships.

To truly master the art of persuasion, one must embrace a customized approach that values the unique motivations and preferences of each individual. This personalized strategy involves active listening and the practice of techniques like mirroring to foster a connection and build trust with others. Such thoughtful engagement not only nurtures trust but lays the groundwork for mutually beneficial relationships, paving the way for more effective and meaningful interactions.

By concentrating on the specific needs and wants of each person, persuaders can more accurately steer them towards choices that resonate with their personal values and goals. This focus ensures that every decision made is not only in the best interest of the individual but also contributes to a sense of satisfaction and fulfillment. The outcome is a rewarding experience that feels genuinely beneficial for all involved, highlighting the true essence of ethical persuasion.

In the realm of persuasion, understanding and leveraging these psychological principles can dramatically enhance one's ability to influence outcomes positively. The application of these tactics across various scenarios, from professional negotiations to daily interactions, underscores their versatility and effectiveness. It is through this strategic application that individuals can truly harness the power of persuasion, achieving goals while maintaining integrity and respect for others' autonomy.

The journey of becoming a persuasive communicator is both challenging and rewarding, offering endless opportunities for growth and learning. By dedicating oneself to mastering these principles and applying them with consideration for the unique perspectives of others, one can achieve remarkable success. The art of persuasion, when practiced thoughtfully and ethically, has the power to transform relationships, facilitate mutual understanding, and create lasting positive impacts in both personal and professional spheres.

Overcoming Objections

Objections from potential customers should be embraced as golden opportunities, not deterrents. These moments offer a unique platform to highlight the exceptional qualities of your product or service, addressing any hesitations head-on. By preparing for common objections with well-thought-out responses, you transform potential stumbling blocks into stepping stones that lead prospects closer to a favorable decision.

Approaching objections with empathy and understanding is key to building trust and rapport with prospects. Acknowledging their concerns sincerely, rather than brushing them aside, shows that you value their perspective and are committed to finding solutions that meet their needs. Providing tangible proof, such as success stories from satisfied customers, can further dispel doubts and underline the unique advantages of what you're offering, setting it apart in the competitive market.

Recognizing objections as a natural aspect of the sales conversation underscores the importance of a positive and proactive engagement strategy. When a prospect raises concerns, it often means they are genuinely considering your product or service and how it might benefit them. Viewing these moments as opportunities to enrich the dialogue not only helps in addressing specific concerns but also in demonstrating the depth of value and reliability your solution brings to the table.

Embracing objections rather than fearing them can significantly enhance the quality of your interactions with prospects. It allows for a deeper exploration of their needs and how your offering can meet those needs, fostering a stronger, more meaningful connection. This approach not only alleviates immediate concerns but also positions your product or service as a reliable and valuable solution, thereby increasing the chances of a successful sale.

Navigating objections with grace and confidence is an art that can significantly impact the outcome of your sales efforts. By seeing each objection as a chance to further elucidate the benefits of your offering, you not only overcome barriers but also build a foundation of trust and credibility with your prospects. This strategic approach paves the way for more engaged conversations, stronger relationships, and ultimately, successful sales outcomes.

Conclusion

Embarking on the journey to excel in sales is a continuous endeavor that intertwines personal growth with the enhancement of professional capabilities. It requires a steadfast commitment, relentless perseverance, and a dedicated pursuit of excellence in each encounter. Those who thrive in the sales arena are those who adopt a mindset geared towards growth, viewing every hurdle not as a setback but as a stepping stone towards mastery and self-improvement. This perspective, when married with a keen insight into the needs and desires of their audience, empowers sales professionals to fine-tune their strategies, ensuring impactful engagements.

The essence of successful selling lies in the ability to weave compelling narratives and master the subtle art of persuasion. Stories have a unique power to connect with individuals on a deeply emotional level, facilitating a bond and fostering trust more effortlessly. When sales professionals adeptly navigate through objections, they not only exhibit a deep empathy towards the customer's reservations but also reinforce this trust. These competencies are not just vital for achieving immediate sales triumphs; they lay the groundwork for enduring relationships and ongoing business, unlocking a sales professional's true potential.

In the realm of sales, developing a profound understanding of one's audience is paramount. It's about listening intently, observing keenly, and responding thoughtfully to the expressed and unexpressed needs of the customer. Such an approach not only enhances the relevance of your offering but also elevates the customer's experience, making it more personal and meaningful. This depth of engagement is what distinguishes the exceptional sales professional from the ordinary, turning interactions into opportunities for lasting impact.

Cultivating the skills of storytelling and persuasion requires patience, practice, and a willingness to learn from every experience. Each conversation is an opportunity to refine these skills, to learn what resonates with people and what doesn't. This iterative process of learning and adaptation is what sharpens a sales professional's ability to influence effectively, making each story told more captivating and each argument more persuasive. Over time, these skills become second nature, enabling sales professionals to navigate complex sales landscapes with grace and efficacy.

The journey to sales mastery is one of continuous learning, personal development, and strategic adaptation. It's about embracing the challenges that come your way, learning from every interaction, and constantly seeking ways to better understand and connect with your audience. By committing to this path of perpetual growth and refinement, sales professionals unlock the door to not just achieving their goals but surpassing them, paving the way for a career not only marked by success but defined by it.

CASE STUDIES: Mastering the Art of Selling

Case Study 1: Software Solutions Inc. - Technology Sector

Background:

Software Solutions Inc. is a company that specializes in providing comprehensive software services for businesses, including customized solutions for data management, analytics, and cloud-based services. Despite having a strong product lineup, the company struggled with sales due to high market competition and a lack of effective sales strategies.

Challenge:

The primary challenge was differentiating their offerings in a saturated market and effectively communicating the value proposition to potential clients. Additionally, the sales team lacked a cohesive strategy and relied on outdated sales techniques that did not resonate with modern buyers.

Strategy Implemented:

The company embarked on a comprehensive overhaul of its sales strategy with a focus on:

- **Training and Development:** Implementing a rigorous training program for the sales team, emphasizing consultative selling techniques and a deep understanding of customer needs.

- **Customer Relationship Management (CRM):** Adopting a state-of-the-art CRM system to better track customer interactions, manage leads, and personalize follow-up communications.

- **Value Proposition Communication:** Refining how the company communicated its value proposition, focusing on the unique benefits of their solutions and how they address specific customer pain points.

Results:

Over the course of 12 months, Software Solutions Inc. saw a significant improvement in sales performance. The trained sales team was better equipped to engage with clients meaningfully, leading to a 25% increase in closed sales and a 40% increase in lead conversion rates. The CRM system allowed for more effective lead management and follow-up, contributing to a higher customer satisfaction rate.

Case Study 2: Fashion Forward - Retail Sector

Background:

Fashion Forward is a boutique fashion brand known for its innovative designs and sustainable practices. Despite having a loyal customer base and strong brand identity, the company faced challenges in expanding its market presence and increasing sales due to intense competition and changing consumer preferences.

Challenge:

The main challenges included staying relevant in a fast-paced industry, attracting new customers, and enhancing the in-store experience to increase sales.

Strategy Implemented:

Fashion Forward implemented several key strategies to address these challenges, including:

- **Experiential Retailing:** Redesigning store layouts to create more engaging and immersive shopping experiences, incorporating technology like virtual try-ons and interactive displays.

- **Digital Marketing and Social Media:** Leveraging digital marketing and social media platforms to engage with a broader audience, showcase their unique value proposition, and drive online sales.

- **Customer Loyalty Programs:** Introducing a loyalty program that rewards repeat customers with exclusive deals, early access to new collections, and personalized shopping experiences.

Results:

These strategies led to a marked improvement in Fashion Forward's sales and brand visibility. The experiential retailing approach attracted more foot traffic, increasing in-store sales by 30%. The enhanced digital marketing efforts resulted in a 50% growth in online sales, while the loyalty program helped improve customer retention rates by 20%.

Both case studies demonstrate the importance of adapting sales strategies to meet the changing needs and preferences of the market. By focusing on customer relationships, leveraging technology, and continuously evolving their sales approaches, both Software Solutions Inc. and Fashion Forward were able to overcome their sales challenges and achieve significant growth.

Examples:

1. **Zig Ziglar,** a legendary figure in the realm of motivation and sales, is celebrated for his profound insights into sales techniques that have inspired countless individuals worldwide. Through his dynamic speaking engagements and bestselling books, Ziglar has left an indelible mark on the sales industry, shaping the way people approach selling and personal development.

2. **Mary Kay Ash,** the visionary behind Mary Kay Cosmetics, not only revolutionized the beauty industry but also championed a movement empowering women through direct selling. Her legacy transcends mere entrepreneurship, as she paved the way for women to achieve financial independence and success on their own terms, leaving an enduring impact on generations of aspiring businesswomen.

3. **Salesforce,** a trailblazer in customer relationship management (CRM), continues to redefine the landscape of sales and marketing with its innovative solutions. Renowned for its user-friendly interface and cutting-edge technologies, Salesforce remains at the forefront of empowering businesses to forge stronger connections with their customers and drive sustainable growth.

4. **Grant Cardone**, a dynamic entrepreneur and sales luminary, has garnered widespread acclaim for his transformative teachings on mastering the art of selling. From bestselling books to electrifying seminars, Cardone's insights into sales psychology and strategy have empowered individuals and businesses alike to elevate their sales performance and achieve unprecedented levels of success.

5. **Apple,** synonymous with innovation and excellence, has not only redefined technology but also revolutionized sales and marketing strategies. With its iconic product launches and unparalleled brand loyalty, Apple continues to captivate consumers worldwide, setting the gold standard for effective salesmanship and brand positioning in the digital age.

Top Five Takeaways

1. **Foster a mindset of abundance and resilience** by recognizing opportunities even in challenging situations. Embrace the belief that there is always room for growth and success, regardless of setbacks.

2. **Develop a deep understanding of your audience's needs** and motivations through active listening and research. Tailor your approach to address their specific pain points and desires, fostering stronger connections and rapport.

3. **Create captivating narratives** that not only capture attention but also emotionally resonate with your audience. Use storytelling techniques to illustrate how your product or service can solve their problems and improve their lives.

4. **Hone your skills in persuasion and influence** by studying psychological principles and applying them ethically in your sales interactions. Build trust and credibility by aligning your recommendations with the interests and goals of your prospects.

5. **Embrace objections as valuable opportunities to provide further value** and address concerns. Approach objections with empathy and a problem-solving mindset, demonstrating your commitment to understanding and meeting your prospect's needs.

Actions to Take

1. **Practice active listening and empathy** during sales conversations, seeking to understand your prospect's perspective and concerns deeply. This approach fosters trust and allows for more meaningful engagement.

2. **Invest in ongoing learning and professional development** to stay abreast of industry trends and sales techniques. Continuously improving your skills equips you to adapt to changing market conditions and maintain a competitive edge.

3. **Cultivate a robust network of mentors and peers** within the sales industry who can offer guidance, support, and fresh perspectives. Leveraging the collective knowledge and experience of your network can help you overcome challenges and seize opportunities.

4. **Harness the power of technology and data analytics** to streamline your sales process and enhance efficiency. Utilize tools and metrics to identify trends, optimize your approach, and deliver more personalized experiences to your prospects.

5. **Regularly monitor your progress and performance metrics**, adjusting your strategy as needed to achieve your sales goals. By staying proactive and responsive, you can continually refine your approach and drive better results.

Actions Not to Take

1. **Avoid resorting to high-pressure tactics** or manipulative techniques in your sales interactions. Building trust and fostering genuine relationships should always take precedence over short-term gains.

2. **Never neglect follow-up with prospects** or fail to provide adequate support post-sale. Building lasting relationships requires ongoing communication and support to ensure customer satisfaction and loyalty.

3. **Resist the temptation to focus solely on closing the deal** without considering the long-term implications for customer satisfaction and retention. Prioritize building mutually beneficial relationships that extend beyond the initial transaction.

4. **Do not ignore feedback from prospects** or dismiss market dynamics that may require adaptation. Embrace feedback as a tool for growth and be willing to pivot your approach based on changing circumstances and customer needs.

5. **Guard against allowing fear of rejection** to undermine your confidence and performance. Embrace rejection as a natural part of the sales process and use it as an opportunity to learn and improve.

Chapter 15: Cultivating Customer Relationships and Loyalty

In the dynamic landscape of modern business, building robust customer relationships and fostering unwavering loyalty form the cornerstone of success. It's about transcending the superficiality of mere transactions to cultivate deep, meaningful connections that stand the test of time. In a world brimming with choices and fierce competition, the capacity to forge genuine bonds with customers is not just beneficial—it's essential for survival and growth. This requires a keen understanding of customer needs, an unwavering commitment to exceed their expectations, and the consistent delivery of value that aligns with their desires and preferences.

Our exploration in this chapter ventures into the art of nurturing customer relationships and loyalty, unveiling the fundamental principles that transform ordinary transactions into lasting partnerships. We will unravel strategies for engaging with customers, tailoring experiences to their unique needs, and fostering trust through unwavering transparency and reliability. The emphasis lies in fostering a customer-centric culture that places the satisfaction and well-being of customers at the forefront, thereby converting them into ardent champions of your brand.

In the journey toward building enduring customer relationships, the focus must be on understanding the nuanced dynamics of customer interactions. By personalizing the customer experience, businesses can create a sense of belonging and connection that resonates on a personal level. This not only enhances customer satisfaction but also deepens their loyalty, making them more likely to return and advocate for your brand.

Creating a culture that prioritizes customer satisfaction requires a shift in mindset, from viewing customers as transactions to seeing them as valuable partners in your business's journey. This involves listening to their feedback, anticipating their needs, and being proactive in addressing their concerns. Such a culture not only nurtures loyalty but also fosters a positive brand image that attracts new customers.

The path to long-term success and prosperity in today's competitive business environment lies in building strong, genuine relationships with customers. By focusing on understanding their needs, exceeding their expectations, and consistently delivering exceptional value, businesses can establish a loyal customer base that not only sustains but also propels their growth. This chapter serves as a guide to mastering the art of customer relationship and loyalty, essential for any business aiming to thrive in the modern marketplace.

Inspirational Quote

> *"Your most unhappy customers are your greatest source of learning."* - Bill Gates

Understanding Your Customers

Understanding your customers transcends the basic gathering of demographic data like age, gender, and geographical location. It requires a deep dive into their unique needs, aspirations, and the challenges they confront in their daily lives. This journey towards understanding demands active listening, where the aim is to fully grasp their perspective before sharing your own, ensuring that every interaction is an opportunity to learn more about what truly matters to them.

Embracing your customers' viewpoints empowers you to foresee their needs and exceed their expectations in ways they hadn't imagined. Such a forward-thinking stance is not just about delivering products or services that align with their desires but also about cultivating meaningful connections that stand the test of time. It's a commitment to viewing the world from their standpoint and letting that insight shape your business strategies, thereby not just fulfilling their current needs but also surprising them with innovations they'll love in the future.

By making empathy and understanding the cornerstone of your business approach, you transform each customer interaction into a treasure trove of insights. These insights become the blueprint for tailoring your offerings to better align with customer expectations, thereby elevating the customer experience to new heights. It's about going beyond the surface to understand the heart and soul of your customer's needs.

Adopting a customer-centric mindset is a game-changer that positions your business for unparalleled success. It's the difference between a company that simply sells and one that truly serves its customer base. By prioritizing the customer's needs and perspectives, you unlock the potential for groundbreaking innovations and create a loyal community of customers who feel seen and understood.

The essence of truly understanding your customers lies in the ability to listen deeply, empathize profoundly, and anticipate their needs with precision. This ethos not only sets the foundation for exceptional product and service development but also forges a strong, enduring bond between your business and its customers. It's a strategic approach that ensures your business not only meets the mark but sets new industry standards, creating delightful experiences that customers cherish long into the future.

Consistent Communication

At the heart of every thriving relationship lies consistent communication, a principle that holds paramount importance in business dealings with customers. Through the strategic use of personalized communication channels—be it personalized emails, direct phone calls, or vibrant social media interactions—businesses can significantly demonstrate their appreciation and support for their clientele. A proactive approach in keeping customers informed, engaged with content tailored to their preferences, and open to their feedback, underscores the commitment to value each customer's unique journey with your brand.

Effective customer communication transcends mere frequency of contact, focusing instead on the richness and relevance of each interaction. It's about forging more than just transactions; it's about creating meaningful connections that deepen the bond between a business and its customers. By inviting and thoughtfully responding to feedback, companies not only boost customer satisfaction but also cultivate loyalty, laying the groundwork for a thriving community centered around their brand.

Building such a community hinges on recognizing the importance of two-way communication. Regular updates, relevant content sharing, and welcoming feedback facilitate a dialogue where both parties feel heard and valued. This dynamic communication fosters a relationship where customers are more than just passive recipients; they are active participants in a shared journey with your brand.

The ultimate aim is to foster a vibrant ecosystem around your brand, one where customers do not merely transact but genuinely feel a part of the brand's narrative. Achieving this requires a commitment to not only listen but to act on customer feedback, thereby enhancing their experience and loyalty. Such an approach not only enriches customer relationships but also sets a foundation for sustained business growth.

The essence of impactful customer communication lies in its ability to create a sense of belonging and appreciation among customers. By prioritizing meaningful engagement and nurturing a two-way dialogue, businesses can transform customer interactions into lasting relationships. The path to a loyal customer base and a robust brand community is paved with consistent, relevant, and engaging communication that resonates with the hearts and minds of those you serve.

Delivering Exceptional Service

In the world of business, delivering exceptional service is not just an action but a testament to the value placed on customer relationships. These distinguished organizations go beyond the norm in every interaction, aiming not just to meet but to soar past customer expectations. They empower their teams to quickly and effectively solve problems, turning potential dissatisfaction into golden opportunities for engagement and satisfaction.

This proactive stance on customer service does more than resolve issues; it transforms challenges into opportunities to showcase the company's unwavering commitment to excellence. It's a strategic approach that speaks volumes, proving that every customer matters and that the business is always ready to go the extra mile. Through this, they build a bridge of trust and reliability that customers feel and appreciate deeply.

The magic of consistently exceeding customer expectations lies in the creation of a solid foundation for enduring loyalty. Such dedication not only cultivates a positive brand reputation but also encourages customers to return, time and again. The ripple effect of this high level of service is powerful, turning satisfied customers into vocal advocates for the brand.

When customers become champions of the brand, they share their exceptional experiences far and wide, attracting more people to the business. This cycle of positive feedback and repeat business is the cornerstone of sustained success and growth. It demonstrates that at the heart of every thriving business is a commitment to not just satisfying customers but delighting them.

The pursuit of exceptional service is a journey that redefines success in business. It's about making every interaction a reflection of the company's dedication to excellence, fostering long-term relationships that are built on trust, loyalty, and mutual respect. This commitment not only elevates customer satisfaction but also propels the business toward new heights of achievement and growth.

Building Trust and Credibility

Trust forms the cornerstone of every successful relationship, be it in our personal lives or in the professional sphere. To cultivate such trust, one must embody integrity, embrace transparency, and exhibit unwavering reliability in every action and decision. By fostering an environment where honesty prevails, and where mistakes are openly acknowledged and rectified promptly, we lay the groundwork for trust to flourish, highlighting its importance in strengthening connections.

Integrity is not just a moral compass but a beacon that guides all our interactions. It demands a commitment to truthfulness, ensuring that our actions consistently reflect our words. This alignment between what we say and do is pivotal, as it cements our reputation as individuals and professionals who can be relied upon, thereby nurturing trust in every relationship we build.

Transparency is the lens through which the authenticity of our intentions is viewed. By being open in our communications and actions, we invite others to see the sincerity of our endeavors. This openness not only builds trust but also encourages a culture of mutual respect and understanding, which are indispensable for any thriving relationship.

Reliability is the promise of consistency, a vow that we are dependable in all circumstances. When our actions mirror our commitments, we become a pillar of support for those counting on us. This reliability fosters a sense of security and confidence among peers, customers, and partners, serving as the bedrock upon which trust is built and maintained.

The essence of building and sustaining trust lies in our ability to remain true to our words, transparent in our intentions, and steadfast in our reliability. These principles are the foundation upon which lasting relationships are built, both personally and professionally. By adhering to these values, we not only enhance our credibility but also create a legacy of trustworthiness that transcends the boundaries of time and circumstance.

Going the Extra Mile

Standing out is not just an advantage but a necessity for enduring success. Elevating your customer service to go above and beyond in preemptively meeting the needs of your clientele distinguishes your brand in a profound and unforgettable manner. When you unveil solutions before your customers even recognize the need, you exhibit not just exceptional service but a visionary approach to problem-solving.

This forward-thinking strategy does more than address immediate concerns; it lays down a bedrock of trust and dependability, cornerstones for fostering lasting customer loyalty. Such a commitment to proactive problem-solving shows your customers they are valued partners, not merely transactions. This cultivation of trust ensures that customers feel secure and appreciated, encouraging their continued patronage and advocacy for your brand.

Personalizing your offerings to align with the unique preferences of each customer underscores a deep-seated respect and appreciation for their individuality. This approach signals a shift from mere transactions to meaningful relationships, showcasing your dedication to their complete satisfaction. By implementing thoughtful gestures, whether through a personalized note or an unexpected gift, you elevate the customer experience to new heights.

These tokens of appreciation do more than delight; they forge an emotional connection, transforming customers into passionate advocates for your brand. Such personalized experiences foster a sense of belonging, making each customer feel like an integral part of a larger community. This emotional investment is invaluable, as it not only secures a loyal customer base but also inspires word-of-mouth promotion, further expanding your reach.

Distinguishing your brand in today's competitive landscape requires a blend of foresight, personalization, and genuine appreciation for your customers. By proactively addressing needs, personalizing experiences, and showing heartfelt appreciation, you not only set your brand apart but also build a loyal community of customers. These strategies not only ensure your immediate success but pave the way for sustained growth and leadership in your market.

Conclusion

Cultivating customer relationships goes beyond the traditional business strategy, becoming a profound commitment to empathy, integrity, and genuine concern for customer well-being. This philosophy requires an in-depth understanding of customer needs and preferences, alongside consistent communication and exceptional service. By building a foundation of trust, businesses can create meaningful and lasting connections with their customers, enhancing loyalty and fostering a sense of community.

The heart of strengthening customer connections is the realization that it's about more than transactions; it's about crafting transformative relationships that offer mutual benefits. By going the extra mile, businesses demonstrate a dedication to surpassing customer expectations, thereby transforming the customer experience into something extraordinary. This commitment not only strengthens bonds but also cultivates a resilient relationship that supports mutual growth and success.

This approach to customer relationships is not just beneficial; it's essential in today's competitive marketplace. By prioritizing customer needs and delivering unparalleled service, businesses can distinguish themselves, creating a unique value proposition. This strategy not only attracts new customers but also retains existing ones, building a loyal customer base that is the cornerstone of long-term success.

In adopting this customer-centric philosophy, businesses embark on a journey of continuous improvement. They become more attentive to feedback, more adaptable to change, and more innovative in their solutions. This dynamic approach ensures that the business remains relevant and responsive to customer needs, fostering a culture of excellence and innovation.

The cultivation of deep customer relationships is a testament to a business's commitment to excellence and integrity. It's a strategy that not only drives business success but also contributes to a better, more connected world. By valuing and nurturing these relationships, businesses can achieve more than just financial success; they can make a lasting impact on the lives of their customers and the communities they serve.

CASE STUDIES: Cultivating Customer Relationships and Loyalty

Case Study 1: A Grocery Chain's Personalized Shopping Experience

Background:

A regional grocery chain recognized the importance of enhancing customer loyalty in a highly competitive market. The chain aimed to cultivate deeper relationships with its customers by leveraging data analytics and personalization.

Challenge:

The grocery chain faced the challenge of differentiating itself from competitors, including big-box retailers and online grocery services. They needed to find a way to make shopping more personal and rewarding for their customers to encourage repeat business.

Solution:

The grocery chain implemented a data-driven loyalty program that used customers' purchase histories to offer personalized discounts, recommendations, and rewards. They developed a mobile app that allowed customers to access these personalized offers, manage shopping lists, and receive notifications about sales on previously purchased items. The app also included a feature for customers to scan items as they shopped, streamlining the checkout process.

Results:

The personalized shopping experience led to a significant increase in customer engagement. The grocery chain saw a 20% increase in app downloads within the first six months and a 15% increase in average customer spend among loyalty program members. The personalized offers encouraged customers to try new products and increased the frequency of visits. Customer feedback highlighted appreciation for the tailored discounts and the convenience of the mobile app features.

By investing in personalized customer experiences and leveraging technology to meet customer needs, the grocery chain strengthened its customer relationships and loyalty. This approach not only differentiated the chain from its competitors but also demonstrated the power of personalization in building lasting customer relationships.

Case Study 2: An Online Retailer's Community Engagement Strategy

Background:

An online retailer specializing in outdoor equipment aimed to increase customer loyalty by building a community around the outdoor lifestyle. The retailer recognized that its customers were not just buying products but were also looking for ways to connect with others who shared their interests.

Challenge:

The retailer needed to enhance its value proposition beyond just selling products. The goal was to create a sense of belonging among customers, encouraging them to become not just repeat buyers but also active members of a community.

Solution:

The retailer launched an online platform that included forums, blogs, and social media groups where customers could share experiences, offer advice, and discuss outdoor activities. They also organized virtual and in-person events, such as workshops on outdoor skills and sponsored hikes, to bring the community together. The retailer integrated this community aspect into its loyalty program, offering points for participation that could be redeemed for discounts on future purchases.

Results:

The community engagement strategy led to a marked increase in customer loyalty and retention. The retailer observed a 30% increase in customer engagement on its platform and a 25% increase in repeat purchases within the first year. The community forums and events facilitated deeper connections among customers, leading to organic brand advocacy and increased word-of-mouth referrals.

By creating a community around its brand and products, the online retailer was able to cultivate stronger customer relationships and loyalty. This case demonstrates the effectiveness of building a community as a means to engage customers beyond transactions, fostering loyalty through shared experiences and interests.

Examples

1. **Zappos:** Zappos, an online shoe and clothing retailer, gained prominence for its exceptional customer service and wide selection of products. With a focus on creating a seamless shopping experience, Zappos offers a diverse range of brands and styles to cater to various tastes and preferences, ensuring customers find exactly what they're looking for with ease.

2. **Amazon:** Amazon, a global e-commerce giant, has revolutionized the way people shop online by offering an extensive range of products, competitive pricing, and fast delivery options through its Prime membership program. Beyond retail, Amazon has diversified into various sectors such as cloud computing, entertainment streaming, and smart home technology, cementing its position as a leading innovator in the digital age.

3. **Nordstrom:** Nordstrom, a luxury department store chain, is renowned for its upscale fashion offerings, impeccable customer service, and elegant shopping environments. With a focus on curating high-quality merchandise and providing personalized styling advice, Nordstrom caters to discerning shoppers seeking premium brands and a luxurious shopping experience.

4. **Southwest Airlines:** Southwest Airlines, a major low-cost carrier, has earned a reputation for its affordable fares, friendly service, and no-frills approach to air travel. By prioritizing efficiency and simplicity, Southwest has become a favorite among budget-conscious travelers, offering convenient routes and flexible booking options to destinations across the United States and beyond.

5. **Disney:** Disney, a multinational entertainment conglomerate, is synonymous with magic, storytelling, and beloved characters that have captivated audiences for generations. From its iconic theme parks and blockbuster films to its expansive media empire, Disney continues to enchant audiences worldwide with its timeless tales and innovative entertainment experiences.

Top Five Takeaways

1. **Understand your customers' needs and preferences:** Take the time to conduct thorough market research and gather insights into what your customers truly desire. Utilize techniques such as surveys, interviews, and data analysis to gain a comprehensive understanding of their preferences, enabling you to tailor your products or services accordingly.

2. **Communicate consistently and transparently:** Establish clear channels of communication with your customers and ensure that you provide regular updates and information about your products, services, and any relevant changes. Transparency builds trust and fosters loyalty among your customer base, ultimately leading to stronger relationships and increased satisfaction.

3. **Deliver exceptional service at every touchpoint:** From the moment a customer interacts with your brand to post-purchase support, strive to exceed expectations at every stage of their journey. Train your staff to provide attentive, knowledgeable assistance and streamline processes to minimize friction, leaving a lasting positive impression on your customers.

4. **Build trust through honesty and reliability:** Uphold integrity in all your interactions with customers by delivering on promises and admitting mistakes when they occur. Consistently providing reliable products and services builds credibility and fosters a sense of trust, which is essential for long-term customer loyalty and advocacy.

5. **Go the extra mile to surprise and delight your customers:** Look for opportunities to exceed customer expectations by offering unexpected perks, personalized recommendations, or special promotions. By consistently delivering delightful experiences, you can create memorable moments that differentiate your brand and cultivate strong emotional connections with your customers.

Actions to Take

1. **Invest in customer relationship management (CRM) software:** Implementing a robust CRM system enables you to centralize customer data, track interactions, and personalize communication effectively. By utilizing CRM tools, you can streamline processes, enhance customer engagement, and ultimately drive business growth through improved relationship management.

2. **Train your team in effective communication and customer service skills:** Provide ongoing training and development opportunities to empower your staff with the necessary skills and knowledge to deliver exceptional customer service. Investing in your team's professional development not only improves customer satisfaction but also boosts employee morale and retention.

3. **Solicit feedback regularly and act upon it:** Establish mechanisms for collecting feedback from customers, such as surveys, reviews, or suggestion boxes, and demonstrate a commitment to addressing their concerns and suggestions promptly. By actively seeking and responding to feedback, you show customers

that their opinions are valued, fostering a culture of continuous improvement and customer-centricity.

4. **Personalize your offerings based on individual preferences:** Leverage customer data and insights to tailor your products or services to the specific needs and preferences of individual customers. Whether through personalized recommendations, targeted marketing campaigns, or customized experiences, personalization demonstrates attentiveness and enhances the overall customer experience, driving loyalty and retention.

5. **Express genuine appreciation for your customers' loyalty:** Show gratitude to your customers for their continued support and patronage through personalized thank-you notes, exclusive offers, or loyalty rewards programs. By acknowledging and rewarding loyalty, you reinforce positive behavior and strengthen the emotional bond between your brand and its customers.

Actions Not to Take

1. **Neglecting to listen to customer feedback:** Avoid dismissing or ignoring customer feedback, as it provides valuable insights into areas for improvement and opportunities for innovation. Failing to listen to your customers can lead to dissatisfaction, disengagement, and ultimately, loss of business.

2. **Overpromising and underdelivering:** Resist the temptation to make exaggerated claims or promises that your products or services cannot fulfill. Managing customer expectations is essential for building trust and credibility, so it's important to be honest and realistic about what you can deliver.

3. **Being inconsistent in your communication and service:** Strive for consistency in your communication and service delivery across all touchpoints to maintain a cohesive and reliable brand experience. Inconsistencies can erode trust and confuse customers, leading to dissatisfaction and churn.

4. **Ignoring the importance of building trust and credibility:** Recognize that trust is the foundation of any successful customer relationship and prioritize actions that build credibility and reliability. Ignoring this fundamental aspect can damage your reputation and undermine customer loyalty over time.

5. **Taking your customers for granted:** Avoid complacency and always treat your customers with respect, appreciation, and attentiveness. Taking customers for granted can lead to apathy, resentment, and ultimately, loss of business as customers seek out brands that value and prioritize their needs.

Part Four: Finance and Operations

Finance and operations are the vital pillars that uphold an organization, working in harmony to fuel growth and efficiency. Finance provides the necessary capital for operations, which in turn generate revenue, sustaining the financial health of the company. Their alignment enhances profitability and ensures strategic plans are effectively executed, leading to sustainable growth.

Chapter 16: Managing Finances and Budgets

Taking control of your finances is not just about working through numbers; it's about taking the reins of your financial future. No matter your current position on the financial spectrum, gaining a deep understanding of budgeting and financial management can unlock doors to greater stability, independence, and happiness. With commitment to applying practical financial strategies and nurturing a positive financial outlook, you can navigate towards a future filled with wealth and abundance.

This section is designed as a roadmap to equip you with the tools and insights necessary to achieve financial wellness and prosperity. Immersing yourself in effective financial practices and cultivating an empowering financial mindset will guide you toward a more secure and satisfying financial journey.

By embracing the principles outlined here, you're not just managing money; you're setting the stage for a life where financial worries are minimized, and opportunities for growth are maximized. Understanding and applying these concepts will illuminate the path to financial freedom, allowing you to make informed decisions that lead to a prosperous future.

Each strategy and perspective shared in this guide is aimed at fostering a holistic approach to financial management. By integrating these practices into your daily life, you'll find yourself on a path to financial empowerment, equipped to meet challenges and seize opportunities with confidence and clarity.

Embarking on this financial journey is about more than just improving your bank balance; it's about transforming your life. With dedication, a willingness to learn, and the implementation of these strategies, achieving financial prosperity is not just a possibility, but an inevitable outcome of your efforts toward personal and financial growth.

Inspirational Quote

> *"Financial freedom is available to those who learn about it and work for it."* - Robert Kiyosaki

Setting Clear Goals

Embarking on a path to financial prosperity begins with the articulation of distinct and precise financial ambitions. Crafting these goals—be it eradicating debt, accumulating funds for a future home, or securing a robust retirement fund—imbues your fiscal voyage with both direction and intent. With your targets set, delineating them into manageable, actionable steps becomes your next endeavor. Establishing a timeline for each aspiration not only aids in task prioritization but also ensures steadfast adherence to your financial blueprint.

The significance of maintaining focus on your financial targets cannot be overstated as you navigate through your economic expedition. It's imperative to continually remind yourself of the underlying motives fueling your financial dreams, as this reinforces your resolve and propels you forward. This constant reflection and dedication to your goals, coupled with the flexibility to adapt your strategy when necessary, paves the way for significant strides towards achieving financial stability and satisfaction.

In the pursuit of financial success, it's essential to break down your overarching objectives into smaller, achievable milestones. This methodical approach not only simplifies the journey but also provides frequent moments of accomplishment, boosting your confidence and commitment to the long-term vision. Celebrating these small victories keeps the journey rewarding and motivates you to persist through challenges.

Creating a financial plan is akin to drafting a roadmap for a journey to prosperity. It requires not just the identification of destinations (goals) but also plotting the course (actionable steps) with care and precision. This roadmap should be revisited and refined periodically to ensure it remains aligned with your evolving financial landscape and life goals, ensuring that every step taken is a step towards fulfillment and success.

The journey towards financial achievement is both a test of perseverance and a testament to the power of strategic planning. By setting clear goals, remaining focused, breaking down objectives into actionable steps, and adjusting your plan as necessary, you forge a path of financial enlightenment. This disciplined and intentional approach transforms the daunting into the attainable, leading you towards a future of financial independence and prosperity.

Creating a Budget

A budget stands as a beacon of financial stability, illuminating the path toward mastering your economic landscape. It begins with a diligent examination of your income and expenditures, shedding light on your fiscal habits. This deep dive into your finances unveils opportunities to optimize spending, thereby channeling resources into achieving your dreams, be it establishing a safety net, eliminating debt, or accumulating wealth for the future.

Embracing a budget requires a balance between precision and adaptability, acknowledging that life's financial demands can shift unexpectedly. This flexibility within your budgetary framework ensures you can weather financial storms without veering off course. It's about crafting a financial strategy that evolves with you, keeping you on track towards your aspirations despite the ebb and flow of economic tides.

The essence of budgeting lies in its ability to transform complex financial decisions into manageable, strategic actions. By identifying potential savings without compromising your quality of life, you empower yourself to make informed choices that propel you closer to your financial milestones. It's a process of continuous refinement, seeking efficiencies that bolster your financial foundation.

Moreover, a well-structured budget acts as a compass, guiding your financial journey with intention and purpose. It's not merely about curtailing expenses but nurturing a mindset geared towards growth and resilience. Through this lens, budgeting becomes an ongoing dialogue with your finances, fostering a relationship where each decision is a step towards financial empowerment.

The journey of budgeting is one of empowerment, self-awareness, and foresight. Regularly revisiting and fine-tuning your budget ensures it remains a faithful navigator, aligning your financial practices with your long-term visions. In this way, a budget is not just a tool but a lifelong companion on the road to financial serenity and success.

Embracing Frugality

Frugality is not about denying oneself the joys of life but about embracing the wisdom of making mindful financial choices. It's a journey of recognizing opportunities to streamline expenses without diminishing one's quality of life. Through deliberate spending, one learns to distinguish between what is truly necessary and what is merely desirable, leading to a more effective allocation of financial resources.

At the heart of frugal living lies the principle of valuing and prioritizing meaningful experiences above the accumulation of material goods. This approach not only enhances personal fulfillment but also cultivates a sense of contentment from being more connected with life's true riches. It's an invitation to discover joy and satisfaction in the abundance of the present, focusing on what genuinely enriches our lives.

Cultivating gratitude for what we already possess and finding delight in the simpler pleasures of life are fundamental to adopting a frugal mindset. Such a perspective shift prompts us to cherish the resources we have, encouraging a lifestyle of contentment with fewer material possessions. It's a transformative experience that deepens our appreciation for the everyday and the ordinary.

Embracing frugality is far more than a strategy for financial savings; it is a commitment to aligning our spending with our deepest values. This alignment brings about a sense of satisfaction that comes from living a life that is both intentional and meaningful. It's about making choices that reflect what we truly value, leading to a richer, more fulfilling existence.

The path of frugality is one of discovery, leading us to a deeper understanding of our personal desires and the value of simplicity. It's not merely a means to an end but a way of living that celebrates efficiency, mindfulness, and the joy of experiencing life to its fullest. By choosing frugality, we choose a life defined not by the quantity of our possessions but by the quality of our experiences and relationships.

Building Multiple Income Streams

Cultivating a diverse array of income streams is a vital step toward achieving financial security and opening doors to new possibilities. Exploring a mix of side projects, freelance work, or avenues for generating passive income can significantly enhance your primary earnings. Moreover, investing in yourself through ongoing education and skill development can greatly increase your earning potential. This strategy not only enriches your financial landscape but also reduces the risk of dependency on a single income source, offering a more stable and prosperous future.

Embracing the journey toward financial diversification requires aligning your income ventures with your personal passions and strengths. Adopting an entrepreneurial spirit and being open to new opportunities can lead to unexpected paths of income. Strategically diversifying your income sources enables you to leverage various opportunities while providing a safety net against the fluctuations of any one stream. This forward-thinking approach enhances your financial durability and fosters a mindset geared towards lifelong learning and success.

In today's dynamic world, the ability to adapt and expand your financial base is more important than ever. Diversifying your income not only secures your financial well-being but also encourages personal and professional growth. Through commitment to self-improvement and a keen eye for opportunities, you can substantially elevate your financial status and quality of life.

By broadening your financial horizons, you not only safeguard against the uncertainties of life but also give yourself the freedom to pursue your dreams with confidence. This empowerment comes from knowing you have created a solid financial foundation that can support your ambitions and withstand the tests of time. It's about building a life where your finances are a springboard to achieving your goals, not a barrier.

The pursuit of multiple income streams is about more than just financial gain; it's a journey towards self-reliance, resilience, and fulfillment. By weaving together different financial strands, you craft a tapestry of security that allows for exploration, creativity, and personal fulfillment. This holistic approach to income diversification is not just a financial strategy; it's a blueprint for a rich and rewarding life.

Investing Wisely

Investing represents a powerful avenue for building wealth over time, offering a beacon of financial growth and stability. It begins with a step of education - understanding the landscape of investment options such as stocks, bonds, real estate, and mutual funds. Embarking on this path with small, manageable investments allows one to gradually expand their portfolio, gaining confidence and expertise along the way.

The wisdom of diversification cannot be overstated in the investment world. It acts as a safeguard, spreading investments across various asset classes and sectors to reduce risk and harness opportunities from different market dynamics. This strategy not only minimizes potential losses but also sets the stage for a more robust and resilient investment portfolio.

Discipline is the cornerstone of successful investing. The journey through the financial markets is often marked by volatility, requiring investors to maintain a steady hand and a clear vision. Avoiding the pitfalls of emotional decision-making and staying true to a strategic investment plan are essential practices for navigating these waters successfully.

Investors are encouraged to view the fluctuations of the market as natural phases rather than deterrents. By focusing on long-term objectives and resisting the urge to react impulsively to short-term market movements, one can maintain a course that is both prudent and promising. This disciplined approach is instrumental in transforming the challenges of today into the successes of tomorrow.

The path to achieving financial goals is paved with the principles of education, diversification, and discipline. By committing to these foundational strategies, investors empower themselves to navigate the complexities of the investment landscape with confidence and clarity. This commitment not only fosters personal growth and financial acumen but also paves the way for a future of financial freedom and prosperity.

Conclusion

Embarking on the journey of financial management is not merely about numbers; it's a path towards self-discovery and empowerment. By setting clear, achievable goals, you lay down a foundation for financial success that directs every decision and action towards your aspirations. This roadmap not only guides you but also inspires discipline and focus, illuminating the path to your dreams with clarity and purpose.

Creating a budget transcends simple arithmetic; it's an exercise in mindfulness and strategic planning. This critical tool enables you to meticulously track your spending, spotlight areas ripe for improvement, and judiciously allocate resources. With every dollar accounted for, you transform your financial landscape into a meticulously curated garden, where every seed of expenditure is planted with intention, promising a harvest of financial stability and growth.

Embracing frugality is not about austerity; it's about making informed choices that align with your core values and financial goals. This philosophy encourages living within your means, prioritizing your expenditures, and adopting a mindset of thoughtful consumption. Such an approach not only safeguards your financial well-being but also enriches your life with simplicity and contentment, free from the clutches of unnecessary material burdens.

Diversifying your income streams is akin to building a resilient financial ecosystem, one that thrives on variety and adaptability. This strategy cushions you against economic fluctuations, reducing your reliance on a single income source. Moreover, wise investments allow your capital to flourish, creating avenues for passive income and fostering long-term wealth. In this way, you secure a financial buffer that shields you from life's uncertainties, ensuring peace of mind.

Integrating these financial practices into your life is a powerful act of taking charge of your financial destiny. It's about crafting a legacy of abundance and prosperity for yourself and your loved ones. With each step forward, you're not just managing money; you're building a future where financial freedom and personal fulfillment go hand in hand, offering a life replete with possibilities and joy.

CASE STUDIES: Managing Finances and Budgets

Case Study 1: Small Business Budget Management

Company: XYZ Bakery

Background:

XYZ Bakery is a small family-owned business located in a bustling neighborhood. They specialize in artisanal bread and pastries, catering to both retail customers and local restaurants. Despite a loyal customer base, the bakery has been facing financial challenges due to rising ingredient costs and increased competition from chain bakeries.

Challenge:

The bakery's owners noticed a decline in profits and realized that they needed to improve their financial management practices. They were struggling to maintain inventory levels, control expenses, and accurately forecast revenue.

Solution:

1. **Budget Creation:** The bakery's owners implemented a detailed budget that outlined expected revenues and expenses for each month. They divided expenses into categories such as ingredients, labor, utilities, and marketing.

2. **Expense Tracking:** They started diligently tracking all expenses using accounting software. This helped them identify areas where costs could be reduced, such as renegotiating supplier contracts and optimizing staffing schedules.

3. **Revenue Forecasting:** To improve revenue forecasting, the bakery started analyzing sales data from previous months and identifying trends. This allowed them to adjust production levels accordingly, minimizing waste and maximizing profits.

4. **Contingency Planning:** Recognizing the importance of being prepared for unexpected expenses, the owners set aside a portion of their profits each month as a contingency fund. This buffer helped them cover unforeseen costs without jeopardizing the business's financial stability.

Outcome:

By implementing these financial management strategies, XYZ Bakery was able to stabilize its finances and increase profitability. The owners gained better insight into their cash flow, allowing them to make more informed decisions about pricing, inventory management, and marketing efforts. As a result, the bakery regained its competitive edge and continued to thrive in the local market.

Case Study 2: Personal Finance Management

Individual: Sarah Johnson

Background:

Sarah Johnson is a recent college graduate who has just started her first job as a marketing assistant at a small firm. While excited about her new career, Sarah is also feeling overwhelmed by her financial responsibilities. She has student loans to repay, monthly rent and utilities to cover, and various other expenses such as groceries, transportation, and entertainment.

Challenge:

Sarah realizes the importance of managing her finances effectively to achieve her long-term goals, such as buying a home and saving for retirement. However, she is unsure where to start and how to prioritize her spending.

Solution:

1. **Budgeting:** Sarah begins by creating a monthly budget that outlines her income and expenses. She allocates a portion of her salary to cover essential expenses such as rent, utilities, and loan payments, while setting aside some money for savings and discretionary spending.

2. **Debt Repayment Strategy:** Sarah develops a strategy for repaying her student loans by allocating extra funds each month towards the principal balance. She also explores options for refinancing her loans to potentially lower her interest rates and reduce her overall repayment term.

3. **Emergency Fund:** Recognizing the importance of having a financial safety net, Sarah starts building an emergency fund to cover unexpected expenses such as medical bills or car repairs. She aims to save at least three to six months' worth of living expenses in a separate savings account.

4. **Long-Term Goals:** Sarah sets specific, achievable long-term financial goals, such as saving for a down payment on a home or contributing to a retirement account. She researches different investment options and seeks advice from a financial advisor to develop a personalized investment strategy.

5. **Monitoring and Adjusting:** Sarah regularly monitors her spending and savings habits to ensure that she stays on track with her financial goals. She makes adjustments to her budget as needed, reallocating funds to different categories or cutting back on discretionary expenses when necessary.

Outcome:

Through diligent budgeting and careful financial planning, Sarah is able to take control of her finances and work towards her long-term goals. She pays off her student loans ahead of schedule, builds a substantial emergency fund, and starts investing for the future. With a solid financial foundation in place, Sarah feels more confident about her financial future and is better equipped to handle any challenges that may arise.

Examples

1. **Warren Buffett,** renowned for his investment prowess and business acumen, is widely regarded as one of the most successful investors of all time. With his patient approach to value investing and long-term perspective, Buffett has amassed a substantial fortune and built Berkshire Hathaway into a conglomerate with diverse holdings spanning various industries.

2. **Dave Ramsey,** a prominent financial expert and best-selling author, is known for his straightforward advice on personal finance and debt management. Through his books, radio show, and Financial Peace University, Ramsey empowers individuals to take control of their money, get out of debt, and build wealth for the future.

3. **Suze Orman,** a respected financial advisor and television personality, is acclaimed for her practical guidance on money management and retirement planning. Through her books, television appearances, and online resources, Orman educates audiences on topics such as saving, investing, and creating a secure financial future.

4. **The FIRE Movement (Financial Independence, Retire Early)** is a lifestyle movement gaining traction among individuals seeking financial freedom and early retirement. Advocates of FIRE prioritize aggressive saving, frugal living, and strategic investing to accumulate wealth quickly and achieve financial independence at a young age.

5. **The Bill & Melinda Gates Foundation,** established by billionaire philanthropists Bill and Melinda Gates, is one of the world's largest private charitable foundations. With a mission to enhance healthcare, reduce poverty, and expand

educational opportunities globally, the foundation invests in initiatives aimed at addressing pressing societal challenges and improving human well-being.

Top Five Takeaways

1. **Set clear financial goals** by outlining specific objectives such as saving for a down payment on a house or establishing an emergency fund for unexpected expenses. Clearly defining your financial targets provides direction and motivation for your money management efforts, guiding you towards a more secure financial future.

2. **Create and stick to a budget** that reflects your income, expenses, and financial goals. By diligently tracking your spending and adhering to a budget, you can better manage your finances, avoid unnecessary debt, and work towards achieving your long-term financial aspirations.

3. **Embrace frugality and conscious spending** by prioritizing needs over wants and seeking out cost-effective alternatives without sacrificing quality of life. By adopting a mindful approach to spending, you can cultivate healthier financial habits, increase your savings potential, and achieve greater financial freedom over time.

4. **Build multiple income streams** to diversify your earnings and reduce dependency on a single source of income. Whether through part-time work, freelance gigs, or passive income streams like investments or rental properties, creating multiple revenue streams can enhance your financial stability and resilience in an ever-changing economic landscape.

5. **Invest wisely for the future** by conducting thorough research, seeking professional advice, and diversifying your investment portfolio. By carefully considering factors such as risk tolerance, time horizon, and investment goals, you can make informed decisions that align with your financial objectives and pave the way for long-term wealth accumulation and financial security.

Five Actions to Take

1. **Track your income and expenses**: It's crucial to meticulously monitor both your earnings and expenditures to gain a clear understanding of your financial situation. By consistently tracking these, you can identify areas where you may be overspending and make informed decisions to optimize your financial health.

2. **Define your financial goals**: Take the time to articulate specific, measurable, and achievable objectives for your finances, whether it's saving for a down payment on a house, funding your children's education, or planning for retirement. Clearly defining your goals provides you with direction and motivation, helping you stay focused on your financial journey.

3. **Establish a budget and stick to it**: Creating a budget that aligns with your financial goals allows you to allocate your income effectively and prioritize your spending. However, it's not enough to merely set a budget; discipline and consistency are essential in adhering to it. Regularly review and adjust your budget as needed to accommodate changes in your financial circumstances.

4. **Seek out opportunities to increase your income**: Explore various avenues for boosting your earnings, whether through side hustles, career advancement, or entrepreneurial ventures. By actively seeking out opportunities to increase your income, you can accelerate your progress towards achieving your financial goals and improve your overall financial stability.

5. **Educate yourself about investing and start investing:** Take the initiative to learn about different investment vehicles, risk management strategies, and long-term financial planning. Armed with knowledge, you can confidently navigate the world of investing and leverage it to grow your wealth over time. Start investing early, even if it's with small amounts, to benefit from the power of compounding and build a secure financial future.

Five Actions Not to Take

1. **Overspend beyond your means**: When you consistently overspend, you're essentially living beyond your financial capabilities, which can lead to mounting debt and financial stress. It's crucial to track your expenses, create a budget, and prioritize spending on essentials to avoid falling into a cycle of overspending.

2. **Ignore your financial situation**: Turning a blind eye to your financial situation can be detrimental in the long run, as it prevents you from addressing any issues or making necessary adjustments. Regularly reviewing your income, expenses, debt, and savings allows you to stay informed and make informed financial decisions that align with your goals.

3. **Rely solely on one source of income**: Depending entirely on one source of income can leave you vulnerable to financial instability if that income stream is disrupted. Diversifying your sources of income, such as through investments,

side hustles, or passive income streams, provides a safety net and enhances your financial resilience.

4. **Make impulsive investment decisions:** Making impulsive investment decisions without conducting thorough research or consulting with financial advisors can result in significant financial losses. It's essential to approach investments with a well-thought-out strategy, considering factors like risk tolerance, investment goals, and market trends to make informed decisions that align with your financial objectives.

5. **Neglect to save for emergencies and the future:** Failing to save for emergencies and the future leaves you vulnerable to unexpected expenses and prevents you from building financial security. Establishing an emergency fund and regularly contributing to retirement accounts are vital steps toward safeguarding your financial well-being and achieving long-term financial stability.

Chapter 17: Understanding Financial Statements

Understanding financial statements is akin to mastering the language of business, empowering both individuals and organizations with the insight needed to make informed decisions, overcome challenges, and achieve financial success. This expertise is essential in navigating the complex world of finance, playing a key role in driving sustainable growth and development. It equips stakeholders with the knowledge to foresee opportunities and risks, ensuring a prosperous future.

In this chapter, we embark on an enlightening journey to decode the complexities of financial statements, revealing the rich insights they hold. By dissecting the intricacies of balance sheets, income statements, and cash flow statements, we will equip you with the ability to assess financial health, discern trends, and craft strategic plans for the future. This journey will transform your understanding, turning complex data into actionable knowledge.

Delving into financial statements opens the door to a world of strategic foresight and operational insight. It's not just about numbers; it's about understanding the story behind them—where a company has been, where it's going, and how it's getting there. This narrative is critical for anyone looking to navigate the financial paths of their personal or organizational journey successfully.

As we peel back the layers of financial statements, we uncover the core of business strategy and financial planning. Each line item and figure speaks volumes about a company's operational efficiency, financial stability, and potential for growth. This deep dive enables individuals and businesses alike to align their strategies with their financial realities, fostering informed decision-making and strategic agility.

By the end of this chapter, the language of financial statements will no longer be a barrier but a bridge to greater understanding and success. Armed with this knowledge, you will be poised to make strategic decisions, identify investment opportunities, and steer towards financial prosperity with confidence. This is not just about financial literacy; it's about empowering yourself with the tools for a brighter, more secure financial future.

Inspirational Quote

"Financial literacy is the key to unlocking the doors of economic empowerment."

The Basics of Financial Statements

Financial statements are the backbone of a company's financial transparency, serving as a window into its fiscal vitality. These documents, encompassing the balance sheet, income statement, and cash flow statement, offer a detailed view of a firm's assets, liabilities, equity, revenue, expenses, profits, and cash management at specific intervals. They are vital resources for stakeholders such as investors, creditors, and management teams, providing the foundational data required to assess the organization's operational success and financial standing.

The essence of understanding these financial documents cannot be overstated for those engaged in the nuanced art of financial analysis and decision-making. Through the balance sheet, one gains a clear picture of a company's financial stability and operational prowess, while the income statement offers insights into its ability to generate profit and sustain growth. Meanwhile, the cash flow statement is a critical indicator of how well a company manages its cash - the lifeblood of its operations - highlighting its proficiency in meeting obligations and funding expansion.

Delving into the intricacies of these financial statements equips stakeholders with the knowledge necessary for robust financial planning and strategic analysis. It lays a solid foundation for stakeholders to navigate through the complexities of investment decisions, lending considerations, and overarching management strategies. This mastery is instrumental in fostering an environment of informed decision-making, where each choice is backed by a thorough understanding of financial health and potential.

In an era where financial acumen is paramount, the ability to decipher and utilize the information presented in financial statements becomes a key differentiator. It not only empowers stakeholders to gauge a company's current financial position but also to forecast its future trajectory. This understanding is critical in sculpting sound investment strategies, identifying viable growth opportunities, and steering clear of potential pitfalls.

Financial statements are not just obligatory documents; they are the lighthouses guiding the corporate vessel through the often turbulent waters of the financial seas. For investors, creditors, and managers alike, they serve as the compasses by which to chart a course towards sustained profitability and success. In cultivating a deep appreciation and comprehension of these financial reports, stakeholders arm themselves with the power to shape the future of their enterprises with confidence and precision.

Decoding the Balance Sheet

A balance sheet stands as a beacon of insight, illuminating the financial stature of a company at a specific juncture. It meticulously catalogues the company's assets, liabilities, and shareholders' equity, offering a panoramic view of its financial possessions, obligations, and the intrinsic value to its proprietors. This financial portrait is indispensable for stakeholders aiming to gauge the company's financial stability, fluidity, and endurance against fiscal pressures. Through a detailed examination of these elements, stakeholders gain clarity on the company's capacity to fulfill both its imminent and prolonged financial commitments.

Assets serve as the backbone of a company, comprising everything from liquid cash and investments to tangible property and machinery, all of which are essential for revenue generation. Contrarily, liabilities represent the company's financial dues and obligations to external entities, essentially delineating the external claims on the company's assets. Shareholders' equity emerges as the net value of the company, calculated by subtracting liabilities from assets, thereby representing the owner's stake in the company's financial resources. Mastery over the balance sheet's nuances is vital for comprehending a company's operational sustainability, debt management proficiency, and growth potential.

The balance sheet, thus, acts not just as a financial statement but as a roadmap guiding stakeholders through the complexities of the company's fiscal landscape. It reveals the equilibrium between what a company owns against what it owes, providing a clear lens through which the financial health and potential of the business can be assessed. In essence, it is a tool that enables a deep dive into the financial undercurrents that shape a company's journey towards sustainability and success.

Delving into the balance sheet, one can uncover the strategic assets at a company's disposal, ready to be leveraged for wealth creation and competitive advantage. It also exposes the liabilities that must be managed judiciously to ensure financial agility and resilience. The equity portion narrates the story of ownership and investment, encapsulating the trust and financial commitment of the shareholders towards the company's vision and mission.

The balance sheet is not merely a financial document; it is a narrative of strength, potential, and promise. It provides a foundation for strategic decisions, investment considerations, and a comprehensive understanding of the company's financial health. With this understanding, stakeholders are better equipped to make informed decisions, chart strategic directions, and contribute towards the company's enduring success and legacy.

Unveiling the Income Statement

The income statement, often referred to as the profit and loss statement, is a beacon of insight into a company's financial journey over a specific timeframe. It elegantly lays out the tapestry of revenues and expenses, leading to the net income, a clear marker of profitability. This document is pivotal in showcasing the company's prowess in generating income from its fundamental operations, painting a vivid picture of financial vigor and capability.

Furthermore, the income statement serves as a window into the company's operational dynamics, revealing critical trends in revenue generation and cost management. It offers a granular view of how effectively a company navigates its financial landscape, highlighting the levers of profitability. By dissecting this document, stakeholders can unearth valuable insights into the company's financial rhythm and the strategies driving its economic engine.

Delving deeper into the income statement allows stakeholders to grasp the essence of the company's operational efficiency. This scrutiny is vital for pinpointing opportunities for financial optimization and strategic realignment. It empowers investors, creditors, and management alike to base their decisions on a solid understanding of the company's capacity to marshal its resources toward profitable ventures.

The income statement stands as a cornerstone in evaluating a company's financial health. It acts as a guiding light for decisions aimed at bolstering financial outcomes, providing a roadmap for navigating the complex terrain of business finance. Through its detailed exposition of financial results, it aids in steering the company toward sustainable growth and profitability.

The income statement is more than just a financial report; it is a narrative of the company's economic resilience and strategic acumen. It not only chronicles the company's ability to generate income but also illuminates the path to financial enhancement and strategic excellence. As such, it is an indispensable tool for anyone looking to forge a deeper connection with the company's financial ethos and drive towards a prosperous future.

Exploring the Cash Flow Statement

The cash flow statement stands as a beacon, illuminating the path of cash through the veins of a company across a defined period. It meticulously organizes cash movements into three pivotal realms: operating, investing, and financing activities, offering a panoramic view of the company's financial dynamics. This classification not only reveals the pulse of a business's operational cash generation but also how it channels this vital resource into investments and financing strategies, thus painting a comprehensive picture of its financial health and agility.

Grasping the intricacies of the cash flow statement is akin to unlocking a treasure trove of insights into a company's financial robustness and operational prowess. It serves as a barometer for measuring the company's prowess in cash generation, an undeniable testament to its financial solidity and a harbinger of growth potential. The ability to dissect and comprehend these financial flows equips stakeholders with the foresight to assess the company's financial strategies, ensuring a solid foundation for forecasting and decision-making.

The narrative woven by the cash flow statement extends beyond mere numbers; it tells a story of liquidity and the company's adeptness at navigating short-term obligations with the liquidity at its disposal. This narrative is crucial, as it highlights the company's capacity to meet immediate financial commitments, a key indicator of its fiscal prudence and operational efficiency. Through this lens, the cash flow statement is not just a financial document but a mirror reflecting the company's ability to sustain and thrive in the ever-evolving business landscape.

For investors and creditors, the cash flow statement acts as a compass, guiding them through the financial undercurrents of the company. It lays bare the strategies employed in managing cash, offering a clear vista on the company's financial maneuverability and investment allure. This clarity is indispensable for making informed decisions, whether in extending credit, making investment choices, or steering the company's financial governance towards sustainable growth.

The cash flow statement is a cornerstone of financial analysis, a vital tool that encapsulates the essence of a company's financial vitality and strategic acumen. It fosters a culture of transparency and informed decision-making among stakeholders, empowering them to chart the course towards financial sustainability and success. In the grand tapestry of financial reporting, the cash flow statement is a pivotal chapter that narrates the resilience, ambition, and financial intelligence of a company, guiding it towards a prosperous future.

Leveraging Financial Ratios

Financial ratios stand as beacons of insight in the complex seas of financial statement analysis, illuminating paths to understanding, comparison, and benchmarking against the standards of the industry. They encompass a variety of measures, such as liquidity ratios, profitability ratios, and leverage ratios, each offering a unique perspective on a company's financial health, risk exposure, and efficiency in operations. Through these ratios, stakeholders gain a robust quantitative basis for evaluating a company's performance, thereby enhancing the decision-making process with the support of concrete financial metrics.

The power of financial ratios transcends simple number crunching, emerging as a pivotal strategic asset for investors, creditors, and company executives alike. Liquidity ratios, for instance, reveal a firm's capability to fulfill its immediate financial commitments, while profitability ratios highlight its success in generating income over and above its expenditures and other costs. Leverage ratios, meanwhile, provide insights into the balance between a company's debt and its equity, serving as indicators of financial stability and risk level. These tools collectively equip stakeholders with the means to undertake a thorough assessment of a company's financial position, paving the way for informed strategic planning and effective risk management.

In the realm of business, the strategic use of financial ratios can significantly influence the trajectory of success. By leveraging such analytical tools, stakeholders can identify trends that signal growth opportunities or potential challenges, enabling proactive responses rather than reactive measures. This strategic approach not only safeguards the company's present interests but also secures its future prosperity by ensuring that decisions are grounded in solid financial understanding.

Moreover, financial ratios facilitate the essential practice of benchmarking, allowing companies to measure their performance against industry peers. This comparison is not just about competition; it's a vital step in understanding where a company stands in the broader market landscape, identifying areas of strength and pinpointing opportunities for improvement. Such insights are invaluable for crafting strategies that drive competitive advantage and sustainable growth.

The judicious application of financial ratios is a cornerstone of sound financial analysis and strategic decision-making. It empowers stakeholders to paint a comprehensive picture of a company's financial health, blending quantitative data with strategic insight. This fusion of information and strategy not only guides a company through the complexities of the financial world but also lays the foundation for enduring success. Through the lens of financial ratios, the path to informed decision-making and strategic foresight becomes clear, showcasing the profound impact of financial intelligence on the journey towards business excellence.

Conclusion

Achieving mastery over financial statements is a cornerstone of financial literacy and empowerment. This skill set unlocks the ability to parse through the intricacies of balance sheets, income statements, and cash flow statements with ease. Such understanding grants individuals and organizations the power to make well-informed choices, illuminating the path to comprehending an entity's fiscal well-being.

Possessing this knowledge positions one to confidently and adeptly navigate the complexities of the business landscape. It transforms the daunting task of financial analysis into a manageable and insightful process. With this clarity, navigating through the economic intricacies becomes a journey of strategic discovery rather than a challenge.

Understanding financial documents is comparable to holding a compass in the vast realm of finance. It equips stakeholders with the tools necessary to evaluate the profitability, liquidity, and overall financial robustness of businesses. This deep dive into financial reporting allows for the anticipation of potential hurdles and opportunities, setting the stage for informed strategic decisions.

This level of financial insight encourages a forward-thinking mindset in financial management. It promotes the adoption of a strategic approach, enabling stakeholders to not just react to financial situations but to anticipate and shape them. Such strategic foresight is invaluable in steering organizations towards sustainable growth and stability.

The ability to interpret and analyze financial statements is more than just a technical skill; it is a critical component of financial empowerment. It fosters a culture of transparency, strategic planning, and proactive management. By embracing this knowledge, individuals and organizations can chart a course towards financial resilience and success, armed with the confidence and precision that comes from true financial understanding.

CASE STUDIES: Understanding Financial Statements

Understanding financial statements is crucial for assessing the financial health and performance of a business. Financial statements provide valuable insights into a company's operations, liquidity, revenue, and expenses. Here are two case studies that illustrate the importance of understanding financial statements.

Case Study 1: TechStart Inc.

Background:

TechStart Inc., a startup specializing in innovative software solutions, aimed to attract more investors to support its expansion. To do this, they needed to demonstrate strong financial health and growth potential through their financial statements.

Challenge:

Despite having innovative products and a growing customer base, TechStart Inc. struggled to manage its cash flow efficiently. This issue wasn't immediately apparent in the income statement due to substantial revenues. However, the cash flow statement and balance sheet told a different story.

Analysis:

- **Income Statement:** Showed increasing revenues year-over-year, suggesting a healthy growing business.

- **Balance Sheet:** Indicated a high level of short-term debt and insufficient cash reserves.

- **Cash Flow Statement:** Revealed that the company was burning through cash much faster than it was coming in, primarily due to high operational costs and significant investments in research and development.

Solution:

By analyzing these financial statements, TechStart Inc. identified the need to manage its expenses more effectively and explore options for restructuring its debt. The company decided to:

- **Cut down** unnecessary operational expenses.

- **Prioritize** projects with the highest return on investment.

- **Negotiate** better terms for its debt.

Outcome:

After implementing these strategies, TechStart Inc. improved its cash position, reduced its reliance on debt, and presented a more attractive financial profile to potential investors. The clearer picture provided by their financial statements helped in securing additional investment for expansion.

Case Study 2: HealthyEats Restaurant Chain

Background:

HealthyEats, a chain of organic restaurants, sought to expand its operations nationally. To achieve this goal, it was crucial to understand its financial performance through its financial statements.

Challenge:

Despite strong sales, profitability was not increasing at the expected rate. The management needed to delve into the financial statements to identify the underlying issues affecting profitability.

Analysis:

- **Income Statement:** Showed steadily increasing revenue but also highlighted rising cost of goods sold (COGS) and operational expenses, which were reducing net income.
- **Balance Sheet:** Revealed a significant amount of inventory being held, tying up valuable resources.
- **Cash Flow Statement:** Indicated that while operations were generating revenue, a large portion of cash was tied up in inventory and not available for expansion efforts.

Solution:

The analysis led HealthyEats to:

- **Implement better inventory management** to reduce waste and free up cash.
- **Renegotiate with suppliers** for better pricing to reduce COGS.
- **Optimize menu prices** and offerings based on profitability analysis.

Outcome:

These steps improved HealthyEats' gross margin and operational efficiency, enhancing its net income and cash flow. The improved financial health, as demonstrated in its financial statements, enabled the company to secure funding for national expansion.

These case studies highlight the importance of understanding financial statements for strategic decision-making. Through comprehensive analysis of income statements, balance sheets, and cash flow statements, businesses can identify strengths, weaknesses, and opportunities for improvement, leading to better financial health and growth prospects.

Examples

1. **Warren Buffett**, a legendary figure in investing circles and the esteemed CEO of Berkshire Hathaway, has built a reputation for his unparalleled expertise in value

investing and long-term wealth creation. With his sage advice and insightful market perspectives, Buffett's strategies have influenced countless investors worldwide, earning him the nickname "The Oracle of Omaha."

2. **Mary Barra,** as the CEO of General Motors, has distinguished herself through her strategic financial acumen and decisive leadership in steering the automotive giant through industry shifts and technological advancements. Her visionary approach to restructuring and investment has positioned General Motors for sustained growth and market leadership in an era of rapid change and innovation.

3. **Jack Welch,** the former CEO of General Electric, is renowned for his exceptional financial acumen and transformative management style, which propelled GE to unprecedented heights during his tenure. Through strategic acquisitions, operational efficiencies, and a relentless focus on shareholder value, Welch solidified his legacy as one of the most influential business leaders of his generation.

4. **Sheryl Sandberg,** the COO of Facebook, is celebrated for her exemplary financial stewardship and strategic insights that have played a pivotal role in the social media giant's growth and resilience amidst evolving market dynamics. Sandberg's leadership has been instrumental in shaping Facebook's monetization strategies and navigating complex regulatory landscapes, reinforcing her reputation as a visionary executive in the tech industry.

5. **Elon Musk,** as the visionary CEO of both Tesla and SpaceX, is renowned for his bold approach to finance and innovation, revolutionizing multiple industries with groundbreaking technologies and audacious ventures. Musk's relentless pursuit of ambitious goals, coupled with his unconventional leadership style, has propelled him to the forefront of the global stage, where he continues to inspire awe and admiration for his visionary thinking and relentless drive to push the boundaries of what's possible.

Top Five Takeaways

1. **Financial statements are vital documents** that offer critical insights into a company's financial well-being, including its profitability, liquidity, and overall performance. By examining the balance sheet, income statement, and cash flow statement, stakeholders can gauge the firm's financial position and assess its ability to meet obligations and pursue growth opportunities.

2. **Understanding the distinct purpose of each financial statement** is crucial. While the balance sheet provides a snapshot of assets, liabilities, and equity at a

specific point in time, the income statement reveals the company's revenues, expenses, and net income over a period, offering insights into its profitability. Similarly, the cash flow statement tracks cash inflows and outflows, highlighting the firm's liquidity and operational efficiency.

3. **Financial ratios serve as powerful tools** for evaluating various aspects of a company's performance and risk. By calculating ratios such as profitability ratios, liquidity ratios, and efficiency ratios, analysts can assess the firm's financial health, identify strengths and weaknesses, and make informed investment or lending decisions.

4. **Achieving financial literacy is essential** for individuals and organizations alike, empowering them to navigate complex financial landscapes with confidence. By gaining knowledge about concepts like budgeting, investing, and managing debt, individuals can make sound financial decisions, while businesses can optimize resource allocation and mitigate financial risks.

5. In today's rapidly changing business environment, **continuous learning and adaptation are paramount** for financial resilience. By staying updated on market trends, regulatory changes, and emerging technologies, businesses can proactively adjust their strategies, seize opportunities, and mitigate threats, ensuring long-term sustainability and success.

Actions to Take

1. **Educate yourself on the fundamentals of financial statements** by enrolling in courses offered by reputable institutions or delving into insightful books authored by finance experts. Online resources, such as tutorials and webinars, can also provide accessible knowledge on balance sheets, income statements, and cash flow statements, empowering you to make informed financial decisions.

2. **Hone your analytical abilities** by systematically examining financial statements from diverse companies spanning various sectors. This hands-on approach allows you to grasp the nuances of financial performance metrics, identify trends, and recognize key indicators of financial health or potential risks within different industries.

3. **Supplement your learning journey** by seeking counsel from seasoned financial professionals or mentors who can offer personalized guidance and share practical insights gleaned from their experiences. Engaging in discussions and seeking feedback can deepen your comprehension of complex financial concepts and refine your analytical techniques.

4. **Stay abreast of evolving accounting standards** and regulatory changes to ensure your interpretations of financial data remain accurate and compliant. Regularly accessing reliable sources, such as industry publications, regulatory updates, and professional forums, enables you to adapt to shifting guidelines and maintain the integrity of your financial analyses.

5. **Enhance your efficiency and precision in financial analysis** by leveraging specialized software or tools tailored for data interpretation and visualization. From spreadsheets equipped with advanced functions to dedicated financial analysis platforms, integrating technology into your workflow can streamline processes, uncover patterns, and facilitate comprehensive insights for strategic decision-making.

Actions Not to Take

1. **Making decisions based solely on intuition** or gut feelings without conducting comprehensive financial analysis can lead to significant risks and missed opportunities in managing finances. It's essential to delve into the numbers, analyze trends, and assess various scenarios to make informed decisions that align with long-term financial goals and mitigate potential pitfalls.

2. Understanding industry-specific dynamics is crucial when interpreting financial statements to grasp the nuances that could affect performance. **Ignoring these dynamics may result in misinterpretation of data** and misguided strategies, hindering the ability to adapt to industry shifts and capitalize on emerging opportunities.

3. **Economic factors and market trends play** a pivotal role in influencing financial performance, and overlooking their impact can lead to costly oversights. By closely monitoring these external forces and their implications on revenue streams, expenses, and overall profitability, businesses can better position themselves to navigate volatility and sustain growth.

4. **While short-term financial metrics provide valuable insights**, solely relying on them for investment decisions may neglect crucial long-term considerations. It's imperative to evaluate factors such as industry trends, competitive positioning, and potential for innovation to ensure investments align with broader strategic objectives and deliver sustainable returns over time.

5. **Neglecting to review and validate financial data** for accuracy and consistency before drawing conclusions can introduce errors and undermine decision-making processes. Thoroughly scrutinizing financial information ensures reliability and

integrity, enabling stakeholders to make well-informed decisions based on a solid foundation of trusted data.

Chapter 18: Securing Funding and Investment

Securing funding and investment is not just a milestone but a transformative force for aspiring entrepreneurs and businesses, propelling dreams into the realm of reality. It's the bridge that converts ambitious visions into concrete achievements, paving a clear path toward success. The journey to secure this vital support may seem formidable at first, yet it's essential to remember that every remarkable journey starts with a bold step forward and a steadfast resolve to overcome obstacles.

Entrepreneurs embarking on this venture must arm themselves with resilience, prepared to confront the intricate challenge of attracting investment. This endeavor demands not just an understanding of the financial landscape but also an unwavering belief in one's vision. It's a test of perseverance, where resilience becomes the key to unlocking opportunities and turning potential into palpable success.

This guide draws on the wisdom and experiences of those who've navigated the journey of securing funding and investment successfully. It offers a beacon of insight for those eager to learn the nuances of raising capital. These stories of triumph serve as a testament to what can be achieved with the right mix of knowledge, strategy, and determination.

By dissecting the strategies that have led to the successful procurement of funding, we aim to equip entrepreneurs with the necessary tools and knowledge to transform their business dreams into tangible outcomes. This exploration is designed to simplify the complexities of financial backing, making the elusive seem attainable for those with the vision and grit to chase their entrepreneurial ambitions.

This chapter is a clarion call to all visionaries looking to carve their niche in the business world. It underscores the importance of not just dreaming big but also embracing the journey with courage, preparation, and an unwavering spirit of persistence. With the right mindset and approach, securing funding and investment can move from being a daunting barrier to an achievable milestone on the road to entrepreneurial success.

Inspirational Quote

"Opportunities don't happen, you create them." - Chris Grosser

Understanding the Landscape

Deep knowledge is a powerful tool that significantly boosts one's chances of securing essential capital. Understanding the myriad funding avenues available, such as bootstrapping, crowdfunding, venture capital, and angel investment, is the first step towards a strategic capital-raising journey. This essential groundwork paves the way for entrepreneurs to wisely choose a funding method that perfectly matches their business model and expansion goals, empowering them to navigate the investment landscape with confidence and precision.

Furthermore, keeping an eye on the latest market trends and investor preferences can sharpen an entrepreneur's pitch, making it more relevant and compelling to potential financiers. Crafting a pitch that resonates with current market realities and investor interests requires not just knowledge of available funding sources but also an in-depth analysis of potential investors' backgrounds and previous investments. This level of preparation not only showcases an entrepreneur's dedication to their venture but also highlights their respect for investors' time and investment philosophies, setting the stage for a more meaningful engagement.

A pitch enriched with comprehensive insights into the funding ecosystem and tailored to the specific nuances of the investment community significantly increases the odds of attracting attention and capital from potential investors. It's essential for entrepreneurs to invest effort into understanding the types of funding accessible and aligning their pitches with the unique preferences and investment track records of the investors they aim to appeal to. This meticulous approach signals a deep commitment to the success of their business and a thoughtful consideration of the investor's perspective and priorities.

Ultimately, a well-prepared pitch that demonstrates a profound understanding of both the specific business needs and the broader investment landscape is much more likely to capture the interest and support of potential investors. Such a pitch not only conveys the viability and potential of the business but also the entrepreneur's strategic acumen and readiness to engage with the investment community on a level that respects their expectations and requirements.

The journey to secure funding is one that demands not just passion and vision but also a strategic and informed approach. Entrepreneurs who arm themselves with a comprehensive understanding of the funding environment, tailor their pitches to the market and investor preferences, and demonstrate a respectful and strategic engagement with potential backers are those who stand the best chance of turning their business dreams into reality. This strategic blend of knowledge, preparation, and respect forms the cornerstone of successful funding endeavors, guiding entrepreneurs through the complex yet rewarding process of securing investment.

Crafting a Compelling Narrative

A captivating narrative is essential when seeking investment, acting as a bridge to connect with potential investors' minds and hearts. By weaving a story that not only showcases your business idea but also reflects your passion and commitment, you create an engaging and memorable pitch. Highlighting the problem your business solves, your unique approach, and the impact you envision invites investors into your world, allowing them to see the value and potential of your venture.

Investors are drawn to the energy and vision behind a project as much as they are to its innovative aspects. Demonstrating your dedication and the growth potential of your business is crucial. A narrative rich in understanding of the market dynamics, the obstacles you anticipate, and your strategies for navigating these challenges speaks volumes. It's this blend of personal engagement and strategic foresight that can tip the scales in your favor.

Remember, you're not just offering an idea; you're inviting investors to be part of a journey. Your story should encapsulate not just what your business does but why it matters and how it resonates on a personal level. Crafting a narrative that balances technical insights with emotional resonance can transform a pitch into a compelling invitation to invest.

In the realm of investment, the power of a well-told story cannot be underestimated. It serves not just as a presentation of facts but as a testament to the vision and spirit of the entrepreneurs. By articulating your dedication and the transformative potential of your solution, you forge a deeper connection with potential investors.

Securing investment is about building relationships based on trust, belief, and shared vision. A narrative that skillfully combines passion with pragmatism, challenges with solutions, and visions with actionable plans is key. Such a story not only captures the imagination of investors but also instills confidence in your ability to realize your ambitious goals, significantly enhancing your chances of success.

Building Relationships

Investing in a new venture is not only about scrutinizing the numbers; it's fundamentally about trust. Entrepreneurs must invest their time in building meaningful connections with potential investors, a task that goes beyond mere financial discussions. Engaging in networking events, setting up casual meetings over coffee, and leveraging existing relationships are essential steps toward showing your genuine self. These interactions are critical in fostering a sense of authenticity and transparency, laying the groundwork for trust and confidence in your vision.

Building a relationship with investors is a nuanced art that involves more than just exchanging numbers. It's about creating a bond that goes deeper than the surface, allowing investors to truly understand your business vision and how you operate. When entrepreneurs are transparent about their business, including its strengths and areas needing improvement, they open the door for investors to become not just funders, but true partners in the entrepreneurial journey.

This approach to securing investment is holistic, prioritizing the establishment of genuine connections over mere financial transactions. By engaging investors on a personal level, entrepreneurs can provide a deeper insight into their business's mission and operational strategies. This openness not only helps in securing the necessary financial support but also ensures the investors' long-term commitment and guidance, vital for the venture's success.

The journey to attract investment, therefore, is as much about building relationships as it is about business acumen. Demonstrating authenticity and transparency with prospective investors is key to building trust and confidence in your proposal. Such a foundation of trust not only facilitates the acquisition of financial backing but also garners enduring support and advice from investors who truly believe in the potential of your venture.

The goal is to transform potential investors into committed partners who offer more than just financial support. By fostering meaningful connections and demonstrating a transparent and honest business ethos, entrepreneurs can secure not only investment but also invaluable guidance and support. This holistic approach ensures a robust foundation for the venture, underpinned by a network of investors who are genuinely invested in its success.

Demonstrating Traction

In the realm of investment, the principle that actions resonate more profoundly than words is universally acknowledged. Demonstrating progress through the development of a prototype, the results of beta testing, or early sales figures significantly bolsters the credibility of a startup. This concrete evidence acts as a powerful endorsement of the business concept's potential and viability, offering investors the confidence that the idea is not just promising but also practical and supported by real-world evidence.

Investors are constantly on the lookout for enterprises that not only propose innovative ideas but also exhibit the ability to bring them to fruition. The achievement of significant milestones, such as unveiling a functioning prototype or achieving initial market penetration, signifies that the entrepreneur has the essential skills and ingenuity to overcome the hurdles of the business landscape. Such demonstrations of progress are vital in fostering trust with prospective investors by mitigating perceived risks and highlighting the entrepreneur's dedication to transforming their vision into a tangible reality.

Thus, early successes are crucial in attracting investment, as they serve to illustrate the concept's appeal to the market and the team's capacity for effective execution. These achievements provide a solid foundation for building a compelling narrative around the startup, one that is rooted in evidence and results rather than mere projections and promises. By showcasing these early wins, entrepreneurs can effectively communicate their commitment to their business and its success, making a compelling case for investment.

This approach not only helps in securing the necessary funding but also establishes a strong rapport with investors, paving the way for future collaborations and support. It underscores the importance of tangible results in the early stages of a startup's journey, positioning it as a credible and promising venture in the eyes of potential backers. Ultimately, the ability to demonstrate early traction through tangible outcomes is a testament to the entrepreneur's vision, execution skills, and the potential for significant impact in their chosen market.

In the competitive landscape of startups, the mantra of 'show, don't tell' becomes a guiding principle for entrepreneurs seeking to captivate the interest and confidence of investors. By prioritizing the achievement of measurable milestones and the presentation of concrete evidence of progress, startups can distinguish themselves in a crowded marketplace. This strategy not only attracts investment but also lays the groundwork for sustained growth and success, affirming the critical role of early achievements in the entrepreneurial journey.

Embracing Resilience

Securing funding for your venture is a journey marked by its challenges and complexities. Yet, it is the resilience and unwavering spirit that transform these obstacles into stepping stones towards success. Embracing a positive mindset and learning from each setback paves the way for overcoming difficulties with grace and determination.

Adversity and rejection, often encountered along this path, are not just obstacles but invaluable teachers. Each "no" is a lesson that sharpens your strategy and refines your approach, making you more adept at navigating the journey. It's crucial to view these rejections as opportunities for growth, pushing you closer to your ultimate goal.

The process of securing funding is a testament to the power of perseverance and positive thinking. Every setback is a chance to reassess and come back stronger, armed with new insights and strategies. This journey is not just about finding financial support but also about personal and professional growth.

Remember, each rejection carries with it the seeds of opportunity and improvement. By embracing each "no" as a step closer to a "yes," you cultivate a mindset geared towards success. It's this perspective that will guide you through the complexities of securing funding, turning potential discouragements into catalysts for advancement.

Securing funding is more than a mission—it's a journey of resilience, learning, and relentless pursuit of your goals. Keeping your eyes on the prize with a positive outlook and a steadfast determination is key to navigating this path. Let every challenge inspire you to push forward, refine your approach, and inch closer to achieving your vision.

Conclusion

Securing funding and investment extends far beyond the mere acquisition of financial resources; it fundamentally involves garnering belief and confidence from potential investors. This belief encompasses faith in your vision for the future, confidence in your capacity to realize that vision, and recognition of the significant value your endeavor contributes to the world. The journey to successfully obtaining investment requires a comprehensive understanding of the investment landscape, coupled with the ability to articulate a compelling narrative about your business. It is essential to cultivate strong relationships with potential investors, showcase tangible progress and traction in your business activities, and maintain a resilient mindset in the face of challenges.

In navigating the path to secure investment, entrepreneurs must engage in strategic planning and execution. Crafting a compelling narrative that clearly communicates the uniqueness and potential of your business idea is critical. This involves not just presenting facts and figures, but also telling a story that connects with investors on an emotional level, demonstrating the impact your business will have. Building a solid foundation of relationships within the investment community, demonstrating the progress and potential for growth of your business, and showing an unwavering commitment to overcoming obstacles are all pivotal steps. By embodying resilience and adaptability, entrepreneurs can significantly increase their chances of securing the necessary funding and support to propel their ventures forward.

CASE STUDIES: Securing Funding and Investment

Case Study 1: Tech Startup Secures Series A Funding

Background:

A promising tech startup specializing in artificial intelligence for healthcare applications struggled to move beyond initial seed funding. Despite a strong product concept and a small but dedicated user base, the startup needed significant investment to further develop its technology and expand its market presence.

Challenge:

The primary challenge was convincing investors of the scalability and potential profitability of the product in a competitive market. Additionally, the startup had to demonstrate a clear path to market expansion and a sustainable business model.

Strategy:

The startup's founders decided to focus on a few key strategies to attract Series A funding:

1. **Proof of Concept:** They enhanced their product to provide tangible results and demonstrate its effectiveness in real-world healthcare settings.

2. **Market Research:** Conducting in-depth market research, they identified a niche market within healthcare where their technology could not only succeed but dominate.

3. **Financial Modeling:** They developed a detailed financial model showing potential revenue, growth projections, and a path to profitability within five years.

4. **Networking:** Leveraging industry contacts, the founders pitched their startup at various tech and healthcare conferences, gaining visibility among potential investors.

5. **Pitch Development:** They refined their pitch to highlight the startup's unique value proposition, technology's impact on healthcare, and the strategic plan for growth and profitability.

Outcome:

The startup successfully secured Series A funding from a consortium of investors impressed by the product's potential impact on healthcare and the detailed plan for growth. The investment allowed the startup to expand its team, further develop its technology, and begin aggressive market expansion. Within two years, the startup had significantly increased its user base and was on track for a profitable future.

Case Study 2: Local Bakery Expands Through Crowdfunding

Background: A local bakery known for its organic and gluten-free baked goods sought to expand its operations and open a second location. Despite having a loyal customer base and solid sales figures, traditional bank financing was difficult to obtain due to the small size of the business and the perceived risk of expansion.

Challenge:

The bakery needed to raise capital to finance the opening of a new location, including leasehold improvements, equipment purchases, and initial operating costs. The challenge was to secure funding without incurring high-interest rates or giving up equity.

Strategy:

The bakery decided to pursue a crowdfunding campaign, appealing directly to its customer base and community for support. Key strategies included:

1. **Community Engagement:** They launched a marketing campaign highlighting the bakery's community involvement and the benefits the new location would bring to another part of town.

2. **Rewards-Based** Crowdfunding: Instead of offering equity, the bakery offered rewards for different levels of investment, including free baked goods, baking classes, and private events.

3. **Social Media Campaign:** Utilizing social media platforms, the bakery shared their expansion plans, goals, and progress of the crowdfunding campaign, encouraging shares and engagement.

4. **Transparency:** They were open about the financial needs of the expansion, how funds would be used, and the projected benefits for the bakery and the community.

Outcome:

The crowdfunding campaign was a success, surpassing its funding goal within a few weeks. The community's support not only provided the necessary capital but also increased the bakery's visibility and customer base. The second location opened to great fanfare and has been thriving, contributing significantly to the bakery's overall growth and success.

These case studies illustrate the diverse approaches businesses can take to secure funding and investment, highlighting the importance of a clear strategy, effective communication, and engagement with potential investors or the community.

Examples

1. **Elon Musk,** the visionary entrepreneur behind SpaceX, has revolutionized the aerospace industry with his ambitious goals of colonizing Mars and making space travel more accessible to humanity. Through SpaceX, Musk has successfully developed reusable rocket technology, significantly reducing the cost of space exploration while pushing the boundaries of innovation in space technology.

2. **Sara Blakely,** the founder of Spanx, disrupted the fashion industry by introducing innovative shapewear solutions that empower women and promote body positivity. Blakely's journey from self-made entrepreneur to billionaire businesswoman serves as an inspiration to aspiring female leaders worldwide, demonstrating the power of perseverance and creative problem-solving in achieving entrepreneurial success.

3. **Mark Zuckerberg,** the co-founder and CEO of Facebook, has transformed the way people connect and communicate globally through his social media platform. With a relentless focus on user experience and technological innovation, Zuckerberg has built Facebook into a multifaceted digital ecosystem, shaping the modern landscape of social networking and online communication.

4. **Jeff Bezos,** the founder of Amazon, has redefined retail and e-commerce with his relentless pursuit of customer-centric innovation and operational excellence. Under Bezos's leadership, Amazon has evolved from an online bookstore into the world's largest online marketplace, offering an extensive range of products and services while pioneering advancements in logistics and cloud computing.

5. **Brian Chesky,** Joe Gebbia, and Nathan Blecharczyk, the co-founders of Airbnb, have transformed the hospitality industry by creating a platform that enables individuals to rent out their properties to travelers worldwide. Through Airbnb, Chesky, Gebbia, and Blecharczyk have democratized travel, fostering a sense of community and cultural exchange while providing economic opportunities for hosts around the globe.

Top Five Takeaways

1. **Knowledge is paramount** when seeking funding and investment opportunities. Understanding market trends, financial strategies, and risk management techniques empowers entrepreneurs to make informed decisions that attract investors.

2. **Crafting a compelling narrative** is essential to captivate investors and stakeholders. By articulating your vision, highlighting your values, and illustrating your dedication, you create a storyline that resonates with your audience and garners support for your venture.

3. **Building meaningful relationships** with potential investors goes beyond mere transactions. It involves fostering trust, cultivating mutual respect, and demonstrating genuine interest in their goals, which lays the foundation for long-term partnerships and collaborative success.

4. **Demonstrating early** traction not only validates your business idea but also enhances your credibility in the eyes of investors. Whether it's securing initial customers, generating revenue, or achieving milestones ahead of schedule, tangible progress showcases your ability to execute and increases investor confidence in your venture's potential.

5. **Embracing resilience is crucial** for entrepreneurs navigating the unpredictable journey of building a business. By maintaining a positive mindset, learning from failures, and adapting to challenges, you demonstrate your ability to overcome obstacles and emerge stronger, which instills confidence in investors about your ability to navigate adversity and achieve success.

Five Actions to Take

1. **Research and understand different funding options:** Take the time to delve into various funding avenues available for your business, from traditional loans to venture capital funding and crowdfunding platforms. By understanding the nuances of each option, you can make informed decisions that align with your business goals and financial needs.

2. **Develop a compelling business narrative:** Craft a captivating story that communicates your vision, mission, and the value proposition of your business to potential investors. By weaving together your unique selling points, market insights, and future projections, you can paint a vivid picture that resonates with investors and inspires confidence in your venture.

3. **Network and build relationships with potential investors:** Cultivate meaningful connections within the investor community by attending networking events, joining industry associations, and leveraging online platforms. Building genuine relationships based on trust and mutual respect can open doors to valuable investment opportunities and strategic partnerships for your business.

4. **Showcase early traction and successes:** Highlight key milestones, customer testimonials, and revenue growth to demonstrate the viability and potential of your business. By showcasing tangible results and success stories, you can instill confidence in investors and position your venture as a promising investment opportunity worthy of their consideration.

5. **Learn from failures and persist despite setbacks:** Embrace failures as learning opportunities and use them to iterate and improve your business strategy. By adopting a resilient mindset and persevering through challenges, you can demonstrate your ability to adapt, innovate, and ultimately achieve long-term success in the face of adversity.

Five Actions Not to Take

1. **Thorough Preparation for Pitches:** Before presenting your ideas to investors, take ample time to research, refine, and rehearse your pitch. Crafting a compelling narrative and anticipating potential questions demonstrates your dedication and increases your chances of success.

2. **Balanced Approach with Investors:** While it's crucial to showcase enthusiasm for your venture, remember to strike a balance and avoid coming across as overly aggressive or pushy. Building rapport and fostering genuine connections with investors can lead to more fruitful partnerships in the long run.

3. **Constructive Use of Feedback:** Embrace feedback and criticism from investors and stakeholders as valuable insights for improvement. Rather than dismissing it, leverage constructive criticism to refine your business strategy and strengthen your pitch for future opportunities.

4. **Realistic Projections:** While optimism is essential for entrepreneurial endeavors, temper it with realism when presenting financial projections. Providing conservative estimates and acknowledging potential challenges demonstrates prudence and credibility to potential investors.

5. **Integrity in Fundraising:** Uphold your values and integrity throughout the fundraising process, even when facing pressure or temptation. Maintaining

transparency and ethical conduct not only builds trust with investors but also lays a solid foundation for the long-term success and sustainability of your venture.

Chapter 19: Optimizing Supply Chain and Logistics

Efficiencey is the cornerstone of success, setting the stage for a journey filled with challenges that inspire innovative thinking. This arena is not just about improving processes and cutting costs but about embracing a comprehensive strategy that integrates innovation, encourages teamwork, and strengthens resilience. Such an approach paves the way for achieving heights of success previously thought unattainable. By embracing this mindset, companies can turn challenges into opportunities for breakthroughs and transform setbacks into lessons that spur growth.

As we traverse this intricate landscape, it's vital to view each obstacle not as a barrier but as a stepping stone to greater excellence and creativity. This outlook prompts us to tackle problems head-on, using inventive thinking and precise strategy to uncover solutions. Adopting this mindset allows organizations to do more than just endure; it enables them to flourish, converting potential risks into chances for growth and progress.

This approach lays the foundation for a future where the supply chain and logistics sectors are not only more efficient and resilient but also perfectly attuned to the ever-changing demands of the global marketplace. It's a vision where collaborative innovation leads the way, transforming the way we think about challenges and opportunities alike. In this evolving environment, resilience becomes our most valuable asset, guiding us through uncertainty and leading us toward a brighter, more adaptable future.

In embracing these principles, businesses position themselves at the forefront of their industries, ready to navigate the complexities of tomorrow with confidence and agility. It is through this lens that we can see each challenge as an invitation to innovate and each obstacle as a chance to redefine our limits. The path forward is marked by a commitment to excellence, a dedication to collaboration, and a relentless pursuit of innovation.

Our greatest advancements lie not in the avoidance of challenges, but in our response to them. By fostering an environment that values creativity, strategic planning, and resilience, we unlock the full potential of our organizations. This journey is not just about reaching new milestones in efficiency and productivity; it's about setting new standards for what is possible in the world of supply chain and logistics, inspiring a future where challenges are the catalysts for innovation and growth.

Inspirational Quote

> *"Success in supply chain and logistics isn't just about moving goods from point A to point B; it's about transforming challenges into triumphs and turning dreams into reality."*

Embracing Innovation

In the dynamic world of supply chain and logistics, innovation acts as the driving force behind transformative progress. It is through the embrace of novel technologies and methods, such as the deployment of automated warehouses, that the sector experiences a leap in efficiency, accuracy, and speed in managing inventories. This revolution in operational procedures not only sets a new bar for excellence but also redefines competitiveness, paving the way for a future where innovation is the benchmark.

The integration of cutting-edge solutions like blockchain for tracking systems has ushered in an era of unmatched transparency and security in the movement of goods worldwide. Such advancements not only streamline operations but also build a foundation of trust and reliability across the global supply chain. The willingness to adopt these innovations opens doors to limitless opportunities, empowering organizations to lead in an ever-evolving marketplace with confidence and integrity.

In the quest for innovation, the supply chain and logistics sector confronts and overcomes modern challenges, including the imperative for sustainability and the reduction of carbon emissions. The application of artificial intelligence and machine learning for route optimization and waste reduction exemplifies how technology can foster environmentally friendly practices. This not only contributes to the well-being of our planet but also highlights the role of innovation in creating a more sustainable future.

The adoption of Internet of Things (IoT) technology further exemplifies how real-time monitoring and asset management can enhance operational decision-making and efficiency. Such technological advancements enable a seamless, more responsive supply chain ecosystem, ensuring that companies remain at the forefront of industry developments. As a result, organizations that prioritize innovation are not just participants but leaders in shaping the sustainable, efficient future of logistics and supply chain management.

The journey towards innovation in supply chain and logistics is about more than just adopting new technologies; it's about fostering a culture of continuous improvement and strategic foresight. Those who commit to this path of innovation will not only navigate the challenges of today but also shape the solutions of tomorrow. In doing so, they will define the future of the industry, leading with initiatives that are smart, sustainable, and ahead of their time, setting a standard for others to follow.

Cultivating Collaboration

In the ever-evolving world of supply chain and logistics, the pursuit of efficiency is not just a goal but a necessity, where each challenge beckons a door to innovative solutions. This arena offers a unique opportunity for growth, pushing beyond the boundaries of mere cost-cutting and process improvement. It invites a comprehensive strategy that embraces new ideas, encourages teamwork, and strengthens adaptability, setting the stage for achieving unparalleled success. With this approach, companies can turn every hurdle into a catalyst for innovation and every setback into a step forward.

Collaboration stands out as a vital key to elevating operations within the supply chain and logistics sector. By fostering strong connections with suppliers, distributors, and other essential partners, businesses create a unified network. This network becomes a cornerstone for enhancing efficiency and minimizing vulnerabilities, transforming the supply chain into a more agile and responsive entity. Such partnerships not only refine processes but also enable quick adjustments to shifts in market demands and consumer needs.

By forging these powerful alliances, a seamless exchange of information and resources is established, improving coordination and decision-making across the board. Companies benefit from the collective wisdom and capabilities of their network, optimizing every link of the supply chain. This collaborative spirit significantly reduces the risks tied to disruptions and paves the way for a more robust operation. As a result, a cohesive and well-coordinated supply network is essential for staying ahead in the competitive global marketplace and securing sustained success.

Adopting a holistic mindset towards supply chain and logistics management transforms traditional challenges into opportunities for growth and innovation. It's about seeing the bigger picture and working together to create a more efficient, resilient, and adaptable operation. This vision not only propels businesses forward but also redefines what's possible, pushing the boundaries of success in the supply chain and logistics domain.

The dynamic nature of supply chain and logistics demands an approach that is innovative, collaborative, and resilient. By embracing these principles, businesses can navigate the complexities of the modern market with agility and confidence. This not only ensures operational excellence but also fosters a culture of continuous improvement and strategic innovation, laying the foundation for long-term achievement and prosperity.

Prioritizing Sustainability

Sustainability has evolved into a fundamental pillar of contemporary life and business, transcending its former status as merely an optional extra. Embracing eco-friendly measures and actively working to diminish our carbon footprint are critical actions for safeguarding our planet's future vitality and health. These initiatives are instrumental in counteracting the detrimental impacts of climate change and conserving precious natural resources for the generations to come, while also cultivating a culture of responsibility and care for our environment.

Moreover, weaving sustainability into the fabric of business operations can significantly bolster long-term prosperity and resilience. Companies that champion environmental considerations often witness a transformative improvement in how consumers view them, which can translate into heightened loyalty and a distinct competitive edge. By adopting sustainable methods, businesses can achieve considerable savings, thanks to more efficient use of resources and reduced waste. This strategic alignment with sustainability signals not only a commitment to environmental stewardship but also a savvy recognition of its importance for enduring success in today's dynamic marketplace.

The journey towards sustainability is marked by the dual benefits of ecological preservation and economic opportunity. It presents a compelling case for businesses and individuals alike to reassess their practices and align them with principles that support the well-being of our planet. As we forge ahead, it becomes increasingly clear that sustainable practices are not just beneficial but essential for a thriving future.

Adopting a sustainable mindset fosters a deeper connection with our environment, encouraging a lifestyle that respects the delicate balance of nature. This approach not only aids in reducing the adverse effects of human activity on the planet but also enriches our lives with a greater sense of purpose and fulfillment. It is a testament to our ability to live harmoniously within our means, ensuring that the beauty and bounty of the Earth are preserved for future generations to enjoy.

The commitment to sustainability is a reflection of foresight, innovation, and responsibility. It embodies a comprehensive understanding of the intricate interdependencies within our ecosystem and the critical role we play in shaping its future. By embracing sustainability, we pave the way for a healthier planet, more resilient economies, and a legacy of stewardship that honors the profound connection between humanity and the natural world.

Nurturing Talent

At the heart of every successful supply chain lies its most vital asset: its people. Their creativity, dedication, and relentless pursuit of excellence fuel the machinery that keeps the supply chain thriving. Investing in comprehensive training and development initiatives unlocks the full potential of this invaluable resource, significantly amplifying their contributions to the organization's success. This commitment to nurturing talent not only arms employees with the skills needed to tackle present challenges but also primes them for the inevitable evolutions of the sector.

When employees are empowered with knowledge and skill enhancement opportunities, they become catalysts for innovation and perpetual growth within their organizations. This support in career advancement cultivates a sense of belonging and motivation among team members, encouraging them to seek and implement strategies that refine operations and introduce groundbreaking solutions. Such an environment, rich in encouragement and opportunities for growth, is fundamental in cultivating a workforce that is not only proficient but also pioneering.

A well-educated and skillful team is the cornerstone of an inventive and continuously advancing supply chain. Their ability to adapt and overcome the intricate challenges of the supply chain landscape is what sets a company apart in today's competitive market. By ensuring that every member of the team is equipped with the necessary tools and understanding, organizations can navigate the complexities of the industry with agility and confidence.

The investment in employee training and development goes beyond mere skill acquisition; it is a testament to an organization's commitment to excellence and resilience. This foresight in preparing the workforce for future challenges ensures that the company remains at the forefront of industry advancements, ready to seize new opportunities as they arise. It is through this strategic development of its people that a supply chain can truly achieve lasting success and sustainability.

The continuous investment in the growth and development of supply chain professionals is not just beneficial—it's imperative for the enduring prosperity of the operation. Such an approach not only equips teams with the necessary competencies to excel in their current roles but also prepares them to lead the industry into the future. By fostering a culture of continuous learning and improvement, organizations can ensure that their supply chain operations are not only effective and efficient today but also poised for innovation and success tomorrow.

Harnessing Resilience

The significance of resilience cannot be overstated. It stands as a beacon of strength, guiding us through the unpredictable waves of change and challenge. Armed with resilience, individuals and organizations gain the fortitude to navigate through tumultuous times, adapting seamlessly to new realities. This capacity for endurance is not innate; rather, it is meticulously cultivated through the development of detailed contingency plans. Such strategic foresight empowers us to confront the unexpected with confidence, ensuring the continuity of our endeavors despite the hurdles that may arise. Our preparedness is our shield, safeguarding our goals and operations from the storms of uncertainty.

The ability to remain flexible and agile in the face of change is a cornerstone of enduring success and growth. Agility, the swift adaptability to the shifting sands of our external environment, acts as our rudder, steering us clear of potential setbacks. It is this very flexibility that transforms challenges into stepping stones, paving the way for innovation and progress. In embracing change, we not only safeguard our current state but also lay the foundation for future advancements. This dynamic approach to obstacles enhances our resilience, enabling us to emerge from adversity not just unscathed but fortified, ready to embrace the opportunities that lie ahead.

The journey of resilience and agility is one of continuous improvement and learning. Each challenge we encounter is an opportunity to refine our strategies, hone our skills, and expand our capabilities. This process of constant evolution fosters an environment of innovation and creativity, where every setback is viewed as a chance to grow stronger and wiser. By adopting this mindset, we cultivate a culture of resilience that permeates every level of our organization, making us more robust and adaptable than ever before.

Moreover, resilience and agility are not solitary pursuits; they thrive on collaboration and shared vision. By fostering a supportive environment where ideas and strategies can be openly discussed and refined, we amplify our collective strength. This synergy not only accelerates our ability to adapt and overcome but also enriches our journey with diverse perspectives and insights. Together, we can face any challenge, turning obstacles into opportunities for collective growth and success.

The path to resilience and agility is marked by preparedness, adaptability, continuous learning, and collaboration. These principles serve as our compass, guiding us through the complexities of the modern world with grace and strength. By embodying these values, we not only navigate the present challenges with confidence but also pave the way for a future brimming with possibilities. Let us embrace resilience and agility as our guiding lights, illuminating the path to success and fulfillment in an ever-changing world.

Conclusion

It is important to understand that the quest for optimization is a continuous journey, not a destination. This path requires a steadfast dedication to perpetual growth and enhancement, anchored in an eager approach towards innovation and a robust culture of teamwork. By prioritizing sustainability, nurturing talent, and cultivating resilience, we lay down the foundation for achieving extraordinary success.

Our endeavors in this intricate domain underscore the significance of being adaptable and welcoming new technological advancements with open arms. This attitude prepares us to tackle obstacles, capitalize on opportunities, and remain at the forefront of a competitive arena. The collective aim for excellence creates a vibrant ecosystem that promotes creativity, and the exchange of knowledge and best practices.

Focusing on sustainable practices, we not only boost operational effectiveness and customer satisfaction but also make a positive impact on the environment and society. Such initiatives are vital for fostering a healthier planet and ensuring the well-being of future generations. It's through these efforts that we can make a lasting difference, highlighting our commitment to not just business success but also to global stewardship.

Incorporating cutting-edge technologies and innovative strategies is paramount to navigating the complexities of supply chain and logistics efficiently. This proactive approach enables us to adapt to market dynamics swiftly, ensuring that we are always a step ahead. It's through this forward-thinking mindset that we unlock new horizons, setting the stage for groundbreaking achievements.

As we journey through this challenging yet rewarding landscape, our unwavering commitment to improvement, collaboration, and sustainability guides us. These principles are the keystones of a prosperous and resilient future, ensuring that the legacy we build today will inspire and benefit generations to come. Through collective effort and shared vision, we are not just reaching our goals but also shaping a future where both business and community thrive.

CASE STUDIES: Optimizing Supply Chain and Logistics

Case Study 1: Implementing Real-time Tracking in E-commerce Logistics

Background:

An e-commerce company was facing challenges in managing its supply chain efficiency, leading to delays in deliveries and increased costs. The primary issue was the lack of real-time visibility into the logistics process, making it difficult to track shipments and predict delivery times accurately.

Solution:

The company decided to implement a real-time tracking system for its supply chain and logistics operations. This system utilized GPS tracking, IoT devices, and a cloud-based logistics platform to monitor the location and status of shipments in real time.

Additionally, the company integrated this system with its existing ERP (Enterprise Resource Planning) system to enhance data accuracy and operational efficiency.

Implementation:

- **GPS and IoT Deployment:** The company equipped all its delivery trucks and containers with GPS trackers and IoT sensors. These devices provided real-time data on vehicle location, speed, and environmental conditions.

- **Cloud-Based Logistics Platform:** A cloud-based platform was adopted to collect and analyze data from the GPS and IoT devices. This platform offered features like route optimization, predictive analytics, and automated alerts for any delays or issues.

- **ERP Integration:** Integrating the real-time tracking system with the ERP allowed for seamless data flow across the supply chain, improving inventory management, order processing, and customer service.

Outcomes:

- **Improved Delivery Times:** The real-time visibility into the logistics process enabled the company to optimize routes, reduce delays, and improve overall delivery times by 25%.

- **Cost Reduction:** Better route planning and inventory management led to a significant reduction in fuel consumption and warehousing costs, saving the company approximately 15% in logistics expenses.

- **Enhanced Customer Satisfaction:** The ability to provide customers with accurate delivery times and real-time updates on their orders significantly improved customer satisfaction and loyalty.

Case Study 2: Streamlining Supply Chain through Vendor Managed Inventory (VMI)

Background:

A manufacturing company was struggling with inventory management issues, leading to stockouts and overstock situations. These challenges were causing production delays and increased holding costs, impacting the company's bottom line.

Solution:

To address these issues, the company implemented a Vendor Managed Inventory (VMI) program with its key suppliers. VMI is a supply chain initiative where the supplier is responsible for maintaining the inventory levels at the buyer's location at the agreed-upon levels.

Implementation:

- **Partnership and Collaboration:** The company collaborated closely with its suppliers to establish trust and set clear expectations for the VMI program.

- **Technology Integration:** The implementation involved integrating the company's inventory management system with the suppliers' systems to enable real-time data exchange about stock levels, consumption patterns, and replenishment needs.

- **Continuous Monitoring and Adjustment:** Both parties agreed to regularly review performance metrics and adjust inventory levels, reorder points, and delivery schedules as needed to optimize the supply chain.

Outcomes:

- **Reduced Inventory Levels:** The VMI program led to a more efficient inventory management system, reducing stock levels by 30% while avoiding stockouts.

- **Increased Operational Efficiency:** By shifting the responsibility of inventory management to suppliers, the company streamlined its operations, allowing it to focus on core business activities and improve production efficiency.

- **Enhanced Supplier Relationships:** The collaborative approach of the VMI program strengthened the relationships between the company and its suppliers, leading to better communication, improved service levels, and more strategic partnerships.

These case studies demonstrate how adopting innovative technologies and collaborative strategies in supply chain and logistics can lead to significant improvements in efficiency, cost savings, and customer satisfaction.

Examples

1. **Amazon** has built its reputation on pioneering innovative approaches and maintaining efficiency within its supply chain operations. This focus has allowed it to set new standards in delivering customer satisfaction and operational success.

2. **Toyota** is celebrated for introducing the Toyota Production System, a methodology that transformed the principles of manufacturing and logistics across the globe. Its practices have become benchmarks for lean production and efficiency.

3. **Maersk** stands out in the shipping industry for its unwavering dedication to sustainability and achieving operational excellence. The company's efforts in these areas have not only improved its own operations but also set a precedent for environmental responsibility in the maritime sector.

4. **UPS** is known for its advanced logistics solutions and unwavering commitment to ensuring customer satisfaction. By continually investing in technology and innovative services, UPS has maintained its position as a leader in the logistics industry.

5. **Procter & Gamble** is recognized for its extensive supply chain expertise and its dynamic approach to adapting to market changes. This adaptability has enabled the company to consistently meet consumer needs while navigating the complexities of global supply chains.

Top Five Takeaways

1. **To remain competitive and innovative**, it's essential to embrace new ideas and technologies. This proactive approach helps in staying ahead of industry trends and prepares the organization for future challenges.

2. **Encouraging teamwork and cooperation** is crucial for developing a strong network of partners. This collaboration enhances efficiency and allows for the sharing of resources and expertise, leading to greater success.

3. **Prioritizing sustainability** is vital for reducing the environmental footprint of your operations. Implementing eco-friendly practices not only benefits the planet but also improves your company's reputation and long-term viability.

4. **Investing in the professional growth** of your employees is key to building a skilled and motivated workforce. By providing training and development

opportunities, you empower your staff, which in turn drives innovation and productivity within the organization.

5. **Building resilience is essential** for navigating through periods of uncertainty and disruption. By preparing for potential challenges and adapting to changes, your organization can maintain stability and continue to thrive in a volatile market.

Actions to Take

1. **Investing in cutting-edge technologies** is essential for streamlining operations and enhancing efficiency. This strategic move not only reduces costs but also significantly improves productivity across the board.

2. **Establishing solid relationships** with suppliers and distributors is crucial for ensuring a reliable supply chain. These partnerships enable a more seamless flow of goods and services, contributing to overall business stability and growth.

3. **Adopting sustainable practices** across the supply chain demonstrates a commitment to environmental stewardship. This approach not only minimizes the ecological footprint but also aligns with the growing consumer demand for responsible business practices.

4. **Providing continuous training and development** opportunities for employees is key to fostering a skilled and motivated workforce. By investing in the growth of your team, you can enhance their performance and ensure the long-term success of your organization.

5. **Developing comprehensive contingency plans** is vital for mitigating risks that could disrupt operations. By preparing for potential challenges, businesses can ensure continuity and resilience in the face of unforeseen circumstances.

Actions Not to Take

1. By **failing to allocate resources to innovation**, companies risk entering a phase of stagnation where they no longer evolve or keep pace with market demands. This lack of investment in new ideas and technologies can ultimately lead to a decline in competitive advantage and market share.

2. **Choosing to operate in isolation** and not seeking collaborative opportunities can severely limit a company's ability to grow and innovate. Collaboration opens

doors to new ideas, technologies, and markets, enhancing the potential for success and expansion.

3. **Ignoring the importance of sustainability** not only poses risks to the environment but also threatens the company's reputation among consumers and investors who increasingly prioritize eco-friendly practices. This oversight can lead to public backlash and a decrease in customer loyalty, affecting long-term profitability.

4. **Not prioritizing talent development** within an organization can result in a workforce that feels undervalued and disengaged. Without opportunities for growth and learning, employees may lack motivation and commitment, leading to decreased productivity and higher turnover rates.

5. **Failing to prepare for potential disruptions** in the market or operations leaves a business highly vulnerable to unforeseen challenges. Without a contingency plan, companies may struggle to recover from setbacks, risking significant financial loss or even total failure.

Chapter 20: Enhancing Operational Efficiency and Productivity

Achieving operational efficiency and productivity stands at the heart of organizational success. This pursuit aims to elevate output while reducing input, embodying the essence of process optimization and the strategic deployment of resources. It's about leveraging what's available, refining processes, and cutting down on waste to amplify performance and market standing.

This narrative delves into the core principles of enhancing operational efficiency and productivity, offering readers a treasure trove of insights, actionable strategies, and motivation to foster transformative change within their entities. By dissecting various methodologies and sharing success stories, the content arms business leaders and professionals with the necessary tools to soar. It stresses the importance of applying these insights in real-world scenarios, bridging the gap between theory and practice for substantial outcomes.

The journey to operational excellence is a strategic one, requiring a commitment to continuous improvement and innovation. This path is not just about achieving short-term gains but about setting the foundation for long-term success and competitiveness. It calls for a proactive mindset, encouraging organizations to always be in pursuit of better, more efficient ways of operating.

In this exploration, we aim to inspire and guide individuals and organizations towards realizing their utmost potential. The focus is on tangible achievements, fostering an environment where growth, efficiency, and innovation go hand in hand. By embracing these principles, entities can not only enhance their operational capabilities but also secure a formidable position in the competitive landscape.

The essence of this guidance is to catalyze a shift towards operational excellence, promoting a culture of continuous improvement that propels organizations forward. It's about transforming theoretical knowledge into practical success, ensuring that every step taken is a stride towards greater efficiency, productivity, and overall organizational health. Through dedication and strategic action, achieving operational efficiency becomes not just a goal, but a tangible reality, paving the way for sustained success and innovation.

Inspirational Quote

"Excellence is not being the best, it's doing your best. It's the relentless commitment to improvement and the unwavering pursuit of efficiency that transforms ordinary into extraordinary."

Embrace Continuous Improvement

It is essential to embrace the concept that improvement is a continuous journey rather than a final goal. The path towards greater efficiency is punctuated with various milestones, each symbolizing significant progress and invaluable learning opportunities. Daily operations become a fertile ground for recognizing areas that need enhancement, paving the way for more streamlined processes and the elimination of superfluous tasks. This relentless pursuit of betterment not only boosts productivity but also nurtures a forward-thinking mindset geared towards solving problems before they arise.

To maintain a competitive edge and swiftly adapt to market fluctuations, it's imperative for organizations to foster a culture that prioritizes innovation and flexibility. The ability to welcome and adapt to change is key to securing a leading position in the ever-evolving business environment. Encouraging an atmosphere receptive to fresh perspectives and novel approaches empowers companies to tackle the inevitable challenges of expansion and transformation head-on.

By promoting a workplace where innovation and adaptability are at the forefront, businesses can adeptly respond to the fast-paced changes in their industry. This strategic emphasis on continual improvement and flexibility guarantees that organizations are fully prepared to handle the intricacies and uncertainties of their fields. Cultivating such a dynamic environment not only propels companies forward but also solidifies their resilience against future disruptions.

Moreover, this approach to constant enhancement encourages employees to contribute their unique ideas and solutions, fostering a sense of ownership and engagement among the workforce. When team members feel valued and heard, their motivation to contribute to the company's success skyrockets, further accelerating the cycle of innovation and efficiency. This collaborative atmosphere is crucial for sustaining long-term growth and competitiveness.

The journey towards organizational excellence is an unending one, filled with opportunities for refinement and innovation at every turn. By embracing a philosophy of continuous improvement, fostering an adaptable and innovative culture, and encouraging employee engagement, businesses can navigate the complexities of their industries with agility and confidence. This holistic approach not only drives productivity and growth but also ensures that organizations remain resilient and proactive in the face of change.

Empower Your Team

Empowerment is the cornerstone of productivity within any team or organization, acting as a catalyst for growth and innovation. By entrusting team members with autonomy, it nurtures a sense of trust and encourages them to tackle tasks and challenges with a fresh perspective. Providing the necessary tools and resources further empowers individuals to execute their responsibilities with efficiency and effectiveness, leading to a thriving work environment.

When employees feel empowered, they are inspired to take the lead, harness their creativity, and make meaningful contributions that align with the organization's objectives. This proactive stance not only accelerates progress but also enhances the collective output of the team. Empowered employees are pivotal in driving the organization forward, reflecting their commitment and the trust placed in them by their leaders.

Fostering an environment that promotes open communication is vital for true empowerment. It creates a space where every team member feels valued and confident in sharing their ideas, contributing to a culture of collaboration and innovation. This open dialogue is the foundation for a dynamic and adaptive workplace, where creativity flourishes and diverse perspectives are welcomed.

Investing in the professional growth of employees through opportunities for skill development is crucial for sustained empowerment. It motivates individuals to enhance their expertise and remain engaged with their roles, leading to personal and professional fulfillment. Such initiatives demonstrate the organization's commitment to its workforce, reinforcing the employees' sense of value and belonging.

Celebrating achievements and recognizing contributions are integral to building a supportive environment that champions empowerment. It not only boosts morale but also solidifies a sense of community and loyalty among team members. This culture of acknowledgment and appreciation is essential for cultivating a committed and enthusiastic workforce, eager to contribute to the organization's success.

Streamline Processes

In the quest for peak performance, the complexity within organizations can often be a formidable barrier. To overcome this, a deliberate and methodical approach is essential, starting with the identification and removal of bottlenecks and redundancies that hinder smooth operations. By meticulously reorganizing tasks and procedures, businesses can streamline their workflows, paving the way for more effective and efficient operations.

The cornerstone of achieving operational excellence lies in the harmonious blend of simplicity and strategic technology integration. This approach not only minimizes operational friction but also boosts productivity and enhances overall efficiency. The focus on simplification helps in decluttering processes, allowing companies to direct their energies towards innovation and value creation.

Embracing simplicity transforms the organizational landscape, enabling team members to concentrate on their primary duties with renewed focus and clarity. The judicious use of technology acts as a catalyst, automating routine tasks and refining data management systems. This dual strategy not only accelerates decision-making but also minimizes the margin for error, setting the stage for a more agile and responsive organization.

The integration of technology and the pursuit of simplicity serve as the backbone for enhancing an organization's agility. This agility is crucial in today's fast-paced business world, where the ability to adapt swiftly to change can be the difference between success and stagnation. Organizations that commit to streamlining their operations and harnessing the power of technology are better equipped to face the challenges of the modern marketplace.

Such organizations stand at the forefront of innovation and competitiveness. Their proactive approach to simplification and technology adoption marks them as leaders, ready to navigate the complexities of the business world with confidence. This not only ensures their sustained growth but also cements their position as industry pioneers, leading by example in the pursuit of excellence.

Leverage Technology

Technology stands as a beacon of progress, propelling advancements across diverse industries. With the advent of automation, artificial intelligence, data analytics, and cloud computing, a new era of business efficiency and productivity has dawned. These innovations offer businesses the tools to streamline operations, cut costs, and refine their decision-making processes, ushering in a wave of enhanced organizational performance and market competitiveness.

In today's rapidly evolving marketplace, the integration of cutting-edge solutions tailored to an organization's unique goals is paramount. This approach not only optimizes the use of resources but also cultivates an environment ripe for ongoing improvement and innovation. Embracing relevant technological advancements empowers your business to accomplish more with less, leveraging efficiency for greater success.

By strategically aligning technology with organizational objectives, companies unlock the potential for remarkable efficiency gains and operational excellence. This synergy between technology and business strategy fosters a competitive edge, ensuring that your organization remains at the forefront of its industry. It's about making technology work for you, transforming potential challenges into opportunities for growth and achievement.

Moreover, the journey towards technological integration is an investment in the future. It paves the way for sustainable development, enabling businesses to adapt and thrive in the face of changing market dynamics. By staying ahead of technological trends, organizations can secure a position of strength and agility, ready to meet the demands of tomorrow.

The embrace of technology is not just about maintaining relevance; it's about setting the pace for innovation and leadership in your sector. By harnessing the power of modern advancements, your organization can achieve unprecedented levels of success and sustainability. This forward-thinking approach not only benefits your business but also contributes to the broader landscape of industry innovation and global progress.

Foster a Culture of Collaboration

Nno entity can afford the luxury of working in isolation. The true power of collaboration is realized in its unparalleled ability to amplify productivity and streamline the pursuit of common objectives across an organization. It is through the encouragement of interdepartmental cooperation that we can effectively dismantle the barriers to communication and collaborative success, fostering an environment where collective efforts flourish.

Promoting a culture of teamwork across different functions is a catalyst for breaking down traditional barriers. This approach not only nurtures a sense of unity but is instrumental in merging diverse talents and insights. Consequently, this synergy unleashes a wave of creativity and operational excellence, driving the organization to new heights of achievement and innovation.

The magic happens when teams align under a shared vision, transforming the workspace into a breeding ground for endless opportunities and enhancements. This alignment fosters a rich exchange of ideas and skills, culminating in breakthroughs that a singular department could scarcely imagine. The shift from a competitive to a collaborative culture not only propels the organization towards its goals but also cultivates a fulfilling and supportive environment for everyone involved.

A collaborative ethos invites a diversity of perspectives and strengths, paving the way for groundbreaking solutions and superior outcomes. This collective strength surpasses what any individual or department can accomplish alone, marking a significant leap towards organizational excellence. Moreover, such a culture of cooperation significantly uplifts employee morale, satisfaction, and loyalty, contributing to a vibrant and productive workplace.

Fostering a collaborative environment is not just about achieving short-term goals; it's about setting the foundation for sustainable growth and innovation. By encouraging teams to work together and share their unique insights, we unlock a treasure trove of opportunities for improvement and progress. This not only accelerates the organization's journey towards its objectives but also ensures a happier, more engaged workforce, ready to tackle the challenges of tomorrow.

Conclusion

Enhancing operational efficiency and productivity is not just about achieving higher outputs; it's a continuous journey towards excellence, innovation, and empowerment. It demands a steadfast commitment to embracing change, which is essential for organizations striving to stay relevant and competitive in the dynamic business landscape. By fostering a culture of collaboration, companies can unlock the collective expertise and creativity of their workforce, leading to innovative solutions and significant improvements.

The role of technology in this journey cannot be overstated. Modern technological advancements provide incredible opportunities to make processes more efficient, improve accuracy, and aid in decision-making. By thoughtfully integrating these tools, organizations can dramatically improve their operational capabilities and realize their full potential. This not only helps them excel in the current competitive environment but also lays the groundwork for sustainable growth and success in the future.

A culture of collaboration and innovation is the cornerstone of achieving and sustaining high levels of efficiency and productivity. When teams work together, sharing insights and ideas, they can overcome challenges more effectively and find better ways to achieve their goals. This synergy not only enhances the workplace atmosphere but also drives the company forward, making it more agile and adaptable to changes.

Investing in technology and innovation is investing in the future of a company. As organizations navigate through the complexities of the modern business world, adopting and adapting to new technologies is crucial. This strategic approach not only streamlines operations but also opens up new avenues for growth and competitiveness.

The path to enhancing operational efficiency and productivity is multifaceted, involving a commitment to change, collaboration, and technological innovation. Organizations that embrace this journey position themselves for enduring success, staying ahead of the curve in a rapidly evolving business environment. This commitment not only benefits the company in terms of efficiency and growth but also empowers employees, fostering a culture of continuous improvement and innovation.

Unlocking Excellence: A Blueprint for Achieving Business Success   Business Lessons

CASE STUDIES: Enhancing Operational Efficiency and Productivity

Case Study 1: Implementing Lean Manufacturing at XYZ Corp

Background:

XYZ Corp, a mid-sized manufacturer of consumer electronics, faced challenges with high operational costs, inventory management issues, and production delays. The company's leadership recognized the need to enhance operational efficiency and productivity to stay competitive.

Solution:

XYZ Corp decided to implement Lean Manufacturing principles, focusing on waste reduction, process improvement, and value stream mapping. The initiative began with a comprehensive audit of existing processes to identify areas of waste and inefficiency. Key strategies included:

- **Just-In-Time (JIT) Production:** XYZ Corp restructured its manufacturing process to produce goods based on actual customer demand rather than forecasts. This shift reduced inventory costs and minimized the storage space required for raw materials and finished goods.

- **Kaizen Events:** The company organized Kaizen events involving employees from various departments to brainstorm and implement process improvements. These events promoted a culture of continuous improvement and empowered employees to suggest and implement changes that enhanced productivity.

- **5S Methodology:** To create a more organized and efficient workspace, XYZ Corp adopted the 5S methodology (Sort, Set in order, Shine, Standardize, Sustain). This approach helped in reducing the time spent on locating tools and materials, thus speeding up the production process.

Results:

Within a year of implementing Lean Manufacturing, XYZ Corp saw significant improvements in operational efficiency and productivity. Production lead times were reduced by 30%, inventory costs decreased by 25%, and the company reported a 20% increase in overall productivity. Employee engagement and satisfaction also improved due to their active involvement in process improvements.

Case Study 2: Digital Transformation in the Logistics Operations of ABC Logistics

Background: ABC Logistics, a leading logistics and supply chain company, was struggling with inefficiencies in its operations, including manual processes, data inaccuracies, and delays in shipment tracking.

Solution:

To address these challenges, ABC Logistics embarked on a digital transformation journey. The company invested in an integrated logistics platform that leveraged IoT (Internet of Things), AI (Artificial Intelligence), and big data analytics. Key components of the solution included:

- **IoT for Real-Time Tracking:** The company equipped its fleet with IoT devices to enable real-time tracking of shipments. This technology allowed ABC Logistics to provide accurate delivery estimates and improve route optimization.

- **AI-Powered Analytics:** ABC Logistics used AI algorithms to analyze historical data and predict future logistics challenges, such as potential delays or bottlenecks. This predictive analysis helped in proactive decision-making and optimizing operations.

- **Automated Warehouse Management:** The company implemented an automated warehouse management system (WMS) that utilized robotics and AI to streamline picking, packing, and inventory management. This reduced manual errors and increased warehouse efficiency.

Results:

The digital transformation initiative led to remarkable outcomes for ABC Logistics. The company experienced a 40% improvement in delivery times, a 30% reduction in operational costs due to optimized routes and automated processes, and a significant increase in customer satisfaction. Additionally, the real-time data analytics provided insights that helped in strategic decision-making and long-term operational planning.

Both case studies illustrate the importance of adopting modern methodologies and technologies to enhance operational efficiency and productivity. While XYZ Corp focused on process improvement and waste reduction through Lean Manufacturing,

ABC Logistics achieved its goals through digital transformation, showcasing the versatility of approaches to operational excellence.

Examples

1. **Toyota** is celebrated for developing the Toyota Production System, a pioneering approach that drastically improved manufacturing processes and efficiency. This system is a cornerstone of lean manufacturing, setting a global benchmark for operational excellence.

2. **Amazon** employs sophisticated algorithms and automation technologies to streamline its logistics and operational processes. This strategic use of technology enables Amazon to maintain high levels of efficiency and customer satisfaction.

3. **Apple's** reputation is built on its unparalleled ability to integrate hardware and software seamlessly. This integration results in products that offer superior productivity and an enhanced user experience, distinguishing Apple in the tech industry.

4. **Southwest Airlines** prioritizes operational efficiency, allowing it to offer low-cost air travel without compromising on service quality. This focus on efficiency and service has made Southwest a favorite among budget-conscious travelers seeking reliable flights.

5. **Walmart** utilizes advanced data analytics and effective supply chain management to refine its operations and increase efficiency. These strategies enable Walmart to offer competitive pricing and maintain a strong position in the retail market.

Top Five Takeaways

1. **Adopting a mindset of continuous improvement** is crucial for staying competitive and innovative. This approach encourages regular reflection and the pursuit of excellence in every aspect of work.

2. **Empowering your team** involves giving them the autonomy to make decisions and the resources they need to succeed. It boosts morale and promotes a sense of ownership and responsibility among team members.

3. **Streamlining processes** is about eliminating unnecessary steps and making workflows more efficient. By doing so, you can reduce waste, save time, and increase productivity across the board.

4. **Leveraging technology** means utilizing the latest tools and platforms to enhance business operations and deliver better results. It's about staying ahead in a digital world by adopting solutions that drive efficiency and innovation.

5. **Fostering a culture of collaboration** is key to unlocking the collective potential of your team. Encouraging open communication and teamwork leads to more innovative solutions and a stronger, more cohesive organization.

Actions to Take

1. **Investing in employee training and development** is essential for enhancing skills and knowledge. It leads to improved performance and job satisfaction, enabling the workforce to tackle challenges more effectively.

2. **Conducting regular process audits** is crucial for uncovering areas where inefficiencies lie. This practice allows organizations to make informed decisions on how to optimize operations and increase productivity.

3. **Implementing automation and digital tools** can significantly streamline workflows and reduce manual errors. By adopting these technologies, businesses can achieve higher efficiency and better utilize their resources.

4. **Fostering open communication** and collaboration across departments is key to breaking down silos and encouraging a more unified approach to problem-solving. This environment promotes innovation and ensures all team members are aligned with the organization's goals.

5. **Staying updated** on the latest advancements in technology and industry best practices is vital for maintaining a competitive edge. It enables companies to adapt to changes quickly and capitalize on new opportunities for growth.

Actions Not to Take

1. **Overlooking employee feedback** on workflow inefficiencies can lead to missed opportunities for improvement and increased frustration among staff. By not

addressing these concerns, companies risk stagnating and failing to optimize their operations effectively.

2. **Launching new technology without offering adequate training** and support can result in underutilization and resistance from employees. This approach not only wastes resources but also diminishes the potential benefits of technological advancements.

3. **Failing to regularly review and update business processes** as the organization grows and changes can hinder its ability to remain competitive and responsive to market demands. Sticking to outdated methods can slow progress and innovation.

4. **Micromanaging employees** stifles creativity and independence, leading to a decrease in motivation and job satisfaction. It's crucial to trust team members and give them the autonomy to make decisions, fostering a more dynamic and engaged workforce.

5. **Permitting the development of organizational silos** obstructs the flow of information and collaboration across different departments. This isolation can result in inefficiencies and a lack of cohesive strategy, undermining the company's overall success.

Part Five: Innovation and Growth

Innovation stands as the bedrock of progress across all sectors, propelling advancements with its blend of creativity and strategic problem-solving. It encourages companies to explore beyond the known limits, unveiling fresh opportunities and securing a competitive edge. By adopting a culture of innovation, organizations gain the agility needed to adapt swiftly to changing market trends and consumer preferences, ensuring their growth is intertwined with societal advancement, driving economies and communities toward a brighter, more promising future.

Chapter 21: Fostering Creativity and Innovation

Cultivating a culture of creativity and innovation is about more than just coming up with new ideas; it's about creating a space where imagination is not just welcomed but celebrated, and breakthroughs are the norm rather than the exception. Such an environment nurtures innovative thinking, empowering people to break free from conventional boundaries and devise solutions that are as unique as they are effective. In today's rapidly evolving world, the ability to innovate sets apart the leaders and trailblazers from the crowd, making it crucial not just for business leaders and team managers but for anyone keen on personal growth and making a real difference.

Embracing creativity opens the door to endless possibilities and paves the way for transformative change. When individuals and organizations prioritize and encourage creative thinking, they become better equipped to adapt quickly, tackle challenges creatively, and capitalize on new opportunities that come their way. This forward-thinking approach to innovation is key to driving progress, ensuring resilience, and maintaining a competitive edge in a complex and ever-changing global landscape. Thus, incorporating creativity at the heart of one's strategy is essential for anyone aiming for lasting success and a meaningful impact, whether they are at the helm of a global enterprise, leading a small team, or on a personal journey of self-improvement.

Nurturing a creative and innovative mindset is the cornerstone of achieving excellence and standing out in any field. By fostering an environment where creative endeavors are encouraged and celebrated, individuals and organizations can unlock their full potential and lead the way in innovation. This commitment to creativity not only fuels personal and professional growth but also inspires others to explore new horizons and challenge the status quo.

In a world where change is the only constant, the ability to innovate and think creatively becomes the most valuable skill one can possess. It enables individuals and organizations to navigate through uncertainty with grace, turning obstacles into opportunities for growth and development. Embracing this mindset is not just beneficial; it's essential for thriving in today's dynamic environment and leaving a lasting legacy.

The journey towards fostering creativity and innovation is a transformative process that enriches both individuals and organizations. It's a path that leads to discovering new solutions, achieving unprecedented success, and making a positive impact in the world. By championing creativity, we not only enhance our own lives but also contribute to a brighter, more innovative future for all.

Inspirational Quote

"Creativity is intelligence having fun." - Albert Einstein

Embrace Curiosity

Creativity and innovation are not just about coming up with new ideas; they're about creating an environment where imagination is not just welcomed but celebrated, and breakthroughs are the norm. Such an environment nurtures innovative thinking, pushing people to think differently and come up with unique, effective solutions. In today's fast-paced world, the ability to innovate sets apart successful individuals and organizations, making it crucial not only for leaders and entrepreneurs but also for anyone looking to grow personally and make a significant impact.

Embracing creativity opens up a world of endless possibilities and leads the way for transformative changes. It allows individuals and organizations to quickly adapt to new challenges, find innovative solutions to problems, and capitalize on emerging opportunities. This forward-thinking approach to innovation drives progress and ensures resilience and sustainability in a competitive, complex landscape.

By valuing and promoting creative thinking, we enable swift adaptation to change, novel problem-solving, and the seizing of new opportunities. This proactive stance on innovation is key to driving progress and ensuring both resilience and sustainability in a world that's constantly evolving. Whether leading a global enterprise, managing a small team, or on a personal journey of growth, making creativity a core part of one's strategy is essential for long-term success and making a lasting impact.

Incorporating creativity into every aspect of one's strategy is not just beneficial; it's essential for achieving enduring success and making a meaningful difference. It's a commitment to seeing beyond the conventional, to imagining what could be, and to pursuing that vision with vigor and determination. This commitment to innovation and creativity is what enables individuals and organizations to thrive, even in the face of adversity.

Fostering an environment where creativity and innovation are at the forefront is not just advantageous—it's imperative for anyone aspiring to make a significant contribution in their field. It is a foundational element that enables the pursuit of excellence, the achievement of goals, and the realization of one's full potential. In essence, cultivating creativity and innovation is the cornerstone of not just surviving but thriving in the modern world.

Foster a Culture of Collaboration

Innovation flourishes in settings that embrace a variety of perspectives and champion collaborative efforts. By dismantling barriers and fostering a culture of teamwork, we lay the groundwork for groundbreaking achievements. Establishing environments where individuals are motivated to express their ideas and collaborate on each other's contributions is crucial. Such an approach not only enriches the creative process but also enhances the collective capability to solve complex problems and develop innovative solutions.

Encouraging a sense of unity and mutual support among team members is vital for sustaining a culture of innovation. When people feel valued and their input is recognized, it creates a positive cycle of engagement and creativity. This atmosphere allows for the free exchange of ideas, where every suggestion is considered valuable and can be built upon by others. By working together in this inclusive and supportive manner, the team is better positioned to achieve remarkable outcomes that surpass what any individual could accomplish on their own.

Embrace Failure as a Stepping Stone

Failure is not the end; it's an integral part of the journey to creativity and innovation. It offers a chance to glean insights that success often overshadows, providing a deeper understanding of one's path. Embracing failure allows for growth and development that would remain hidden without these challenges, turning fear into a powerful force for forward movement.

Each mistake we make is an opportunity to learn and improve, marking an essential aspect of both personal and professional growth. These missteps are not setbacks but rather milestones that guide us closer to our objectives, clarifying the path ahead. It is crucial to recognize that every major breakthrough has its roots in perseverance through difficulties, with each obstacle serving as a crucial step towards excellence.

By celebrating our failures, we honor the process of discovery and learning. This mindset shift is vital for anyone aiming to achieve significant milestones, as it reframes obstacles as opportunities for enhancement. Adopting this approach ensures continuous progress and fosters a culture of resilience and determination.

Viewing challenges as catalysts for innovation encourages a proactive stance towards problem-solving. It invites an exploratory attitude, where experimentation and the willingness to take calculated risks become the norm. This not only accelerates personal growth but also contributes to a broader culture of creativity and invention.

The journey to success is enriched by the lessons learned from failure. These experiences build a foundation of wisdom and strength, preparing individuals for the complexities of their endeavors. By embracing this perspective, we set the stage for unparalleled achievements, making every setback a valuable part of our story towards greatness.

Cultivate a Bias Towards Action

Ideas are the seeds from which the trees of innovation and change grow, yet they require the nurturing waters of action to sprout and flourish. To bring these seeds to life, it's imperative to foster a mindset that values action above endless contemplation, particularly when faced with the unknown. Embracing this philosophy means breaking ambitious goals into smaller, achievable tasks, thereby charting a clear and attainable path to your ultimate vision. With each step taken, progress is made, and momentum gathers, serving as the driving force that sustains motivation and helps navigate through the barriers that may stand in your way.

Embarking on the journey from concept to reality is much like navigating a path that demands both a sense of direction and unwavering commitment. As you consistently apply yourself, each progressive action not only moves you nearer to your aspirations but also emphasizes the value of steadfastness. This forward momentum is essential for surmounting the inevitable challenges and uncertainties encountered along the path to meaningful achievements.

By adopting a proactive stance and dedicating yourself to continual action, you initiate a cycle of progress and success that accelerates your journey towards your objectives. This approach transforms the daunting into the doable, turning lofty dreams into achievable realities. It teaches us that through persistence and a step-by-step strategy, even the most ambitious visions can be realized.

This methodology of action over contemplation does not just apply to personal goals but is equally effective in professional environments. It encourages a culture of innovation, where ideas are quickly brought to the testing phase, learning is accelerated, and adaptability becomes a core strength. In such a dynamic setting, every team member becomes a pivotal contributor to the collective mission, fostering a sense of ownership and engagement.

The transition from idea to action to achievement is a testament to the power of human will and creativity. It serves as a reminder that with the right mindset, a clear plan, and a commitment to action, there are no limits to what can be accomplished. This journey not only leads to the realization of tangible outcomes but also to personal growth and the satisfaction that comes from making a meaningful impact.

Embrace Change and Adaptability

Innovation thrives in environments that embrace change and exhibit the flexibility to adapt to new realities. This welcoming attitude towards change transforms uncertainty from a barrier into a driving force for growth, promoting a proactive approach over a reactive one. By staying adaptable and agile, individuals and organizations are better equipped to quickly tackle unforeseen challenges and seize new opportunities, demonstrating the power of resilience and openness in the face of change.

Flexibility is not just beneficial; it's a necessity, allowing for the rapid adjustment of strategies and objectives as situations evolve. This agility enables a seamless transition in response to new information or changing market dynamics, ensuring that progress is not only maintained but accelerated. The ability to swiftly realign resources and focus in response to the external environment is a hallmark of successful and innovative entities.

The acknowledgment that change is the only constant underscores the critical role of adaptability in achieving lasting success. Those who accept and embrace the fluid nature of our world find themselves better equipped to navigate its complexities, converting potential roadblocks into opportunities for advancement. This mindset shift from viewing change as a threat to seeing it as an opportunity is what differentiates the trailblazers from the rest.

It is the capacity to pivot and adapt that sets apart the leaders in any field. This adaptability fosters resilience, enabling individuals and organizations to not just survive but thrive amidst constant change. Leaders who embody this philosophy are often at the forefront of innovation, steering their teams through uncharted waters with confidence and vision.

Maintaining resilience and an open mind is essential for anyone aspiring to excel in today's dynamic environment. By embracing change and preparing to adapt to new circumstances, individuals and organizations can unlock their full potential, turning challenges into victories. This approach not only fuels personal and professional growth but also contributes to a culture of continuous improvement and innovation.

Conclusion

Embarking on the path to foster creativity and innovation transcends the mere pursuit of goals; it is an engaging voyage that invites exploration, fosters collaboration, champions resilience, and demands adaptability. At the heart of this journey lies a steadfast dedication to cultivating curiosity, the cornerstone of imaginative thinking and groundbreaking innovations. Through the power of teamwork and the exchange of diverse viewpoints, individuals merge their distinct talents and insights, paving the way for the birth of unique ideas and inventive solutions.

Recognizing and embracing failure as an indispensable part of the learning process is paramount. Such experiences, though seemingly setbacks, are often rich with valuable lessons that pave the way for significant breakthroughs and creative leaps forward. This understanding nurtures a culture where experimentation is celebrated, and the seeds of innovation can flourish, transforming challenges into stepping stones towards success.

The journey from conception to realization necessitates proactive steps to breathe life into ideas. This dynamic approach ensures that creative visions are not just dreamt but are actualized, making a palpable impact on our world. It's the bridge that turns the intangible into the tangible, embodying the true spirit of innovation.

Adaptability, in the face of ever-changing landscapes, stands as a critical pillar of this journey. The ability to pivot, refine, and evolve ideas in light of new insights or obstacles is indispensable for the continuity of innovation. It's this fluidity and flexibility that enable breakthroughs to emerge, even in the most unforeseen circumstances.

By embracing these guiding principles, individuals and organizations not only unlock their inherent creative potential but also make meaningful contributions to their communities and the larger tapestry of our world. It's a testament to the power of collective creativity and the transformative impact it can have on shaping a brighter, more innovative future.

CASE STUDIES: Innovation and Growth

Case Study 1: Tesla, Inc. - Revolutionizing the Automotive Industry

Background:

Tesla, Inc., founded in 2003 by a group of engineers including Elon Musk, aimed to prove that electric vehicles (EVs) could surpass traditional gasoline-powered cars in performance, safety, and sustainability. At a time when EVs were largely dismissed by major automakers, Tesla's innovative approach and commitment to research and development (R&D) have been central to its growth and success.

Innovation: Tesla's innovation strategy encompasses several key areas:

1. **Electric Powertrain:** Tesla developed a high-performance electric powertrain, leading to the launch of the Tesla Roadster in 2008, the world's first electric sports car. This was followed by the Model S, Model X, Model 3, and Model Y, each offering improvements in range, speed, and affordability.

2. **Autopilot and Full Self-Driving (FSD):** Tesla has been a pioneer in integrating advanced driver-assistance systems. Its Autopilot and FSD capabilities, built on machine learning and data collected from Tesla vehicles on the road, aim to bring about fully autonomous driving in the future.

3. **Battery Technology and Production:** The company's focus on battery innovation led to the development of more efficient and cost-effective battery solutions. The establishment of the Gigafactory was a strategic move to secure battery supply and reduce costs through scale.

4. **Direct Sales Model:** Breaking from the traditional dealership model, Tesla opted for direct sales to customers through its showrooms and online platform, enhancing customer experience and reducing overhead costs.

Growth:

Tesla's innovative approach has fueled its growth:

1. **Market Valuation and Sales:** Tesla's market capitalization has grown significantly, making it one of the most valuable automakers globally. Its sales volumes have seen a steady increase, with the Model 3 becoming the world's best-selling EV.

2. **Global Expansion:** Tesla has expanded its manufacturing footprint with Gigafactories in the United States, China, and plans for more in Europe and Asia, enabling it to meet growing global demand.

3. **Energy Solutions:** Beyond vehicles, Tesla has diversified into energy storage and solar energy solutions, furthering its mission to accelerate the world's transition to sustainable energy.

4. **Challenges and Opportunities:** Tesla's journey has not been without challenges, including production delays, regulatory scrutiny, and competition. However, its commitment to innovation remains a key driver of growth, with opportunities in new markets, product lines, and technology advancements.

Case Study 2: Amazon.com, Inc. - Transforming Retail through Technology

Background:

Amazon, founded by Jeff Bezos in 1994 as an online bookstore, has grown into a global e-commerce and cloud computing giant. Its success is attributed to relentless innovation, customer-centricity, and leveraging technology to disrupt and dominate the retail industry.

Innovation:

Amazon's innovative strategies are multifaceted:

1. **E-Commerce Platform:** Amazon revolutionized online shopping with features like customer reviews, personalized recommendations, and Prime membership, offering fast, free shipping and entertainment services.

2. **Amazon Web Services (AWS):** Launched in 2006, AWS became a leader in cloud computing services, providing a broad range of infrastructure and platform services to businesses globally, contributing significantly to Amazon's profitability.

3. **Supply Chain and Logistics:** Amazon's investments in automation, robotics, and artificial intelligence (AI) have streamlined its supply chain and logistics, enabling efficient inventory management, order fulfillment, and delivery, including the ambitious goal of same-day delivery for Prime members.

4. **Consumer Electronics and Digital Services:** Amazon has also diversified into consumer electronics with products like Kindle, Fire Tablet, and Echo smart speakers, integrating its digital services like Amazon Music, Video, and Alexa, the AI-powered virtual assistant.

Growth:

Amazon's growth trajectory reflects its innovative edge:

1. **Market Dominance:** Amazon has become the go-to online retailer for millions worldwide, with a growing market share in not only retail but also in cloud computing through AWS.

2. **Global Expansion:** With operations in numerous countries, Amazon continues to expand its global footprint, adapting its model to local markets while leveraging its technological infrastructure for efficiency and scale.

3. **Financial Performance:** Amazon's revenue and profit have grown exponentially, supported by the diversification of its business model and the scalability of its platform.

4. **Challenges and Opportunities**: Despite its success, Amazon faces challenges, including regulatory scrutiny, competition, and the need to continuously innovate. Opportunities lie in expanding into new markets, further technological advancements, and sustainable practices to address environmental concerns.

These case studies illustrate how Tesla and Amazon have harnessed innovation to drive growth, transforming their industries and setting new standards for performance, customer experience, and sustainability.

Examples

1. **Pixar Animation Studios**: Known for its unparalleled contributions to the animated film industry, Pixar Animation Studios consistently sets new standards for storytelling and technological innovation in animation. Each of Pixar's creations, from the pioneering "Toy Story" to the emotionally rich "Coco," serves as more than just entertainment; they are pivotal cultural touchstones that inspire creativity and bridge generations with their universal themes and imaginative storytelling.

2. **Google:** Google stands as a titan in the global technology sector, having reshaped the way we gather information, communicate, and manage our daily routines with its array of pioneering services and products. The company's relentless drive for innovation, evident in everything from its search engine to advancements in artificial intelligence, has not only altered the digital domain but also fundamentally changed our interactions with the online world, making information more accessible and integrated into everyday life.

3. **Tesla:** Led by the ambitious Elon Musk, Tesla is a driving force in the transition to electric vehicles, spearheading advancements in sustainable transport and energy. Tesla's vehicles, known for their innovative features and exceptional performance, are more than just cars; they are a statement about the future of mobility, marrying sustainability with cutting-edge technology to challenge the traditional automotive market and encourage a move towards environmental responsibility.

4. **Marie Curie:** Marie Curie's pioneering research in radioactivity broke new ground in physics and chemistry, earning her the distinction of being the first woman to receive a Nobel Prize and the only individual to be awarded in two separate scientific disciplines. Her relentless pursuit of knowledge and her groundbreaking achievements have not only carved her name into the annals of scientific history but also continue to serve as a beacon of inspiration for scientists around the world, encouraging perseverance and curiosity in the face of adversity.

5. **Steve Jobs:** As the co-founder of Apple Inc., Steve Jobs was an emblematic figure in the tech world, whose innovative vision and commitment to excellence revolutionized consumer electronics with products such as the iPhone and iPad. Jobs' unique approach to product design, emphasizing simplicity and user experience, catapulted Apple into a league of its own, making it a benchmark for innovation and significantly influencing how technology is integrated into our daily lives.

Top Five Takeaways

1. **Embrace curiosity and never stop learning:** Cultivate a mindset of curiosity, continuously seeking new knowledge and perspectives to fuel personal and professional growth. By embracing curiosity, individuals can uncover innovative solutions and adapt to an ever-changing world, fostering creativity and resilience.

2. **Foster a culture of collaboration and diversity of thought:** Encourage teamwork and inclusivity, recognizing that diverse perspectives lead to more comprehensive problem-solving and innovation. By valuing input from individuals with varied backgrounds and experiences, organizations can foster a culture of creativity and foster a sense of belonging among team members.

3. **View failure as a stepping stone to success:** Shift the perspective on failure from a setback to a valuable learning opportunity, encouraging risk-taking and resilience. By reframing failure as a necessary part of the journey toward success, individuals can develop a growth mindset, learn from their mistakes, and ultimately achieve greater levels of achievement.

4. **Take bold action and iterate along the way:** Embrace a bias towards action, taking calculated risks and iterating on strategies based on feedback and outcomes. By embracing experimentation and iteration, individuals can avoid stagnation, drive innovation, and uncover new opportunities for growth and improvement.

5. **Embrace change and adaptability as opportunities for growth:** Embrace change as a natural part of life and business, remaining flexible and adaptable in the face of uncertainty. By viewing change as an opportunity for growth rather than a threat, individuals can cultivate resilience, embrace new challenges, and thrive in dynamic environments.

Five Actions to Take

1. **Encourage brainstorming sessions and idea sharing:** Foster a culture of creativity and innovation by providing opportunities for team members to brainstorm and share ideas freely. By creating a collaborative environment where all voices are heard and valued, organizations can unlock new insights and drive continuous improvement.

2. **Provide resources for continuous learning and development:** Invest in the growth and development of team members by offering training programs, workshops, and resources that support ongoing learning. By empowering individuals to expand their skills and knowledge, organizations can foster a culture of continuous improvement and adaptability.

3. **Celebrate experimentation and risk-taking:** Recognize and reward individuals who take initiative, experiment with new ideas, and embrace calculated risks. By celebrating innovation and resilience, organizations can inspire creativity and motivate team members to push beyond their comfort zones in pursuit of excellence.

4. **Establish clear goals and encourage action-oriented behavior:** Define clear objectives and key results (OKRs) to guide individuals and teams toward success, encouraging decisive action and accountability. By setting ambitious yet achievable goals, organizations can align efforts, track progress, and drive meaningful results.

5. **Embrace feedback and iterate based on insights:** Create a feedback-rich environment where constructive criticism is welcomed and used to drive continuous improvement. By soliciting feedback from peers, mentors, and stakeholders, individuals can gain valuable insights, identify areas for growth, and refine their approaches for greater effectiveness.

Five Actions Not to Take

1. **Discourage dissenting opinions** or alternative viewpoints: Avoid stifling creativity and innovation by embracing diverse perspectives and encouraging constructive debate. By valuing dissenting opinions, organizations can uncover blind spots, mitigate risks, and make more informed decisions.

2. **Punish failure or mistakes**: Resist the urge to blame or punish individuals for failures or mistakes, recognizing them as valuable learning opportunities. By fostering a culture of psychological safety, organizations can encourage risk-taking and experimentation, driving innovation and growth.

3. **Micromanage creative processes:** Trust team members to take ownership of their work and find creative solutions to challenges, avoiding excessive control or micromanagement. By empowering individuals to make autonomous decisions and take ownership of their projects, organizations can foster a culture of accountability and innovation.

4. **Resist change or cling to outdated methods:** Embrace change as an opportunity for growth and evolution, avoiding complacency or resistance to new ideas. By staying agile and adaptable, organizations can remain competitive in a rapidly changing world, seizing opportunities and driving continuous improvement.

5. **Suppress experimentation or risk-taking behavior:** Encourage individuals to take calculated risks and experiment with new ideas, avoiding a culture of fear or aversion to failure. By creating a safe space for innovation and exploration, organizations can unlock new opportunities, drive creativity, and stay ahead of the curve.

Chapter 22: Harnessing Technology for Competitive Advantage

Technology stands as a beacon of progress and innovation, transforming the way we live and work. It has become an essential pillar for businesses aiming to thrive in the ever-evolving market landscape, where staying ahead is synonymous with constant innovation and adaptation. This narrative highlights the monumental role of technology in driving individuals and organizations to achieve remarkable milestones, illustrating its capacity to redefine success and open doors to unparalleled opportunities.

The integration of technology into every facet of business operations and strategy has revolutionized how entities operate, compete, and grow. By leveraging technological advancements, companies can streamline their processes, enhance productivity, and foster a culture of efficiency and agility. This shift not only simplifies complex challenges but also introduces novel pathways for expansion and innovation, marking a significant leap towards operational excellence and market leadership.

At the heart of this transformation is the symbiotic relationship between technology and progress, a bond that underscores the importance of embracing new digital frontiers. This connection is a powerful catalyst for unlocking potential, enabling both individuals and organizations to venture into territories once deemed unreachable. It's a testament to the transformative power of technology, serving as a bridge to a future where innovation and growth are boundless.

The discourse on technology's impact is a call to action for a proactive embrace of digital advancements, positioning them as the foundation for building a competitive edge in today's dynamic business environment. It encourages a forward-thinking mindset, urging entities to leverage technology not just as a tool, but as an integral component of their strategy for achieving extraordinary success. This approach is pivotal for navigating the complexities of the modern world, ensuring sustainability and resilience in the face of change.

The narrative of technology as a cornerstone of innovation and progress offers a compelling vision for the future. It champions the idea that through the strategic adoption of technological solutions, individuals and organizations can transcend traditional limitations, fostering a landscape of endless possibilities. This perspective is not only inspiring but serves as a roadmap for those aspiring to reach new heights of achievement, heralding a new era of success driven by the transformative power of technology.

Inspirational Quote

"Technology is a double-edged sword—it can be the source of many wonders, but also a weapon of destruction. How we choose to wield it determines our destiny."

Embrace Innovation

Innovation stands as the beacon of progress in the technological realm, marking the foundation upon which various industries build their advancements. By instilling a culture that elevates innovation to a principle, organizations create a fertile ground for groundbreaking ideas and transformative solutions to flourish. It is through the encouragement of teams to venture into uncharted territories, tinker with nascent technologies, and perceive setbacks as pivotal learning moments, that innovation truly gains momentum.

History is replete with instances where major breakthroughs were birthed from the crucible of overcoming obstacles and daring to question the established norms. This legacy underscores the importance of fostering an environment where innovation is not just encouraged but celebrated. Such a culture is instrumental in propelling organizations to transcend conventional boundaries and pave new paths that lead to remarkable achievements.

Embracing innovation as a core value positions organizations at the vanguard of their fields, ensuring they remain ahead in a world characterized by constant change. When individuals are empowered with the freedom to think outside the box, collaborate seamlessly, and adopt innovative strategies, they unlock an infinite realm of possibilities for transformation and growth. This empowerment is the catalyst that ignites the spark of creativity and drive for excellence.

Investing in the cultivation of an innovative mindset is not merely a strategy for gaining a competitive edge; it is a commitment to adaptability and resilience in the face of shifting market demands and consumer expectations. Organizations that prioritize innovation are better equipped to navigate the complexities of the modern marketplace, delivering solutions that are not only cutting-edge but also deeply attuned to the needs of their customers. This proactive approach to innovation is what distinguishes industry leaders from followers.

The journey towards innovation is an ongoing process of exploration, experimentation, and evolution. By championing innovation at every level, organizations can transform challenges into opportunities, setting new standards of excellence and redefining what is possible. In a world that never stands still, the commitment to innovation is what ensures sustained success, driving not just technological progress but shaping the future of society at large.

Adaptability is Key

Being adaptable is not just an advantage but a necessity for survival. The rapid advancement in technology requires companies to stay alert and proactive to prevent becoming outdated. It's crucial to continuously scan the horizon for new trends and align your strategies accordingly, ensuring your business remains at the forefront of innovation. This approach not only prepares you for the future but also positions you to lead it.

Investing in your team's ongoing education and skill development is key to maintaining this adaptability. Such investments empower your workforce, equipping them with the tools and knowledge needed to tackle new challenges and adapt to changes seamlessly. This commitment to learning and growth fosters a resilient and flexible organizational culture, capable of navigating the complexities of today's business environment with confidence.

Change, often perceived as a threat, should instead be seen as a gateway to new opportunities and growth. Progressive companies embrace this reality, leveraging disruption as a catalyst to innovate and sharpen their competitive edge. This mindset transforms potential challenges into stepping stones, propelling the business forward into uncharted territories of success and innovation.

Creating a culture that values adaptability and views change positively is fundamental for businesses aiming for longevity and relevance in a fluctuating market. This culture encourages everyone in the organization to think creatively, approach problems with a solution-oriented mindset, and see beyond the status quo. It's this visionary approach that enables businesses to thrive, turning obstacles into opportunities for development and progress.

Tthe journey towards a thriving, adaptable business is ongoing and ever-evolving. It demands a commitment to continuous improvement, openness to learning, and an unwavering focus on the future. By embracing change, investing in people, and aligning with the pace of innovation, businesses can not only survive but excel, marking their place as leaders in the global marketplace. This path, though challenging, is rich with opportunities for those ready to embark on it, promising a future of success and innovation.

Customer-Centric Approach

Technology has become the bridge connecting customers to businesses, offering a wealth of information and options at their fingertips. Companies that wish to thrive must adopt a customer-first approach in all aspects of their operations. This strategy involves leveraging technology to delve into customer behavior with data analytics, crafting tailor-made experiences, and preemptively meeting their needs. By focusing on the customer journey and consistently adding value, businesses can build lasting bonds and loyalty, standing out in a crowded marketplace.

Embracing technology to gain insights into customer preferences and market trends allows businesses to respond with remarkable agility. This nimbleness not only boosts customer satisfaction but also elevates companies to the forefront of their industries, ready to meet consumer needs even before they emerge. As technological advancements unfold, the dedication to enhancing the customer experience remains crucial for sustained growth and enduring success in the ever-changing business landscape.

Integrating cutting-edge technology into decision-making enables companies to stay ahead, understanding and adapting to customer desires and shifts in the market quickly. This forward-thinking approach secures a competitive advantage, positioning businesses as visionary leaders. It's through this commitment to innovation and customer focus that companies can achieve standout success and navigate the complexities of today's business world with confidence.

Investing in technology to understand and anticipate customer needs transforms the way businesses operate, making them more responsive and customer-oriented. This proactive stance not only meets but exceeds customer expectations, fostering a sense of trust and loyalty. In doing so, businesses not only retain their relevance but also pave the way for future growth and profitability in a digital-dominated era.

The journey towards becoming a customer-centric and technologically adept organization is ongoing and dynamic. It requires a steadfast commitment to putting the customer at the heart of every decision and action. Through this lens, businesses can unlock unparalleled opportunities for innovation, customer satisfaction, and long-term prosperity, setting a new standard for excellence in the digital age.

Foster Collaboration

Organizations today have a golden opportunity to enhance teamwork across geographical divides. By harnessing the power of collaborative tools and platforms, such as project management software and communication apps, they can dismantle the traditional barriers that have segmented teams. This shift not only promotes unity across different departments but also steers them towards achieving shared objectives with a unified vision.

In an era where innovation and inclusivity are paramount, fostering open communication and valuing diverse viewpoints are crucial. Such an environment encourages employees to offer their unique insights and skills, enriching the collective efforts. By tapping into the vast pool of collective intelligence, organizations stand to gain in efficiency, creativity, and overall success, propelling them towards their goals with renewed vigor.

The adoption of modern technology for enhanced collaboration is not just a matter of convenience but a strategic necessity for businesses aiming to excel in the competitive market. Establishing open lines of communication and valuing diverse thoughts pave the way for innovative problem-solving and effective decision-making. This, in turn, instills a strong sense of belonging and dedication among employees, aligning their efforts with the organization's ambitions.

Empowering every individual to voice their ideas creates a culture where everyone feels valued and invested in the company's success. This sense of ownership and participation leads to higher levels of engagement and commitment to the organization's objectives. As a result, businesses not only witness a boost in productivity and innovation but also cultivate a workforce that is passionate and aligned with the company's vision.

By fostering a culture of collaboration and inclusivity, organizations can significantly enhance their operational efficiency and creative output. Such a culture positions companies as agile and forward-thinking, ready to face the complexities of the business world with resilience and creativity. By embracing these principles, businesses can secure a competitive edge, ensuring their growth and sustainability in the ever-evolving corporate landscape.

Ethical Considerations

Prioritizing ethical considerations is not just important—it's imperative. This involves a steadfast commitment to upholding ethical standards throughout the journey of technology development and deployment. These standards are fundamental, covering respect for privacy, the promotion of diversity, and the protection of human rights, ensuring that our advancements benefit society as a whole.

Transparency is a cornerstone of ethical technology use, necessitating open communication with all stakeholders about how technologies are applied and their broader societal impacts. By steadfastly adhering to these ethical principles, organizations can not only achieve their goals but also contribute significantly to societal well-being, reinforcing the importance of ethics in technological progress.

As we venture further into the realm of technological innovation, it becomes clear that maintaining ethical integrity is paramount. This requires a deliberate effort to balance the myriad benefits of technology with essential ethical considerations, ensuring that our technological advancements serve the greater good without compromising moral values.

A commitment to transparency and accountability is crucial in all facets of technology use. This approach fosters trust and ensures that all actions are in harmony with our ethical obligations, setting a standard for responsible innovation.

The true measure of success in the technological domain extends beyond the mere efficacy of solutions. It encompasses their adherence to ethical standards, demonstrating how they contribute positively to society. This holistic approach to technology development not only ensures progress but also guarantees that this progress is aligned with the values that define us as a society, paving the way for a future where technology and ethics go hand in hand.

Conclusion

Leveraging technology for a competitive edge is not just about keeping up with the latest trends or tools; it involves a deep commitment to fostering an innovative, flexible, and ethically responsible culture. This commitment means viewing technology as a catalyst for progress, always being eager to learn, and striving for continuous improvement. It also means incorporating technology into every aspect of operations to boost productivity, streamline efficiency, and elevate performance to new heights.

The strategic application of technology enables businesses and individuals alike to discover and seize new possibilities, making a substantial and positive difference in the world. By simplifying complex processes, accessing untapped markets, or crafting eco-friendly solutions, technology holds the key to significant growth and groundbreaking innovation. To fully embrace these opportunities, it's crucial to not only keep pace with technological evolution but also master the art of utilizing these advancements strategically to fulfill goals and brighten the future.

In the heart of technology lies the power to transform visions into reality, pushing the boundaries of what's possible and driving humanity forward. This transformation requires a visionary approach, where technology is not seen merely as a set of tools, but as a partner in shaping a better tomorrow. By aligning technology with our aspirations, we can unlock unparalleled potential, fostering development that is not only rapid but also sustainable.

Adopting technology with a purpose goes beyond mere implementation; it's about creating value that resonates on a global scale. Through thoughtful integration of technological innovations, we can address pressing challenges, enhance quality of life, and pave the way for a future that is prosperous for all. This journey towards technological empowerment is paved with the principles of ethical use, inclusivity, and a commitment to making a lasting impact.

As we stand on the brink of a technological renaissance, the call to action is clear: embrace technology with an open mind and a determined heart. By doing so, we can redefine the limits of possibility, inspire generations to come, and build a legacy of progress that transcends time. The future is not just about what technology can do for us, but what we can achieve together with technology as our ally, crafting a world where innovation and human values converge for the greater good.

CASE STUDIES: Harnessing Technology for Competitive Advantage

Case Study 1: Amazon's Use of Big Data and AI for Market Domination

Overview:

Amazon, a global leader in e-commerce and cloud computing, has masterfully leveraged technology to gain a competitive edge. Through the use of big data analytics and artificial intelligence (AI), Amazon has optimized every aspect of its business model, from supply chain management to customer service.

Technology Implementation:

- **Big Data Analytics:** Amazon collects vast amounts of data from its customers, including browsing history, purchase patterns, and product preferences. By analyzing this data, Amazon can predict customer behavior, tailor product recommendations, and manage inventory more efficiently.

- **AI and Machine Learning:** Amazon uses AI to enhance its operational efficiency and customer experience. Examples include the Amazon Go store, which uses computer vision and sensor fusion to allow a checkout-free shopping experience, and the Alexa virtual assistant, which provides a seamless user interface.

Results:

- **Customized Shopping Experience:** Amazon's recommendation engine, powered by AI, accounts for a significant portion of its sales by suggesting products to customers based on their browsing and purchase history.

- **Supply Chain Optimization:** Through predictive analytics, Amazon has achieved near-perfect inventory management, reducing waste and ensuring products are in stock when customers want them.

- **Market Expansion:** The technology also enables Amazon to enter new markets and sectors, such as groceries (Amazon Fresh) and healthcare (Amazon Pharmacy), with a significant competitive advantage.

Amazon's strategic use of big data and AI has not only solidified its position as a market leader but also continuously pushes the boundaries of what's possible in e-commerce and beyond.

Case Study 2: Tesla's Innovation in Electric Vehicles and Autonomous Driving

Overview:

Tesla has revolutionized the automotive industry by harnessing cutting-edge technology to produce electric vehicles (EVs) and develop autonomous driving capabilities. Its success is largely attributed to its innovative use of software and hardware technology.

Technology Implementation:

Electric Powertrain Technology: Tesla has developed high-efficiency electric motors and battery systems that outperform traditional internal combustion engines in both power and range.

Autopilot and Full Self-Driving (FSD): Utilizing advanced sensors, cameras, and AI algorithms, Tesla vehicles can navigate with minimal human intervention. Continuous software updates over-the-air (OTA) improve these systems' capabilities and safety features.

Results:

- Market Leadership in EVs: Tesla's technological advancements have made it a frontrunner in the electric vehicle market, setting standards for range, performance, and sustainability.

- Enhanced Safety and Convenience: Tesla's Autopilot and FSD features have not only improved vehicle safety but also offered unprecedented convenience to drivers, positioning Tesla as a pioneer in autonomous driving technology.

- Sustainable Energy Solutions: Beyond vehicles, Tesla's technology extends to sustainable energy products, such as solar panels and battery storage, further diversifying its competitive advantage.

Tesla's strategic focus on technology and innovation has disrupted the automotive industry, leading the transition towards sustainable transportation and autonomous driving. Its commitment to technology as a core business strategy continues to set it apart from traditional automakers.

Examples

1. **Amazon** has fundamentally altered the landscape of e-commerce by leveraging advanced logistics and technology to offer personalized shopping experiences. This has not only made shopping more convenient but also significantly increased customer satisfaction through tailored recommendations.

2. **Tesla** has revolutionized the auto industry by introducing electric vehicles that combine cutting-edge technology with sustainable energy solutions. Their commitment to autonomous driving technology is also paving the way for a future where transportation is both cleaner and safer.

3. **Netflix** has changed the way we consume media by introducing a streaming service that uses sophisticated algorithms to recommend content. This innovation has made it easier for users to discover shows and movies they love, disrupting traditional cable and broadcast models.

4. **Airbnb** has redefined the hospitality sector by creating a platform that connects travelers with unique lodging options around the world. This approach has not only expanded accommodation choices for consumers but also democratized travel by enabling people to rent out their properties.

5. **Google** has maintained its dominance in the search engine market through relentless innovation and has diversified into various sectors, including software, hardware, and cloud computing. Their continuous efforts to improve and expand their services have solidified their position as a technology leader.

Top Five Takeaways

1. **Cultivating an innovative culture** within your organization can significantly accelerate technological advancements and lead to groundbreaking solutions. This culture encourages creativity and risk-taking, which are essential for staying ahead in a competitive market.

2. **Remaining agile and adaptable** is crucial for navigating the rapidly evolving business environment effectively. Companies that can quickly respond to changes and embrace new opportunities are more likely to thrive and outperform their competitors.

3. **Enhancing the customer experience** through technology not only fosters loyalty but also drives growth by meeting and exceeding consumer expectations. Personalization and engagement through digital means can create a more connected and satisfying customer journey.

4. **Promoting collaboration and embracing** diversity of thought are key to unlocking the collective potential of your team. A varied team brings different perspectives and ideas, which can lead to more innovative solutions and a stronger competitive edge.

5. **Adhering to ethical standards** in technology development and usage is vital for building long-lasting trust and credibility with your audience. Ethical considerations should guide decision-making processes to ensure technology benefits society as a whole.

Actions to Take

1. **Investing in the continuous training** and development of your team ensures that their skills remain relevant and competitive. This commitment to professional growth can lead to more innovative ideas and keep your organization at the forefront of technological advancements.

2. **Staying open to and adopting emerging technologies** can position your company to lead rather than follow in industry disruptions. By exploring new tech trends, you can identify opportunities to enhance your products or services and create new value for your customers.

3. **Regularly assessing and upgrading your technology infrastructure** is essential for maintaining a scalable and secure operation. This proactive approach can prevent potential issues and ensure your systems can support growth and change over time.

4. **Implementing comprehensive data privacy and security policies** is crucial for protecting sensitive information and maintaining customer trust. Clear guidelines help safeguard against breaches and ensure ethical handling of data, reinforcing your commitment to stakeholders' safety.

5. **Building partnerships and seeking collaboration** with tech experts and innovative startups can provide valuable insights and access to cutting-edge technologies. These relationships can accelerate your own technological initiatives and keep you ahead of industry trends.

Actions Not to Take

1. **Neglecting cybersecurity** can expose your organization to significant risks, including data breaches and cyber attacks. Prioritizing security measures is essential for protecting your assets and maintaining trust with your customers and partners.

2. **Resisting technological change** and sticking to outdated processes can hinder your company's growth and competitiveness. Embracing innovation and remaining open to new ways of working are critical for staying relevant in today's fast-paced business environment.

3. **Ignoring customer and stakeholder feedback** on technology initiatives can lead to missed opportunities for improvement and innovation. Engaging with your audience can provide valuable insights that drive better decision-making and product development.

4. **Underestimating the importance of diversity** and inclusion within tech teams can limit your organization's creative and innovative potential. A diverse workforce brings a range of perspectives that can enhance problem-solving and lead to more effective solutions.

5. **Compromising on ethical standards** for short-term advantages can have long-lasting negative impacts on your brand and reputation. It's important to weigh the long-term consequences of decisions and strive for integrity in all your technological endeavors.

Chapter 23: Expanding into New Markets and Industries

Embarking on a journey into new markets and industries is an exhilarating adventure filled with opportunities for growth, innovation, and transformation. This daring venture marks a crucial step towards achieving unparalleled success and unlocking untapped potential. As we embark on this path, it is essential to face challenges with unwavering bravery and determination, understanding that each obstacle is a stepping stone towards our goals.

Let us approach this expedition with a spirit of adventure, fearless in our pursuit of the unknown and eager to carve out a unique path towards excellence. The thrill of navigating uncharted waters inspires us to push boundaries and redefine what is possible. This journey is not just about reaching a destination but about the discoveries and innovations we make along the way.

In the face of uncertainties and the complexities that come with exploring new territories, our resolve must remain strong. Our commitment to move forward with tenacity and resilience will guide us through. Adopting a mindset geared towards exploration and adaptability enables us to capture opportunities and tackle challenges with creativity and endurance.

As we plot our course through these unexplored realms, let's stay true to our dedication to innovation and continual growth. This commitment ensures that our voyage towards new frontiers is as rewarding as the achievements that lie ahead. The journey itself enriches us, providing invaluable experiences and insights that fuel our progress.

Let this venture be a testament to our courage, creativity, and unwavering commitment to excellence. As we venture forth, let us remember that the path to greatness is often uncharted, but with perseverance and a pioneering spirit, we can navigate any challenge and emerge victorious. Together, we will explore the vast potential of new markets and industries, paving the way for a future of endless possibilities and achievements.

Inspirational Quote

> "Success is not final, failure is not fatal: It is the courage to continue that counts." - Winston Churchill

Embrace Change

Change is not just inevitable but a powerful force for growth and development. It is the key that unlocks the door to adaptability and innovation, allowing both individuals and organizations to flourish in a world that never stands still. By welcoming change with open arms, we transform uncertainty into opportunity, fostering resilience and a forward-thinking mindset that heralds a future rich with possibilities and achievements.

Recognizing change as a fundamental aspect of existence is the first step toward harnessing its potential. This acknowledgment equips us with the courage and positivity needed to face transitions head-on, turning challenges into stepping stones for success. It encourages us to step out of our comfort zones, inviting a world of exploration and continuous improvement that propels us towards our aspirations.

By integrating change into our lives and work, we unlock a dynamic pathway to progress and excellence. This approach encourages us to question the status quo and venture into uncharted territories, sparking innovation and creativity. It is in this space of transformation that individuals and organizations find the momentum to advance, setting new benchmarks and redefining what is possible.

Embracing change is synonymous with embracing growth. It allows us to evolve with the times, ensuring we remain relevant and competitive in an ever-changing landscape. This mindset of adaptability and openness to new experiences is crucial for personal development and organizational success, laying the foundation for a thriving future.

The acceptance and embrace of change propel us towards unlocking our fullest potential. It is a catalyst for discovery, learning, and achievement, enabling us to navigate the complexities of the modern world with confidence and optimism. In embracing change, we pave the way for a future filled with unparalleled successes and innovations, ready to meet the evolving demands of our personal and professional lives.

Cultivate Innovation

Innovation stands as the cornerstone of enduring success for any organization. It fuels our ability to stand out and advance, setting us apart from our competitors and guiding us toward groundbreaking achievements. Cultivating a culture rich in innovation not only fosters creativity but also drives the continuous development necessary to excel in rapidly evolving markets and sectors. This forward-thinking mindset guarantees our position as industry leaders, consistently exceeding expectations and pushing the limits of possibility.

By embracing innovation, we secure our competitive advantage and unlock new horizons. Creating a supportive atmosphere where novel ideas flourish and experimentation is embraced, we empower our team members to transcend traditional limits. This strategy ensures our agility in adapting to new trends and technologies, establishing us as pioneers in our domain.

Incorporating innovation into the fabric of our organization is crucial for capturing new opportunities and sustaining our edge in the marketplace. It allows us to welcome and nurture groundbreaking ideas, providing the impetus for our teams to challenge the status quo. By doing so, we not only adapt rapidly to changes but also lead the way, defining the future of our industry.

Fostering a culture of innovation elevates our growth potential and reinforces our position as industry leaders. It transforms our approach, encouraging a continuous quest for improvement and the pursuit of excellence. This commitment to innovation not only propels us forward but also cements our reputation as visionaries, inspiring others to follow our lead.

Innovation is the lifeblood of any thriving organization. It is the key to unlocking unparalleled success, driving us beyond conventional boundaries and towards a horizon filled with endless possibilities. By prioritizing innovation, we not only ensure our continued relevance but also shape the future, creating a legacy of excellence and inspiration for generations to come.

Build Strong Relationships

Building strong relationships is the foundation of success in any field. It involves creating authentic connections with clients, team members, and key partners, thereby establishing a supportive network crucial for exploring new territories and industries. Emphasizing the importance of trust and camaraderie in these relationships highlights the essence of teamwork needed to tackle obstacles and achieve shared dreams.

Through dedicated efforts to nurture meaningful bonds, we create powerful alliances that serve as the backbone for enduring growth and success. These partnerships not only make way for the sharing of ideas and resources but also foster a collective determination aimed at reaching mutual objectives. Adopting a culture of cooperation allows us to leverage the combined expertise and capabilities of our allies, enabling us to navigate difficulties and capitalize on opportunities with both confidence and finesse.

Investing time and energy into building these connections pays off by opening doors to uncharted opportunities and innovative solutions. It encourages an environment where challenges are approached with a unified strategy, ensuring a higher likelihood of overcoming them. This approach reinforces the belief that together, we are stronger and more capable of making significant advancements.

Cultivating such relationships requires a commitment to openness, understanding, and mutual respect. It's about more than just networking; it's about building a community of like-minded individuals who are committed to supporting each other's successes. This spirit of collaboration is what propels individuals and organizations to new heights, fostering an atmosphere where collective achievement is celebrated.

The essence of building strong relationships lies in the recognition that our collective efforts are greater than the sum of our individual actions. This philosophy not only enhances our capacity to achieve remarkable outcomes but also enriches our journey towards them. By valuing and investing in our relationships, we pave the way for a future marked by collaboration, resilience, and shared triumphs.

Stay Agile

The key to success lies in the ability to adapt quickly to change. Organizations that champion agility are better equipped to navigate the complexities of the modern market. Adopting a flexible and creative mindset allows businesses to overcome obstacles and seize new opportunities, ensuring they stay ahead of the curve.

Agility in business is not just about speed; it's about being prepared to transform challenges into chances for advancement. By moving away from traditional, rigid practices and towards a culture that values adaptability, companies can respond to market changes with precision and innovation. This strategic flexibility is crucial for maintaining relevance and achieving long-term prosperity in a constantly changing environment.

The adoption of an agile mindset encourages a proactive approach to problem-solving and decision-making. It empowers organizations to experiment, learn from setbacks, and continuously improve. This culture of continuous evolution fosters an environment where creativity and innovation flourish, driving businesses toward unparalleled success.

Incorporating agility into the core of business operations transforms the way challenges are viewed and addressed. It shifts the focus from merely reacting to changes to actively seeking out and leveraging opportunities for growth. This forward-thinking approach ensures companies are not just surviving but thriving, making them more resilient and competitive in the global market.

The journey towards business agility is a transformative process that requires commitment, courage, and collaboration. It's about building a foundation that supports rapid adaptation, encourages innovation, and cultivates a dynamic workforce. With agility as a guiding principle, businesses can look forward to a future filled with endless possibilities, sustained growth, and lasting success.

Never Stop Learning

Valuing knowledge as our greatest treasure is essential. Our unwavering commitment to lifelong learning and perpetual self-improvement strengthens our ability to adeptly maneuver through the complexities of different industries and markets with flexibility and determination. By fostering an environment that prioritizes continual development, we set ourselves at the leading edge of breakthroughs, ready to capitalize on new opportunities and tackle obstacles with assurance.

Each obstacle encountered is an invitation to grow both personally and professionally. Viewing these challenges as stepping stones to advancement opens the door to unparalleled achievements. As we gather new insights and enhance our skills, we increase our potential to innovate, adapt, and flourish amidst the perpetual changes of our surroundings, driving both our personal growth and the progress of our organizations.

The journey of discovery is unending, and each step taken is a stride toward excellence. The pursuit of knowledge not only enriches us but also empowers us to make significant contributions to our fields. In this journey, we become architects of our destiny, sculpting a future that reflects our highest aspirations and values.

Adopting a mindset geared towards embracing challenges as opportunities enriches our professional journey with invaluable experiences. This perspective transforms obstacles into lessons that forge resilience and wisdom, key ingredients for lasting success. Through this transformative process, we become more versatile, ready to navigate the twists and turns of our careers with confidence and strategic foresight.

The essence of our professional journey is defined by our ability to remain students of life, constantly curious and eager to learn. This ethos not only propels us towards our goals but also cultivates a legacy of innovation and excellence. By committing to this path of continuous growth and learning, we pave the way for a future replete with achievements and fulfillment, both for ourselves and for the communities we serve.

Conclusion

As we embark on the exciting journey of exploring new markets and industries, it's crucial that we step forward with bravery, unwavering resolve, and a distinct vision. Embracing change and nurturing a culture of innovation places us in a prime position to adapt and thrive amidst the ever-changing business landscape, opening doors to untapped opportunities. Building and maintaining solid relationships with stakeholders and partners will play a key role in securing our presence and achieving long-term growth in these new ventures.

The ability to stay agile and responsive to the shifting dynamics of the market is essential as we tread into unknown territories. This agility allows us to quickly adapt our strategies and leverage emerging trends, ensuring we remain competitive and relevant. Moreover, a steadfast commitment to ongoing learning is vital, enabling us to stay ahead of industry developments and continually enhance our strategies to better serve our target markets.

Through dedication and a collaborative effort, we are well-equipped to navigate challenges and embrace the successes that await us. This journey is not just about expansion but about transforming our organization and setting new benchmarks in excellence. By keeping our core values at the forefront of our efforts, we are destined to make a significant impact and achieve remarkable outcomes in these new arenas.

Each step we take in this direction is a testament to our team's resilience, creativity, and forward-thinking mindset. It's an opportunity to redefine what's possible, push beyond our limits, and create a legacy that resonates within and beyond our industry. With each challenge we overcome, we grow stronger and more capable of turning visionary ideas into reality.

Let's approach this endeavor with optimism and the conviction that we have what it takes to excel. Together, we have the potential to not only reach but surpass our goals, setting a new standard for innovation and success. Our journey into new markets and industries is more than an expansion; it's a bold step toward defining the future of our organization and making a lasting impact on the world.

CASE STUDIES: Expanding into New Markets and Industries

Case Study 1: Tech Company Expanding into Health Tech

A leading technology company, originally focused on consumer electronics, recognized the growing demand for health and wellness products. Observing the increasing reliance on technology for health management, the company decided to expand into the health tech industry. This decision was fueled by the company's strategic goal to diversify its product portfolio and tap into new revenue streams.

Market Analysis:

The company conducted extensive market research to understand the health tech industry's landscape, identifying key trends such as wearable health monitors, telehealth services, and AI-driven diagnostic tools. They also analyzed consumer behavior, preferences, and the regulatory environment to ensure compliance and adoption.

Product Development:

Leveraging its expertise in consumer electronics, the company developed a line of wearable health devices that monitor vital signs, physical activity, and sleep patterns. They integrated these devices with a mobile app that uses AI to provide personalized health insights and recommendations.

Partnerships and Compliance:

Understanding the importance of credibility and trust in the health sector, the company partnered with established healthcare providers and institutions for clinical validation of their products. They also navigated the complex health regulatory landscape to ensure their products met all compliance standards.

Marketing and Distribution:

The company used a multi-channel marketing strategy targeting both consumers and healthcare professionals. They highlighted the accuracy, ease of use, and benefits of their products in improving health outcomes. Distribution channels included online platforms, retail partnerships, and direct sales to healthcare organizations.

Outcome:

The company successfully entered the health tech market, with its products receiving positive feedback for innovation and reliability. Their entry not only diversified their revenue but also positioned them as a prominent player in the health tech industry, opening doors to further innovation and market expansion.

Case Study 2: Retail Giant Venturing into Sustainable Products

A global retail giant, known for its vast product range and global presence, decided to expand into the sustainable products market. This strategic move was driven by the growing consumer demand for eco-friendly and sustainable goods across various categories, including clothing, home goods, and personal care.

Market Analysis:

The retailer conducted comprehensive analysis to understand consumer attitudes towards sustainability, identifying a significant shift towards eco-conscious buying behaviors. They also studied competitors' offerings to identify gaps and opportunities in the sustainable products market.

Product Sourcing and Development:

The retailer worked closely with suppliers and manufacturers to source sustainable materials and develop products that met strict sustainability criteria. They focused on transparency, ensuring that the sustainability claims of their products were verifiable and communicated clearly to consumers.

Supply Chain Transformation:

Recognizing the importance of sustainability across the value chain, the retailer implemented changes to their supply chain to reduce carbon footprint, enhance energy efficiency, and promote ethical labor practices. This included investing in renewable energy sources and adopting circular economy principles.

Marketing and Customer Engagement:

The retailer launched a targeted marketing campaign to promote their sustainable product line, emphasizing the environmental and social benefits of choosing sustainable products. They also engaged customers through educational content and sustainability initiatives, fostering a community of eco-conscious consumers.

Outcome:

The expansion into sustainable products was met with strong consumer support, enhancing the retailer's brand reputation and loyalty among environmentally conscious consumers. The move not only tapped into a growing market but also aligned the retailer's operations with broader sustainability goals, contributing to positive social and environmental impacts.

Both case studies illustrate how companies can successfully expand into new markets and industries by leveraging their core competencies, understanding market needs, and aligning their strategies with consumer trends and values.

Examples

1. **Amazon** has successfully branched out into various sectors, not just dominating e-commerce but also making significant strides in cloud computing through AWS. This demonstrates Amazon's strategic approach to diversification and its ambition to lead in multiple domains.

2. **Apple** stands at the forefront of innovation, constantly revolutionizing industries such as technology with its iPhones, music through iTunes, and telecommunications with its network advancements. Its success lies in not just creating products but crafting ecosystems that redefine user experiences.

3. **Tesla**, under Elon Musk's visionary leadership, has not only revolutionized the electric vehicle market but also made impactful entries into solar energy and energy storage. This expansion underscores Tesla's commitment to sustainable energy solutions and its aim to be at the center of the green energy transition.

4. **Airbnb** has transformed the hospitality sector by introducing a platform that connects homeowners with travelers, offering an alternative to traditional hotel stays. Its innovative model has reshaped how people travel, offering more personalized and unique accommodation experiences.

5. Google, initially launched as a pioneering search engine, has since diversified into a multitude of industries, including but not limited to digital advertising, cloud services, and the development of autonomous vehicles. This diversification reflects Google's ambition to innovate and lead across the tech landscape.

Top Five Takeaways

1. **Viewing change as an essential driver of growth** can pave the way for unprecedented success and development within any organization. It encourages a forward-thinking mindset that is crucial for staying relevant in today's fast-paced world.

2. **Fostering a culture that prioritizes innovation** ensures that a company remains at the cutting edge of its industry. It's about empowering employees to think creatively and pursue breakthrough ideas that can redefine the market.

3. **Developing and maintaining strong connections** with customers and stakeholders is fundamental to understanding market needs and building loyalty. These relationships are the cornerstone of any successful business, providing valuable insights and support.

4. The ability to **remain flexible and responsive to market dynamics** is a vital characteristic of resilient organizations. Agility allows businesses to navigate obstacles and capitalize on opportunities more effectively.

5. **Embracing a continuous learning** attitude opens up avenues for growth and improvement. It's about constantly seeking new knowledge and understanding emerging trends to stay ahead in the competitive landscape.

Five Actions to Take

1. Before venturing into a new market, it's critical to **conduct comprehensive research to understand the industry landscape**, competition, and customer needs. This preparation is key to identifying opportunities and avoiding costly mistakes.

2. **Investing in state-of-the-art technology** and robust infrastructure is essential for supporting expansion and ensuring operational efficiency. These investments lay the groundwork for scaling up and competing effectively in new arenas.

3. **Assembling a team with diverse skills** and perspectives is crucial for innovation and problem-solving. A talented workforce can drive a company's expansion efforts forward, navigating challenges and seizing new opportunities.

4. **Forming strategic alliances with industry leaders** and relevant stakeholders can provide valuable resources, knowledge, and market access. These partnerships can accelerate growth and enhance a company's competitive edge.

5. **Creating a detailed expansion plan** with specific, measurable objectives helps to focus efforts and track progress. A clear roadmap ensures that the expansion aligns with the company's overall vision and goals.

Five Actions Not to Take

1. **Diving into new markets without adequate planning** or research can lead to failure. It's important to understand the complexities of the market and formulate a strategic approach to mitigate risks.

2. **Ignoring the feedback of customers** and stakeholders can alienate your base and lead to missed opportunities for improvement. Listening and adapting to feedback is crucial for long-term success and customer satisfaction.

3. **Resistance to change and innovation** can stifle a company's growth and render it obsolete. Embracing innovation is essential for staying competitive and relevant in an ever-evolving market.

4. **Expanding without a focused strategy** or spreading resources too thinly can jeopardize both new and existing operations. It's vital to ensure that expansion efforts are sustainable and aligned with the company's core competencies.

5. **Underestimating the value of strong partnerships** and customer relationships can hinder growth. Building and nurturing these relationships is fundamental to expanding successfully and maintaining a competitive advantage.

Chapter 24: Scaling Your Business for Growth

Scaling a business for growth is an exhilarating journey that goes beyond merely increasing sales or expanding operations. It is a comprehensive endeavor that requires vision, determination, and strategic planning. Embracing innovation, seizing new opportunities, and adapting to the ever-changing market dynamics are essential steps on this transformative path, where each decision propels the business closer to its goals of expansion and evolution.

This exploration into the art of scaling businesses unveils the core principles and inspiring stories at the heart of sustainable growth. Through an examination of real-life success stories and the dissection of critical strategies, we aim to offer valuable insights and advice to entrepreneurs and business leaders. This journey through the nuances of growth equips you with the knowledge to navigate the complexities of scaling, blending theoretical insights with practical advice to light the way.

In the realm of business, scaling is akin to embarking on a grand voyage, requiring not just a map, but also the agility to sail through uncharted waters. It demands a balance between the courage to pursue new avenues and the wisdom to fortify your existing foundations. Every step taken is a leap towards transforming your business into a more formidable, resilient entity, capable of weathering the storms of market volatility.

We focus on the pillars of growth and the mesmerizing tales of businesses that have mastered the art of scaling. By dissecting their strategies and principles, we offer a beacon of guidance for those poised to take their enterprises to new heights. This narrative is not just about growth; it's a manifesto on building a legacy of enduring success in the competitive tapestry of today's business world.

Through this discourse, we aim to empower you with the insights and tools necessary for achieving scalable growth. By marrying theoretical concepts with actionable strategies, we illuminate the pathway for businesses to flourish and dominate in their respective domains. This is more than a guide; it's an inspiration for organizations to aim higher, pushing the boundaries of what's possible and redefining the landscape of their industries.

Inspirational Quote

"Success is not final; failure is not fatal: It is the courage to continue that counts." - Winston Churchill

Embrace Innovation

Innovation is not just a buzzword; it's the lifeline that propels organizations towards excellence and distinction in a crowded market. It begins with cultivating a vibrant ecosystem where creativity is nurtured and curiosity is celebrated, allowing every team member to feel empowered to bring their groundbreaking ideas to the table. Such an environment ensures that innovation is not just an occasional spark but a continuous flame that lights the path forward, distinguishing one company from another.

The pursuit of innovation requires an unwavering commitment to staying ahead of the curve, keenly observing emerging technologies and market dynamics. This agility in adapting to change, coupled with the willingness to revisit and refine business strategies, embodies the essence of an innovative culture. Understanding that innovation isn't confined to monumental discoveries but includes incremental advancements as well, underscores the importance of embracing change in all its forms, fostering a culture that thrives on improving every aspect of the business.

By fostering a workplace where every idea is valued and exploration is encouraged, we pave the way for innovation to flourish. This approach not only drives the organization forward but also embeds a deep-seated belief in the potential for change and growth within each employee. It's through this collective endeavor that the seeds of innovation are sown, germinating into strategies and solutions that propel the company into new heights of success.

Acknowledging the power of incremental innovation alongside groundbreaking leaps forward is crucial for sustained progress. Small enhancements, often overlooked, can lead to significant gains in efficiency, customer satisfaction, and overall competitiveness. It's this holistic view of innovation, appreciating both the big and small shifts, that can transform the way a company operates, ensuring it remains adaptable and forward-thinking in an ever-changing landscape.

Embracing innovation at every level of the organization is a testament to a company's commitment to excellence and longevity. It's a strategic choice that sets a firm foundation for growth, resilience, and a competitive edge that's hard to replicate. By championing innovation, businesses not only navigate the complexities of today's market but also light the way for the future, crafting a legacy of success that is built on the bedrock of continuous improvement and creative thinking.

Build a Strong Team

Investing in the right talent is a cornerstone of organizational excellence. When businesses focus on bringing together individuals who are not just aligned in their passion and drive but also bring a variety of skills to the table, they set the foundation for a formidable team. This diversity in talent enables the company to navigate complex challenges and capitalize on new opportunities with agility and creativity.

Nurturing a culture of collaboration is critical for unlocking the potential of every team member. Encouraging open dialogue and shared responsibility allows for a free exchange of ideas, fostering an innovative atmosphere where creativity thrives. This approach not only enhances productivity but also builds a sense of community among team members, making the workplace a breeding ground for groundbreaking ideas.

The establishment of a purpose-driven culture goes a long way in uniting the team under a common vision. When individuals understand how their work contributes to a larger mission, their motivation to succeed skyrockets. This sense of purpose binds the team together, driving them towards shared achievements and enhancing the overall performance of the organization.

Cultivating an environment where everyone feels valued and connected to the company's goals is essential for long-term success. This connection fosters a positive work atmosphere that boosts employee engagement and satisfaction. When team members feel part of something bigger, they are more likely to go above and beyond, contributing to the company's success in meaningful ways.

The key to a thriving organization lies in its people. By investing in recruitment, development, and retention of top talent, fostering a collaborative and purposeful work culture, and valuing each individual's contribution, businesses can achieve unparalleled success. This holistic approach to talent management ensures not only the achievement of organizational goals but also the development of a resilient and innovative workforce ready to face the future.

Focus on Customer Experience

Delivering unparalleled customer experiences is critical for carving out a significant market niche and nurturing enduring loyalty. Companies that excel in this realm actively listen to their customers, always aiming to exceed their expectations, thereby setting themselves apart from the competition and cultivating a devoted following. It is vital to tailor interactions by deeply understanding each customer's unique needs and desires, anticipating their demands, and offering customized solutions that resonate with real value. When customers feel truly heard and valued, they transform into powerful brand ambassadors, enthusiastically sharing their positive experiences and significantly enhancing the company's reputation.

Prioritizing customer satisfaction and engagement is a strategic move that propels an organization's brand image and cements its market position. The commitment to refining the customer experience yields significant benefits, including heightened customer loyalty, an uptick in new customer acquisitions, and expansive business growth. Through an ongoing commitment to improvement and a steadfast focus on the customer, businesses can develop profound connections with their clientele, fostering a sense of loyalty that is both rare and invaluable in today's rapidly changing business landscape.

Embracing a customer-first philosophy is not just a strategy but a culture that permeates every level of an organization. This approach not only enhances the immediate interaction but also builds a foundation for long-term relationships that support business sustainability. By investing in understanding and meeting customer needs, companies can unlock a level of engagement that transcends the ordinary, driving both immediate gains and long-term success.

In this dynamic and ever-evolving business environment, the key to thriving is not just meeting but anticipating customer needs. Innovating and adapting based on feedback ensures that businesses remain relevant and top-of-mind among their target audience. Such a proactive stance on customer experience not only solidifies a company's market position but also sets the stage for future innovations and growth.

The heart of business success lies in the ability to create and maintain happy customers. This philosophy of putting the customer at the center of everything not only drives profitability but also builds a legacy of excellence. As businesses continue to navigate the complexities of the modern marketplace, those that remain steadfast in their commitment to delivering exceptional customer experiences will undoubtedly lead the pack, achieving sustainable growth and unparalleled success.

Scale Strategically

Scaling a business is not just about growth; it's an art that requires careful planning and execution to ensure that expansion is consistent, quality is never compromised, and ethical standards are upheld. To thrive, it is essential to weave scalability into the fabric of your business, ensuring that every process, system, and piece of infrastructure is designed to handle increased demand and support growth. Emphasizing the importance of scalable revenue streams and efficient distribution channels is paramount, as these elements are the backbone of long-term profitability and the overall health of the business.

Adaptability and agility are the cornerstones of a successful scaling strategy, allowing businesses to respond to changes swiftly while staying true to their core values and mission. This balance ensures that as the business grows, it remains reliable and consistent, thereby building trust among stakeholders. It is this trust that forms the foundation of a sustainable relationship with customers, employees, and partners alike.

By prioritizing scalability and flexibility, companies can navigate the complexities of expansion with confidence. Identifying and leveraging scalable opportunities not only drives financial growth but also establishes a robust platform for enduring success. It's about creating a legacy of excellence, where financial stability and sustainable practices go hand in hand.

Staying committed to your core values and mission in the face of growth challenges is what differentiates the extraordinary from the ordinary. This commitment acts as a lighthouse, guiding your business through the rough seas of change and ensuring decisions are made with integrity and transparency. It's this unwavering dedication to what you stand for that fosters a culture of trust and reliability, crucial for thriving in today's dynamic business environment.

Scaling a business is a journey of strategic growth, adaptability, and unwavering commitment to core principles. By focusing on scalable solutions and staying agile, businesses can embrace expansion while maintaining a strong ethical foundation. Remember, the goal is not just to grow, but to grow wisely, ensuring a legacy of success that is both profitable and principled.

Cultivate Resilience

In the pursuit of success, the road is often paved with challenges that test our resolve and endurance. These obstacles, though daunting at first glance, are the very experiences that sculpt our character and amplify our resilience. Viewing each stumbling block as a catalyst for personal growth allows us to transform adversity into a powerful driver of progress, building a foundation of strength that supports us in all our endeavors.

Every setback encountered along the way should be regarded not as a signal of defeat but as a temporary detour towards our ultimate destination. The true measure of success lies in our response to these challenges—the way we adapt, learn from our mistakes, and persist with unwavering determination. This mindset of relentless pursuit and adaptation is what carves the path to achievement and the realization of our dreams.

Maintaining a positive outlook is essential in the face of setbacks, as it enables us to approach problems with creativity and resilience. Instead of being deterred by obstacles, we learn to navigate around them, finding innovative solutions that propel us forward. This proactive stance not only brings us closer to our goals but also enriches our journey with invaluable lessons and experiences.

The resilience to overcome hurdles is fueled by the belief in our potential and the vision of what lies ahead. It requires a steadfast commitment to progress, even when the path seems unclear. By embracing each challenge as an opportunity to learn and grow, we inch closer to our aspirations, fortified by the knowledge and strength gained along the way.

The journey to success is a testament to the human spirit's capacity to overcome. It is a narrative of personal evolution, where each obstacle surmounted adds a chapter of triumph and wisdom. By viewing setbacks as stepping stones, we not only achieve our goals but also emerge as more resilient, knowledgeable, and determined individuals, ready to face the next challenge with confidence.

Conclusion

To scale a business for growth, it's crucial to embrace the journey of continuous learning, adapting, and evolving. This means keeping a keen eye on market trends, understanding consumer preferences, and integrating emerging technologies into your business model. Encouraging a culture of innovation within your team allows for the exploration of new ideas, products, and services, ensuring you remain a step ahead in a competitive landscape.

Building a strong, diverse team is fundamental to the successful execution of growth strategies. A team that brings together varied skills and perspectives can approach challenges more creatively and efficiently, driving your business towards its growth objectives. This collaborative environment is the bedrock of innovation, enabling your organization to navigate the complexities of scaling with confidence and agility.

Customer satisfaction should be at the heart of your growth strategy. Happy customers not only provide repeat business but also act as advocates for your brand, attracting new clients through word-of-mouth. A strategic approach to scaling involves setting clear objectives, prioritizing initiatives that drive the most value, and smartly allocating resources to areas with the highest impact.

Resilience plays a key role in the growth trajectory of any business. The path to scaling is fraught with challenges and setbacks, but with resilience, adaptability, and perseverance, these obstacles become stepping stones towards your goals. Cultivating a resilient mindset within your organization ensures that your team can bounce back from setbacks stronger and more determined.

The journey of scaling a business is a testament to the power of persistence and strategic planning. By staying committed to learning, innovation, and customer satisfaction, while building a resilient and diverse team, your business is well-equipped to navigate the challenges of growth. This approach not only propels your business forward but also establishes a strong foundation for sustained success and leadership in your industry.

CASE STUDIES: Scaling Your Business for Growth

Case Study 1: Tech Startup - Rapid Scaling Through Strategic Partnerships

Background:

A tech startup, specializing in cloud-based project management tools, faced intense competition in a rapidly evolving market. The company had a robust product but needed to scale quickly to capture market share and sustain growth.

Challenge:

The startup struggled to reach a broad customer base due to limited marketing resources and brand recognition. The leadership team realized that without rapid expansion, the company risked being overshadowed by larger competitors.

Strategy for Scaling:

- **Strategic Partnerships:** The company identified potential partners with established customer bases that complemented their product. This included collaborations with larger tech firms, consultancy agencies, and educational institutions to bundle their project management tool with existing services or products.

- **Channel Sales Strategy:** Instead of relying solely on direct sales, the startup developed a channel sales strategy, allowing them to tap into the sales forces of their partners, thus expanding their reach without the need for a large in-house sales team.

- **Enhancing Product Value:** The company continuously improved its product based on feedback from partners and end-users, adding new features and integrations that broadened its appeal.

Outcome:

The strategic partnerships allowed the startup to rapidly scale its user base, leveraging the brand strength and customer networks of its partners. Sales and market penetration increased significantly, with the company securing a solid position in the market. The enhanced product value, combined with the credibility gained through partnerships, led to a sustainable growth trajectory.

Case Study 2: E-commerce Platform - Leveraging Technology for Scalable Growth

Background:

An emerging e-commerce platform was gaining traction but needed to scale operations to handle growing demand and diversify its product offerings to stay competitive.

Challenge: The platform faced operational bottlenecks, such as inventory management, fulfillment processes, and customer service limitations, which hindered its ability to scale efficiently.

Strategy for Scaling:

- **Technology-Driven Operations:** The platform invested in advanced inventory and logistics management software to automate and streamline operations. This technology allowed for real-time inventory tracking, predictive analytics for demand forecasting, and efficient order fulfillment processes.

- **AI and Machine Learning:** To enhance customer experience and operational efficiency, the platform implemented AI-driven chatbots for customer service and machine learning algorithms for personalized product recommendations, significantly improving customer satisfaction and loyalty.

- **Marketplace Expansion:** The platform expanded its marketplace model by inviting third-party sellers to offer their products, increasing the variety of available products without the need for physical inventory. This strategy also included rigorous vetting processes to ensure product quality and seller reliability.

Outcome:

The adoption of advanced technology and the marketplace expansion strategy enabled the e-commerce platform to scale its operations and product offerings rapidly. Operational efficiencies reduced costs and delivery times, enhancing customer satisfaction and repeat business. The platform saw a substantial increase in sales volume and revenue, establishing itself as a competitive force in the e-commerce space.

Both case studies illustrate the importance of strategic planning, leveraging technology, and partnerships in scaling a business for growth. While the approaches differ based on industry and specific challenges, the core principle remains: adaptability and strategic innovation are key to successfully scaling a business.

Examples

1. **Amazon**, a global powerhouse, has established itself as a leader in the online retail space, offering an expansive array of products and services that cater to virtually every need and desire. Its foray into technology, with developments like Alexa and Prime, has fundamentally altered the landscape of e-commerce and cloud computing, enhancing customer experiences through unparalleled convenience and efficiency.

2. **Google** stands as a titan in the tech industry, its name becoming synonymous with internet searches and a gateway to digital exploration. By offering an extensive suite of services, including Gmail, Google Maps, and YouTube, and venturing into advanced fields like artificial intelligence and quantum computing, Google is redefining how we gather information and engage with the online world, continuously expanding the horizons of technological possibility.

3. **Apple**, a symbol of innovation and elegance in technology, has captivated consumers worldwide with its array of sophisticated products such as the iPhone, iPad, and Mac computers. It emphasizes design and user interaction, crafting ecosystems that merge hardware, software, and services into a seamless experience, thus setting a benchmark for style and functionality in the tech industry.

4. **Airbnb** has revolutionized the way we think about travel and accommodation, making it possible for homeowners to offer their spaces to guests from around the world. This platform not only provides a wide selection of places to stay but also enables personalized experiences, fostering connections between hosts and travelers and encouraging the exploration of new cultures and destinations in a more intimate and unique manner.

5. **Tesla** is driving the future of transportation with its commitment to electric vehicles and sustainable energy. By pioneering advancements in battery technology and self-driving cars, Tesla is not just changing the automotive landscape but is also leading the charge towards a more sustainable future, promoting the adoption of clean energy and redefining mobility for generations to come.

Top Five Takeaways

1. **Foster a Culture of Innovation and Creativity:** Encourage an environment where new ideas are valued and creativity thrives, enabling your organization to stay ahead in competitive markets. This approach not only sparks innovation but also attracts forward-thinking individuals who are eager to contribute to groundbreaking projects.

2. **Invest in Recruiting, Developing, and Retaining Top Talent:** Dedicate resources to finding and nurturing the best talent, recognizing that the strength of your team is a critical driver of success. By investing in your employees' growth, you ensure the long-term vitality and competitiveness of your business.

3. **Prioritize Exceptional Customer Experience at Every Touchpoint:** Ensure that every interaction with your company is positive and memorable, from initial contact through post-purchase support. This commitment to excellence in customer service builds loyalty and encourages word-of-mouth referrals.

4. **Scale Strategically by Prioritizing Scalability and Adaptability:** Plan for growth by developing processes and infrastructure that can expand as your business does. Adapting swiftly to market changes and scaling intelligently are key to sustainable success and avoiding the pitfalls of overexpansion.

5. **Cultivate Resilience by Viewing Setbacks as Opportunities for Growth:** Embrace challenges and failures as chances to learn and improve. This mindset fosters resilience, ensuring that your organization can navigate through difficulties and emerge stronger on the other side.

Five Actions to Take

1. **Conduct Regular Brainstorming Sessions to Foster Innovation**: Organize frequent brainstorming meetings to encourage creative thinking and idea generation among your team. This practice not only leads to innovative solutions but also fosters a collaborative culture that values each member's contributions.

2. **Invest in Ongoing Training and Development Programs for Employees:** Commit to the continuous professional growth of your employees through education and skill-building opportunities. Such investments not only enhance individual capabilities but also strengthen the overall expertise of your organization.

3. **Implement a Robust Customer Feedback Mechanism to Gather Insights:** Establish a system for collecting and analyzing customer feedback to better understand their needs and preferences. This information is invaluable for refining your offerings and improving customer satisfaction.

4. **Develop a Scalable Business Model That Can Accommodate Growth:** Design your business model with scalability in mind, ensuring that you can efficiently manage increased demand without compromising on quality or service. This strategic planning is essential for smooth transitions during growth phases.

5. **Cultivate a Resilient Mindset Through Mindfulness Practices or Coaching:** Encourage resilience among your team members through mindfulness or professional coaching, helping them to maintain focus and positivity in the face of challenges. This not only aids personal development but also contributes to a supportive and adaptable organizational culture.

Five Actions Not to Take

1. **Neglecting to Invest in Employee Development and Retention:** Avoid overlooking the importance of nurturing and keeping your talent, as doing so can weaken your team's morale and performance. Employees are your most valuable asset, and their growth directly impacts your company's success.

2. **Ignoring Customer Feedback or Failing to Address Customer Concerns:** Do not disregard the insights and experiences of your customers. Ignoring feedback can lead to dissatisfaction and erode trust in your brand, ultimately affecting your bottom line.

3. **Scaling Too Quickly Without Proper Planning or Infrastructure:** Resist the temptation to expand rapidly without ensuring the necessary systems and processes are in place. Premature scaling can strain resources and lead to operational failures that are difficult to recover from.

4. **Losing Sight of Your Core Values and Mission in Pursuit of Growth:** Always remember the principles and goals that define your organization. Sacrificing your core values for short-term gains can damage your reputation and alienate your stakeholders.

5. **Allowing Setbacks or Failures to Derail Your Long-term Vision and Goals:** Do not let temporary obstacles discourage you or alter your strategic direction. Maintaining focus on your long-term objectives is crucial for overcoming challenges and achieving lasting success.

Chapter 25: Nurturing a Culture of Continuous Improvement

One often faces the formidable challenge of continuous advancement. It demands a deep-seated commitment to cultivating an environment where improvement is not just encouraged but becomes a way of life. This culture transcends simple actions, embedding itself into our very essence and equipping us with the mindset needed to forge ahead, even when faced with adversity.

Acknowledging every step forward, no matter how small, is pivotal in our journey toward excellence. These strides, each unique in their contribution, collectively pave the way to greatness. They serve as reminders that progress, in its many forms, is both valuable and attainable, pushing us to strive for more in all facets of life.

The principle of continuous improvement calls for unwavering dedication and resilience. It's about understanding that growth is an endless journey, characterized by incremental advancements that, while seemingly modest, are incredibly impactful. This perspective not only steels us against challenges but also transforms obstacles into springboards for learning and evolution.

Cultivating a growth mindset is crucial for individuals and organizations alike, as it empowers them to approach hurdles with grit and perseverance. Viewing setbacks as opportunities for development teaches us to embrace the learning process, refining our approach with each lesson learned. This mindset lays the foundation for a path brimming with success, guiding us closer to our highest aspirations.

The commitment to continuous improvement is what fuels our progress and drives us toward achieving our full potential. It's a journey marked by the constant pursuit of betterment, inspiring us to reach beyond our current capabilities and embrace the endless possibilities that await. In this endeavor, our resilience, dedication, and the lessons we gather along the way become our most valuable assets, propelling us forward into a future of limitless potential.

Inspirational Quote

"Excellence is not a destination; it is a continuous journey that never ends." - Brian Tracy

Embracing Change

Change is a relentless force that propels us toward growth and new horizons. It stands as the cornerstone of advancement, urging both individuals and organizations to stretch their boundaries and embrace innovation. By welcoming change, we acknowledge its power to reshape our lives, offering us the chance to refine and enhance our journey.

It takes a bold heart and an open mind to embrace the winds of change. This journey demands not just acknowledgment of change's inevitability but also the courage to face the unknown with resilience and optimism. As we step out of our comfort zones, we are met with unparalleled opportunities to grow, learn, and conquer the challenges that lie ahead, paving the way to unlocking our utmost potential in an ever-changing landscape.

On the flip side, resistance to change can anchor us to a state of complacency, causing us to miss out on invaluable opportunities for personal and professional growth. However, those who welcome change with optimism and readiness are the ones who find themselves ahead, navigating the currents of an ever-transforming world with grace. It's about shifting our perspective to see change not as an obstacle but as a gateway to endless possibilities.

Adopting a positive stance towards change requires a transformation in how we perceive our circumstances. It's about cultivating a spirit of adaptability and determination that empowers us to use change as a stepping stone toward achieving our ambitions. This proactive approach to embracing change not only helps us to accept the inevitability of transformation but also to seek out and utilize these moments as catalysts for personal and professional evolution.

Embracing change, therefore, is more than a passive acceptance; it's an active pursuit of growth. It invites us to continually seek ways to leverage the transformative power of change, ensuring that we remain agile, forward-thinking, and fully prepared to thrive in dynamic environments. By doing so, individuals and organizations alike can not only adapt to the ever-evolving landscape but also lead the charge toward innovation and success.

Cultivating a Growth Mindset

At the heart of continuous improvement and success lies the growth mindset, a powerful belief in the potential for personal and professional evolution. This mindset embraces the idea that through dedication and effort, one's abilities and intelligence can expand, leading to a proactive pursuit of development. It encourages facing challenges head-on, seeking out feedback for growth, and learning from every setback, making it a cornerstone for those aiming to enhance their capabilities.

Adopting a growth mindset propels individuals onto a path of self-improvement filled with excitement and resilience. It transforms the way challenges are perceived, seeing them not as barriers but as stepping stones to greater knowledge and skill. This approach fosters a culture of continuous learning and adaptability, ensuring that setbacks are not endpoints but opportunities for reflection and growth.

To nurture a growth mindset, it's crucial to engage in practices that affirm this perspective. Viewing obstacles as chances to grow, welcoming constructive criticism as fuel for progress, and committing to lifelong learning are key strategies. These actions reinforce the belief in one's ability to develop and thrive, laying the groundwork for achieving remarkable personal and professional milestones.

Embracing a growth mindset means stepping into a journey of self-enhancement with eagerness and determination. This journey is not just about reaching a destination but about valuing the process of growth itself. It enables individuals to unlock their fullest potential and navigate the path to their ambitions with confidence and agility.

Cultivating a growth mindset is about more than just personal gain; it's about contributing to a culture of perseverance, innovation, and resilience. By embodying this mindset, individuals not only elevate their own lives but also inspire those around them to embark on their own journeys of continuous improvement. This shared commitment to growth fosters a community where challenges are embraced, feedback is valued, and every setback is viewed as a lesson, paving the way for a future of collective success and fulfillment.

Fostering Collaboration

At the core of exceptional achievement lies the power of collaboration. It's understood that no one person can reach the pinnacle of success alone. Fostering an atmosphere where teamwork is prized and the exchange of ideas is encouraged creates a fertile ground for collective triumphs. This environment enables individuals to not only bring their unique talents and viewpoints to the table but also to gain from the group's shared knowledge, paving the way for more creative solutions and stronger results.

The synergy of diverse talents within a team, guided by a common purpose, unlocks unparalleled potential and leads to remarkable achievements. Collaboration is the key to tapping into the full spectrum of a team's capabilities and realizing ambitious aspirations. When people come together in a spirit of harmony, they can use their combined strengths to navigate obstacles and seize opportunities with greater efficiency.

A culture of collaboration brings about a deep sense of community and mutual support, enhancing the commitment and enthusiasm of all team members. This sense of unity and shared purpose is vital for sustaining high levels of motivation and engagement across the organization. It's through this spirit of collective endeavor that teams can achieve far beyond what individuals could accomplish on their own.

Embracing collaboration as a foundational value is crucial for maximizing a team's potential and achieving lofty goals. By working in concert, individuals can leverage their distinct abilities to surmount challenges and make the most of opportunities more effectively. Moreover, a collaborative ethos nurtures a feeling of belonging and mutual aid, boosting the overall morale and drive within the team.

By making collaboration a core principle, organizations can create a dynamic and welcoming environment where everyone is encouraged to contribute to mutual successes. This approach not only enriches the work experience for each team member but also propels the organization towards its objectives with renewed vigor and creativity. Through the collective efforts of its people, an organization can achieve extraordinary outcomes and set new standards of excellence.

Encouraging Innovation

Innovation stands as the cornerstone of progress and a critical factor for maintaining competitiveness. It's essential to nurture an environment that encourages creative thinking and allows for continuous experimentation. By equipping individuals with the necessary resources, steadfast support, and the freedom to experiment, we lay the groundwork for groundbreaking ideas and novel solutions to emerge.

The act of embracing calculated risks is a testament to the commitment towards innovation, guiding us into unexplored territories and beyond the confines of conventional wisdom. This adventurous spirit is crucial for unearthing innovative solutions that tackle complex challenges head-on. It's through this bold exploration that we uncover new paths to success, demonstrating the transformative power of innovation in overcoming obstacles.

Providing the right tools and fostering a conducive atmosphere for innovation empowers individuals to excel and bring their diverse insights to the forefront. This strategy not only ignites creativity but also instills a deep sense of ownership and pride in their contributions. The ripple effect of this empowerment is a vibrant culture of innovation, where every member feels valued and motivated to push the boundaries.

Incorporating innovation as a foundational principle is essential for driving growth and ensuring resilience in an ever-changing landscape. It's the organizations and communities that place a premium on creativity and experimentation that lead the charge in making significant breakthroughs. These pioneers set the stage for a future marked by remarkable advancements and enduring prosperity.

By fostering a culture that places a high value on innovation, we are paving the way for a brighter, more sustainable future. This commitment to nurturing creativity and encouraging experimentation is what propels us forward, ensuring that we remain adaptable and thrive amidst the complexities of the modern world. In embracing this ethos, we unlock the potential for extraordinary achievements and set a new standard for excellence in every endeavor.

Celebrating Progress

Creating a culture of celebration within any organization is a cornerstone of fostering an environment where every achievement, no matter its size, is valued. When we take the time to recognize every win, from the monumental to the minor, we create a vibrant atmosphere that honors dedication and hard work. This act of acknowledgment, whether it's for an individual's effort or a team's success, not only elevates morale but also cements a sense of unity and collaborative spirit among colleagues.

By celebrating achievements, we send a clear message: perseverance and commitment are essential components of success. Highlighting these milestones encourages employees to stay driven and passionate about their roles. This cycle of positive reinforcement doesn't just boost job satisfaction; it also fosters a mindset geared towards growth, viewing every challenge as a stepping stone for further development and learning.

The power of recognizing accomplishments extends beyond mere motivation. It acts as a beacon, inspiring both individuals and teams to aim for excellence and continuous improvement. In an environment where every effort is celebrated, the drive to exceed expectations and push boundaries becomes ingrained in the organization's culture. This commitment to excellence is what sets apart thriving organizations from the rest.

Moreover, the act of celebrating progress is a testament to the value of hard work and dedication. It reinforces the belief that with persistence and commitment, any goal is achievable. This not only keeps employees engaged and motivated but also instills a sense of pride in their work and the contributions they make towards the organization's success.

Fostering a culture of celebration within an organization is instrumental in building a foundation of recognition, appreciation, and continuous advancement. Celebrating wins, regardless of their size, cultivates a positive and motivating environment that encourages growth, learning, and excellence. This approach not only enhances job satisfaction and team cohesion but also propels the organization towards achieving its vision and goals in an atmosphere ripe with opportunity and recognition.

Conclusion

Embracing change and nurturing a mindset geared towards growth stand as crucial pillars. By opening ourselves to new challenges and seizing opportunities to evolve, we can transcend our current limitations and tap into our latent potential. This journey is further enriched by creating an inclusive space where different viewpoints are not just heard but celebrated, fostering innovation and enabling us to solve complex problems in novel ways.

Organizations that dedicate themselves to continuous learning and celebrate each step forward set the stage for extraordinary achievements. Encouraging a culture of experimentation, where lessons are drawn from every outcome, empowers a team to navigate the ever-changing business landscape with agility and confidence. This ethos of perpetual improvement paves the way for both individuals and companies to reach new heights of success and make a lasting impact.

By fostering an environment where growth is at the forefront, individuals can unlock a world of possibilities. This commitment to development not only propels us forward but also inspires those around us to strive for their best. In turn, this collective ambition can drive remarkable progress and innovation, making what once seemed insurmountable within reach.

The path to realizing our dreams and contributing meaningfully to society is built on the foundation of adaptability and continuous learning. By valuing diverse insights and encouraging risk-taking, we can break new ground and achieve breakthroughs that redefine what's possible. This journey of growth and discovery is not just about reaching a destination but about shaping a legacy of resilience, creativity, and collaboration.

The journey towards fulfillment and success is a continuous loop of embracing change, learning, and collaboration. By adopting a growth mindset and fostering an environment that celebrates diversity and innovation, we unlock endless opportunities for personal and professional development. This approach not only elevates individual potential but also propels organizations to achieve unparalleled success, leaving a positive mark on the world.

CASE STUDIES: Nurturing a Culture of Continuous Improvement

Case Study 1: Toyota - Embracing the Kaizen Method

Background:

Toyota, the global automotive leader, has long been celebrated for its approach to continuous improvement, primarily through the implementation of the Kaizen method. Kaizen, a Japanese term meaning "change for the better," focuses on the philosophy of continuous, incremental improvement and is a cornerstone of Toyota's corporate culture.

Implementation:

At Toyota, Kaizen is more than just a productivity tool; it's a way of life. The company encourages all employees, from assembly line workers to top management, to engage in problem-solving and to contribute ideas that enhance efficiency, quality, and worker satisfaction. This approach is operationalized through regular team meetings, suggestion systems, and continuous training programs. Employees are trained to identify "muda" (waste) and are empowered to suggest ways to eliminate it.

Results:

The implementation of Kaizen at Toyota has led to significant improvements in production efficiency, quality, and employee satisfaction. For example, small, continuous improvements have allowed Toyota to reduce production times and minimize inventory, thereby reducing costs and increasing profitability. Moreover, by involving employees in the decision-making process, Toyota has fostered a sense of ownership and accountability, leading to higher job satisfaction and lower turnover rates.

Key Takeaways:

Toyota's success with Kaizen illustrates the importance of fostering a culture that values continuous improvement. Key factors include employee empowerment, ongoing training, and leadership commitment to the philosophy.

Case Study 2: General Electric - Implementing Six Sigma

Background:

General Electric (GE), one of the largest and most diversified conglomerates, adopted Six Sigma in the mid-1990s. Six Sigma is a data-driven approach and methodology for eliminating defects in any process, from manufacturing to transactional and from product to service.

Implementation:

Under the leadership of then-CEO Jack Welch, GE embarked on an ambitious plan to train its employees in Six Sigma principles. Welch recognized the importance of quality as a competitive edge and mandated Six Sigma training for all technical employees. This initiative was known as "Quality is Job 1." GE implemented various Six Sigma tools, such as DMAIC (Define, Measure, Analyze, Improve, Control), to identify and remove causes of defects and minimize variability in manufacturing and business processes.

Results:

GE reported multibillion-dollar savings as a result of its Six Sigma initiatives. Beyond financial gains, Six Sigma helped GE improve customer satisfaction by enhancing the quality and reliability of its products and services. The initiative also played a crucial role in shaping GE's culture, making quality improvement and efficiency top priorities for all employees.

Key Takeaways:

GE's experience with Six Sigma demonstrates the power of a structured, data-driven approach to continuous improvement. Critical success factors include top-down commitment, comprehensive training, and integration of quality improvement measures into the company's culture.

Conclusion:

Both Toyota and GE demonstrate that nurturing a culture of continuous improvement requires a clear strategy, dedicated leadership, and the involvement of all employees. While the specific tools and methodologies may differ, the underlying principles of employee empowerment, customer focus, and ongoing learning are universal.

Examples

1. **Toyota** is widely recognized for its revolutionary Toyota Production System, which places a strong emphasis on kaizen, or continuous improvement, as a core principle. This approach has not only transformed manufacturing practices worldwide but also serves as a benchmark for operational excellence in various industries.

2. **Elon Musk** has become synonymous with cutting-edge innovation, through his leadership at companies like SpaceX and Tesla, where he challenges conventional thinking and drives advancements in space exploration and electric vehicles. His visionary approach has catalyzed significant breakthroughs, reshaping industries and inspiring a new generation of entrepreneurs.

3. **Carol Dweck's** groundbreaking work on the growth mindset has illuminated the power of believing in the ability to develop skills and intelligence through effort and perseverance. Her research emphasizes that embracing challenges and learning from failures are crucial steps toward achieving one's full potential.

4. **Google** has institutionalized innovation by allowing its employees to dedicate 20% of their working time to pursue projects they are passionate about. This policy has led to the development of some of Google's most successful products and services, underlining the importance of personal interest and autonomy in driving creativity.

5. **Mahatma Gandhi** exemplified the principle of continuous improvement through his lifelong dedication to nonviolent resistance and social reform. His philosophy and actions have left a lasting legacy, demonstrating that persistent, peaceful efforts can lead to profound social change and justice.

Top Five Takeaways

1. **Viewing change as an** opportunity rather than a threat is essential for growth and development. This perspective encourages adaptability and resilience in the face of new challenges and environments.

2. **Developing a growth mindset**, as highlighted by Carol Dweck, enables individuals to see challenges as opportunities to learn and improve, rather than insurmountable obstacles. This approach fosters perseverance and innovation.

3. **Successful collaboration** brings together diverse perspectives and skills, significantly enhancing the potential for achieving shared goals. It creates a synergistic environment where collective efforts lead to greater accomplishments.

4. **Encouraging creativity and innovation** is pivotal for progress and staying competitive. By valuing and nurturing new ideas, organizations can break new ground and lead in their respective fields.

5. **Celebrating each milestone and progress**, no matter how small, reinforces a culture of positivity and continuous improvement. It motivates individuals and teams to maintain momentum and strive for excellence.

Five Actions to Take

1. **Setting specific, measurable goals** provides direction and focus for continuous improvement efforts. It helps individuals and teams to align their actions with broader organizational objectives.

2. **Providing consistent feedback and support** is crucial for fostering a culture of growth and learning. It ensures that individuals and teams feel valued and understood, facilitating their development and engagement.

3. **Creating a culture that encourages taking risks** and experimenting with new ideas is essential for innovation. This environment allows individuals to explore possibilities without fear of failure, leading to breakthroughs and advancements.

4. **Acknowledging and rewarding contributions** to continuous improvement not only boosts morale but also reinforces the value placed on innovation and progress within the organization.

5. **Leading by example** and demonstrating a personal commitment to growth and development inspires others to adopt similar values. It establishes a leadership model that promotes a culture of continuous improvement and excellence.

Five Actions Not to Take

1. **Resisting change** and clinging to outdated practices can stifle growth and innovation. It's important to remain open and flexible, adapting to new information and circumstances.

2. **Dismissing feedback or constructive criticism** closes off opportunities for improvement and learning. Valuing diverse perspectives and being open to feedback are key components of a growth-oriented culture.

3. **Stifling creativity and discouraging new ideas** can prevent the discovery of novel solutions and innovations. Encouraging a free exchange of ideas supports a dynamic and forward-thinking environment.

4. **Neglecting to recognize and celebrate achievements** can demotivate individuals and teams, making it harder to maintain momentum in continuous improvement efforts.

5. **Allowing complacency to take root** undermines the drive for progress and excellence. It's crucial to continuously seek ways to improve and challenge the status quo to foster a vibrant and dynamic organizational culture.

Epilog

In the epilogue of "Unlocking Excellence," we reflect on the journey embarked upon by both the readers and the characters within the book's narrative. As we conclude this enlightening exploration into the realms of business, entrepreneurship, and leadership, it's crucial to pause and acknowledge the profound lessons learned and the transformative insights gained.

Throughout these pages, we've delved into the intricacies of strategic planning, innovation, and adaptability, learning that success in business often hinges on the ability to navigate uncertain terrain with resilience and determination. We've witnessed the triumphs and tribulations of visionary leaders who dared to challenge the status quo and carve their paths to success through sheer perseverance and unwavering commitment to their goals.

Yet, amidst the tales of triumph, we've also encountered moments of failure and setbacks—essential reminders that the path to mastery is paved with obstacles and hurdles. However, it is in these moments of adversity that true resilience is forged, and invaluable lessons are learned. As we bid farewell to the characters we've come to admire and the stories that have inspired us, let us carry forward the wisdom gleaned from their experiences into our own endeavors.

As the final chapter of this book draws to a close, it's essential to recognize that true success in business extends beyond mere financial gain. It encompasses integrity, ethics, and a commitment to making a positive impact on the world around us. Whether it's through fostering inclusive workplaces, championing sustainability initiatives, or giving back to our communities, the mark of a truly successful business lies in its ability to create value beyond the bottom line.

In closing, let us remember that the journey towards mastering success is an ongoing pursuit—one that requires continuous learning, growth, and adaptation. As we turn the last page of this book, let it serve as a catalyst for our own aspirations and ambitions, igniting within us the drive to pursue excellence in all our endeavors. And so, as we step boldly into the future, may we carry with us the lessons learned from these pages, empowering us to thrive in the ever-evolving landscape of business and beyond.

Glossary of Terms

These terms are fundamental to understanding the financial and operational aspects of a business and are used regularly in the corporate world.

1. **Account Payable:** The amount a company owes to its suppliers or vendors for goods and services purchased on credit.
2. **Account Receivable:** The amount of money owed to a business by its customers for goods or services provided on credit.
3. **Asset:** Anything of value owned by a business, including cash, inventory, property, equipment, and intangible assets like patents or trademarks.
4. **Assets:** The total resources owned by a company, which can be categorized as current assets, fixed assets, and intangible assets.
5. **Audit Committee:** A subgroup of a company's board of directors responsible for overseeing financial reporting and disclosure processes.
6. **Auditor:** An independent professional who examines and verifies a company's financial records to ensure accuracy and compliance with regulations.
7. **Balance Sheet:** A financial statement that provides a snapshot of a company's financial position by listing its assets, liabilities, and shareholders' equity at a specific point in time.
8. **Board of Directors:** A group of individuals elected by shareholders to oversee the management of a corporation and make major decisions on their behalf.
9. **Budget:** A financial plan that outlines expected revenues and expenses over a specific period, typically one year, to help guide decision-making and control spending.
10. **Business Sectors:** Different segments of the economy where businesses operate, such as technology, healthcare, finance, and retail.
11. **Capital:** Financial resources used to start, operate, or expand a business, including funds raised from investors or generated through earnings.
12. **Capitalization Table:** A document that outlines the ownership structure of a company, including the distribution of shares among shareholders and any outstanding equity or securities.

13. **Cash Conversion Cycle:** The time it takes for a company to convert its investments in inventory and other resources into cash flow from sales.

14. **Cash Flow:** The movement of money in and out of a business, including cash inflows from sales and cash outflows for expenses, investments, and financing activities.

15. **CFO (Chief Financial Officer):** The senior executive responsible for managing a company's financial operations, including financial planning, reporting, and risk management.

16. **C-Level Executive:** Senior executives in a company, typically including the CEO, CFO, COO (Chief Operating Officer), and CTO (Chief Technology Officer), who hold top management positions.

17. **Debt:** Money borrowed by a company from lenders or creditors, which must be repaid with interest over a specified period.

18. **Depreciation:** The gradual decrease in the value of an asset over time due to wear and tear, obsolescence, or other factors.

19. **EBITDA:** Earnings Before Interest, Taxes, Depreciation, and Amortization, a measure of a company's profitability that provides insight into its operational performance.

20. **Economies of Scale:** Cost advantages gained by a company when it increases its scale of production, leading to lower average costs per unit.

21. **Fiscal Year:** A 12-month accounting period used by a company for financial reporting and budgeting purposes, which may or may not coincide with the calendar year.

22. **Forecast:** An estimate or projection of future financial performance based on current data, trends, and assumptions.

23. **Goodwill:** The intangible value attributed to a company's reputation, brand, customer relationships, and other factors that contribute to its overall worth.

24. **Gross Margin:** The difference between a company's revenue and the cost of goods sold, expressed as a percentage of revenue, indicating its profitability before operating expenses.

25. **HR (Human Resources):** The department within a company responsible for managing employee-related matters, including recruitment, training, compensation, and benefits.

26. **Industries:** Broad categories of businesses grouped based on similar products, services, or activities, such as manufacturing, transportation, hospitality, and telecommunications.

27. **Inflation:** A sustained increase in the general price level of goods and services in an economy over time, reducing the purchasing power of money.

28. **Interest Rate:** The cost of borrowing money or the return on investment earned on savings or investments, expressed as a percentage.

29. **Internal Rate of Return (IRR):** A financial metric used to evaluate the profitability of an investment by calculating the discount rate that makes the net present value of future cash flows equal to zero.

30. **Investment Bank:** A financial institution that assists companies and governments in raising capital by underwriting or acting as an intermediary in issuing securities, such as stocks and bonds.

31. **Investor:** An individual or institution that provides capital to a business or investment opportunity with the expectation of receiving a return on their investment.

32. **Inventory:** The goods and materials held by a business for resale or use in production, including raw materials, work-in-progress, and finished goods.

33. **Joint Venture:** A business arrangement in which two or more parties collaborate to undertake a specific project or venture, sharing risks, resources, and profits.

34. **Key Performance Indicator (KPI):** Quantifiable metrics used to evaluate the success or performance of a business, department, or individual against predefined goals or objectives.

35. **Lenders:** Individuals or institutions that provide loans or credit to borrowers, expecting repayment with interest over a specified period.

36. **Leverage:** The use of borrowed funds or financial instruments to increase the potential return on investment, amplifying both gains and losses.

37. **Liabilities:** Financial obligations or debts owed by a company to creditors, suppliers, or other parties, including loans, accounts payable, and accrued expenses.

38. **Loan:** A sum of money borrowed from a lender with the expectation of repayment, typically with interest, over a specified period.

39. **Market Capitalization:** The total value of a company's outstanding shares of stock, calculated by multiplying the current share price by the total number of shares outstanding.

40. **Minority Interest:** Ownership stake in a company held by shareholders who own less than 50% of its outstanding shares, often resulting from strategic investments or acquisitions.

41. **Net Income:** The profit or earnings of a company after deducting all expenses, taxes, and interest payments from total revenue.

42. **Net Present Value (NPV):** A financial metric used to evaluate the profitability of an investment by calculating the present value of its expected cash flows, discounted at a specified rate.

43. **Owner's Equity:** The residual interest in the assets of a business after deducting liabilities, representing the owner's investment in the company.

44. **Private Equity:** Ownership interest in companies that are not publicly traded, typically held by private equity firms or accredited investors.

45. **Profit Margin:** The ratio of a company's net income to its revenue, expressed as a percentage, indicating its profitability relative to sales.

46. **Quality Assurance (QA):** The process of ensuring that products or services meet specified standards of quality and comply with regulatory requirements.

47. **Return on Investment (ROI):** A measure of the profitability of an investment, calculated as the ratio of the net profit generated to the initial cost of the investment, expressed as a percentage.

48. **Sarbanes-Oxley:** A U.S. federal law enacted to improve corporate governance and financial reporting transparency, requiring companies to implement internal controls and disclosure procedures.

49. **Securities and Exchange Commission (SEC):** A U.S. government agency responsible for regulating securities markets and protecting investors by enforcing securities laws.

50. **Share Owners:** Individuals or entities that own shares of stock in a corporation, entitling them to a portion of the company's profits and voting rights at shareholder meetings.

51. **Shareholder:** A person or entity that owns shares of stock in a corporation, representing ownership in the company and entitling them to dividends and voting rights.

52. **Total Enterprise Value:** The total value of a company, including its market capitalization, debt, minority interest, and preferred equity, representing the cost of acquiring the entire business.

53. **Undercapitalization:** A situation in which a company lacks sufficient capital or financial resources to support its operations, growth, or investment needs.

54. **Valuation:** The process of determining the worth or value of a business, asset, or investment, often based on financial analysis, market trends, and comparable transactions.

55. **Valuation Multiples**: Ratios or metrics used to estimate the value of a company relative to its financial performance, such as price-to-earnings (P/E) ratio or enterprise value-to-EBITDA (EV/EBITDA) ratio.

56. **Venture Capital:** Financing provided to startups or early-stage companies by investors in exchange for an equity stake, with the expectation of high returns on successful ventures.

57. **Wall Street:** A metonym for the financial markets and institutions located in New York City, including the New York Stock Exchange (NYSE) and investment banks, often used to refer to the financial industry as a whole.

58. **Working Capital:** The difference between a company's current assets and current liabilities, representing its ability to meet short-term financial obligations and fund operational activities.

59. **Yield:** The income generated by an investment, typically expressed as a percentage of the investment amount, such as dividend yield or bond yield.

60. **Zero-Based Budgeting (ZBB**): A budgeting approach in which all expenses must be justified for each new budget period, starting from zero base, regardless of previous budgets or allocations.

About the Author

George Bickerstaff is a well-known business leader who has made significant contributions to healthcare, finance, and information technology. He attended Rutgers University and earned degrees in industrial engineering and business administration. Later, he continued his education at Harvard Business School.

George began his career as an industrial engineer but later transitioned to the finance sector. He achieved rapid success in companies like General Electric, Dun and Bradstreet, and Novartis Pharma AG.

After a successful corporate journey as the Chief Financial Officer of six companies, George co-founded M.M. Dillon & Co., an investment bank specializing in helping healthcare and technology companies. In this role, he offered valuable strategic, operational, and financial guidance to many growth-focused companies worldwide.

Under George's leadership, his companies experienced remarkable growth by introducing innovative products and services that helped their stakeholders. His leadership principles emphasized teamwork, clear goals, and adaptability, leading to transformative changes in his ventures.

In addition to his corporate roles, George's ability in corporate governance, strategic planning, and finance made him a respected board member of over twenty global companies. His significant contributions to The Global Leaders network highlight his influence on the global business arena.

Beyond his business accomplishments, George is known for his philanthropic efforts, particularly in healthcare improvement and children's rights advocacy. He served as the Chairperson of the International Vaccine Institute and as Vice Chair of the International Centre for Missing & Exploited Children.

George Bickerstaff's visionary leadership, strategic ability, and unwavering commitment to excellence serve as an inspiration to appearing leaders, showcasing the profound impact one individual can have on industries and society.

George Bickerstaff

https://www.linkedin.com/in/bickerstaff/

Made in the USA
Middletown, DE
26 March 2024

51722464R00176